Making Law Matter

Making Law Matter

Environmental Protection
and Legal Institutions in Brazil

Lesley K. McAllister

STANFORD LAW BOOKS
An imprint of Stanford University Press
Stanford, California

Stanford University Press
Stanford, California

©2008 by the Board of Trustees of the Leland Stanford Junior University.
All rights reserved.

Printed in the United States of America on acid-free, archival-quality paper

Library of Congress Cataloging-in-Publication Data

McAllister, Lesley K. (Lesley Krista), 1970-
  Making law matter : environmental protection and legal institutions in Brazil / Lesley K. McAllister.
    p. cm.
  Includes bibliographical references and index.
  ISBN 978-0-8047-5823-9 (cloth : alk. paper)
  1. Environmental law--Brazil. 2. Brazil. Ministério Público Federal. I. Title.
  KHD3421.M433 2008
  344.8104'6--dc22   2008006698

Typeset by Bruce Lundquist in 10/14 Minion

For Nathan and Erin

Contents

Illustrations and Tables

Preface

THIS BOOK IS ABOUT Brazilian prosecutors who function much like public interest environmental lawyers in other countries. They sue polluters and the government to enforce environmental laws. They accuse environmental agencies of shirking their duties because of political pressure. They form alliances with local environmental groups and the media. They attend professional meetings to share strategies about how to be more effective environmental advocates. Several of the country's most recognized experts on Brazilian environmental law come from their ranks. As I argue in these pages, the work of these prosecutors is making environmental law matter in Brazil.

A story about prosecutors who act like environmental advocates—and who do a decent job of it—seems unlikely. Yet, while it has not been my goal or approach, I am confident that a public choice theorist could explain the behavior of Brazilian environmental prosecutors. As individuals and as an institution, prosecutors receive substantial public attention and acclaim for their environmental work. Headline enforcement cases, particularly those against the government, reinforce the notion that prosecutors are politically independent from the government and that they play a vital role in representing public interests. This redounds to the institution in the form of public legitimacy and, ultimately, the preservation of its substantial powers. Also, prosecutors are paid very well and new positions are filled through competitive civil service exams that attract many of the best young lawyers in the country. While corruption is always a possibility, prosecutors may be more resistant than many other governmental employees because of their favorable working conditions and status in the legal profession.

The incentives of Brazilian prosecutors are structured such that they tend to take environmental law seriously and act in ways that make environmental law have an impact in society. Many of the advances in environmental law implementation and enforcement in the past two decades can be directly linked to the work of Brazilian prosecutors. Considering the weakness of capacity in environmental policy in most developing countries, this is something that deserves to be studied and replicated if possible.

NOT ENOUGH SCHOLARLY ATTENTION has been paid to environmental law in developing countries. For many years, the prevailing idea was that countries would get environmental law after they get economic development. We are all on a similar course of development, it was assumed, and developing countries were not developmentally ready for environmental law. When they became ready, developing countries would simply learn from developed countries that had already passed through that phase of development.

This viewpoint is no longer tenable. There is no uniform course of development—no six stages, no linear progression, no universal road map to the economic and environmental good life. Moreover, there is a need for effective environmental laws in developing countries immediately, not just sometime in the future. Regardless of economic development, environmental quality matters to people's health and people's lives. Moreover, environmental problems increasingly transcend national borders, and their solutions will require that environmental laws be capable of being implemented and enforced in developing countries as well as developed countries. The question of how well environmental protection works in developing countries is one of considerable practical and scholarly importance.

The Brazilian case shows that involvement of legal institutions is a route toward enhancing the effectiveness of environmental law. What is special about legal institutions? Why should they be involved in environmental protection? Legal institutions can operate in ways that make societal actors both know the law and follow the law. When a prosecutor files a headline environmental case, the public as well as the defendant learn more about what the law requires of them. When the judge decides an environmental case, the law is interpreted to clarify its meaning and applicability. Prosecutions and court decisions also compel compliance with the law. The legal system is harnessed to bring force to environmental laws.

Environmental protection in developing countries can benefit from the involvement of legal institutions. Legal institutions have not generally been players in environmental protection, but there are many reasons they could and should be. In many countries, as in Brazil, courts and prosecutors are relatively strong institutions. Moreover, in many countries, legal reforms have occurred to improve the legal system's capacity to resolve cases quickly and efficiently, often through specialized or alternative courts or through compromise and settlement. Legal institutions may have greater capacity in the area of enforcing laws than the executive branch. Environmental protection in developing countries stands to benefit from tapping into this capacity.

Legal institutions in developing countries should become involved in environmental protection because impunity for offending environmental laws visibly erodes the rule of law. The rule of law suffers when environmental laws are flouted, and making environmental law matter is part of constructing the rule of law. Legal institutions also stand to gain by increasing their involvement in environmental law enforcement. Environmental problems garner national and international attention, and when legal actors force the executive branch to improve environmental protection, they can send a strong signal of their political independence (see Farber 2002).

Brazil stands out as a country where legal institutions have forged a path toward environmental rule of law. Prosecutorial institutions have prioritized environmental protection and have developed ways to resolve cases flexibly through negotiation and settlement. Many judges have also become receptive to environmental cases, and prosecutors advocating for environmental protection in the courts often prevail. Environmental protection became a legal issue of consequence, and the consequences of environmental law were strengthened.

THIS BOOK IS BASED primarily on fieldwork conducted in Brazil from October 2001 through May 2002. I spent four months in the state of São Paulo and two months in the state of Pará. In each state, I became a participant observer in the Ministério Público and environmental agencies through internships that provided access to the internal workings of these institutions and the views of their members (Wolcott 1995; Bernard 1995). My role as a participant-observer also allowed me to obtain a variety of quantitative data that were produced for internal use regarding organizational characteristics and enforcement activities.

In each state, research consisted of the observational and informal conversational methods of participant observation, the development of key informant relationships, archival research in institutional and university libraries, and over a hundred semistructured interviews (Fetterman 1998; Emerson, Fretz, and Shaw 1995; Spradley 1979). In addition to prosecutors and agency officials, I interviewed scholars, leaders of environmental groups, environmental lawyers, and business and political leaders knowledgeable about or involved in Brazilian environmental law and politics.

My first internship was in the São Paulo Ministério Público's Environmental Prosecution Support Center from October through December 2001. I was able to share an office with the director and his two assistant prosecutors, and this arrangement led to frequent lunch invitations and opportunities to observe their interaction with prosecutors who called or visited for advice on particular cases. I also had extensive contact with the five environmental prosecutors responsible for the city of São Paulo, whose offices were in the same building. As an intern in the support center, I was also able to attend the four-day environmental conference of the São Paulo Ministério Público in November 2001, generally open only to prosecutors and invited guests and speakers. In addition to providing information on how environmental prosecutors exchange and generate knowledge, attendance at this conference afforded many opportunities to informally talk with other state and federal prosecutors active in environmental enforcement.

My second internship was in the São Paulo pollution control agency, CE-TESB, from early January through February 2002. I divided my time between two agency divisions, the enforcement division and the legal division. As described in Chapter 2, CETESB is headquartered in the city of São Paulo and has thirty-four enforcement field offices throughout the state. By spending a week in a field office located in the São Paulo metropolitan area, I was able to accompany field inspectors on visits, review enforcement case files, and have formal conversations with the field office staff. After this experience, I returned to the agency headquarters office to gather additional information from the enforcement officials there and to begin my internship in the legal division of the agency. There I shared an office with the attorney in charge of litigation and, from this vantage point, was able to observe conversations and meetings with agency staff that sought the attorney's advice on particular cases and situations. As an intern in CETESB, I was also able to make a significant number of contacts in São Paulo's Secretariat of the Environment, of which CETESB forms part and which is housed in the same building.

In the state of Pará, I was an intern in the environmental center of the Pará State Ministério Público from mid-April through mid-May 2002. As an intern,

I was invited to attend a variety of meetings that also included agency officials, thus providing an opportunity to understand the interactions between state prosecutors and agency officials. While I was not able to set up an internship in the Pará state environmental agency, several formal interviews and informal discussions with agency officials provided an understanding of the institution and access to internal enforcement data. In the latter half of May 2002, my research focused on the Federal Ministério Público in Pará and the federal environmental agency, IBAMA, in Pará. Information was gathered through interviews as well as research in the administrative files of each institution.

Acknowledgments

Many people and organizations in both Brazil and the United States deserve recognition for making this book happen. Innumerable Brazilian prosecutors lent their time and insight to the research. The enthusiasm that they have for environmental protection made research a pleasure. I want to particularly acknowledge the help of Antonio Herman Benjamin, José Carlos Meloni Sícoli, Luis Roberto Proença, Fernando Akaoui, Raimundo de Jesus Coelho de Moraes, Luis Ismaelino Valente, and Ubiratan Cazetta. Many environmental agency officials were also very willing to share their perspectives. Special thanks go to Sandra Madaglia, Joaquim Ferreira das Neves, Antonio Augusto Costa de Faria, and Selma Bara Melgaço.

Several Brazilian scholars had been thinking and writing about Brazilian prosecutors long before I arrived, and they were very generous in sharing their knowledge. I refer particularly to Rogério Arantes, Catia Aida Silva, Débora Alves, Maria da Gloria Bonelli, Maria Teresa Sadek, Alvino Oliveira Sanches Filho, and Rosângela Cavalcanti. I feel very privileged to have had the opportunity to learn from them.

At University of California, Berkeley, where this project began, I owe special thanks to Bob Kagan, who has been a wonderful mentor and friend at every step in my academic career. I also want to thank Peter Evans, Dick Norgaard, Laura Enríquez, Lawrence Friedman, and Rogelio Pérez-Perdomo for their encouragement and advice. In its various stages, the research was funded by a UC Berkeley Institute of International Studies Hewlitt Pre-Dissertation Travel Grant; a UC Berkeley Center for Latin American Studies Travel Grant; a UC Berkeley Pre-doctoral Fellowship in Social Studies of Science and Technology; an Organization of American States Training Program Grant; a National Science Foundation Law and Social Science Dissertation Improvement Grant;

and an Environmental Protection Agency "Science to Achieve Results" (STAR) Fellowship. I thank these organizations for their willingness to fund difficult-to-categorize research that crosses interdisciplinary and geographic boundaries.

During my time at the University of San Diego (USD) School of Law, I received great support in bringing this work through its final stages. Particularly helpful comments on the text were given by Lynne Dallas, Jack Minan, Kathryn Hochstetler, Robert Percival, Matt Taylor, and Colin Crawford. USD directly supported the completion of the manuscript with a generous summer research grant and a terrific staff of law librarians. Amanda Moran, Kate Wahl, and all the other helpful people at Stanford University Press made the publication process enjoyable.

My final thanks go to my wonderful family. My parents, while sometimes questioning the usefulness of a doctorate, never questioned my decision to pursue one. My husband Andrew was always there for me with ideas and insight—from Berkeley to Brazil to San Diego. I dedicated this book to our children, Nathan and Erin, who remind me daily that future generations are counting on us to leave them with a healthy environment that can support their hopes and dreams as it has ours.

Abbreviations

ABEMA
: Brazilian Association of State Environmental Agencies,
Associação Brasileira de Entidades Estaduais de Meio Ambiente

ATPF
: Authorization for the Transport of Forest Products,
Autorização para Transporte de Produto Florestal

CETESB
: Environmental Sanitation Technology Company,
Companhia de Tecnologia de Saneamento Ambiental
(São Paulo)

CNJ
: National Judicial Council,
Conselho Nacional de Justiça

COEMA
: State Environmental Council,
Conselho Estadual do Meio Ambiente (Pará)

CONAMA
: National Environmental Council,
Conselho Nacional do Meio Ambiente

CONAMP
: National Association of the Ministério Público,
Confederação Nacional do Ministério Público

CONMAM
: Council of Environmental Defense,
Conselho de Defesa do Meio Ambiente (Rio Grande do Sul)

CONSEMA
: State Environmental Council,
Conselho Estadual do Meio Ambiente (São Paulo)

DAE
: Department of Water and Sewage,
Departamento de Aguas e Esgotos (São Paulo)

DAIA   Department of Environmental Impact Evaluation,
             Departamento de Avaliação dos Impactos Ambientais
             (São Paulo)

DEPRN   State Department of Natural Resource Protection,
             Departamento Estadual de Proteção de Recursos Naturais
             (São Paulo)

EIA   Environmental Impact Study,
             Estudo de Impacto Ambiental

FEEMA   State Environmental Engineering Foundation,
             Fundação Estadual de Engenharia do Meio Ambiente
             (Rio de Janeiro)

IBAMA   Brazilian Institute of the Environment and Renewable Natural
             Resources,
             *Instituto Brasileiro do Meio Ambiente e dos Recursos Naturais
             Renováveis*

IBAMA/PA   Pará state office of IBAMA

IBDF   Brazilian Institute of Forestry Development,
             Instituto Brasileiro de Desenvolvimento Florestal

IBGE   Brazilian Institute of Geography and Statistics,
             Instituto Brasileiro de Geografia e Estatística

IMAZON   Institute of Amazonian Peoples and Environment,
             Instituto de Homem e Meio Ambiente da Amazônia

IPAM   Environmental Research Institute of the Amazon,
             Instituto de Pesquisa Ambiental da Amazônia (Pará)

MMA   Ministry of the Environment,
             Ministério do Meio Ambiente

PMFS   Sustainable Forest Management Plan,
             Plano de Manejo Florestal Sustentável

RIMA   Environmental Impact Report,
             Relatório de Impacto Ambiental

SECTAM   State Secretariat of Science, Technology and the Environment,
             Secretaria de Estado de Ciência, Tecnologia e Meio Ambiente
             (Pará)

SEMA   Special Secretariat for the Environment,
           Secretaria Especial do Meio Ambiente

SEMAM   National Environmental Secretariat,
           Secretaria Nacional do Meio Ambiente

SISNAMA   National Environmental System,
           Sistema Nacional do Meio Ambiente

SMA   State Secretariat of the Environment,
           Secretaria de Estado do Meio Ambiente (São Paulo)

STF   Federal Supreme Court,
           Supremo Tribunal Federal

STJ   Superior Court of Justice,
           Superior Tribunal de Justiça

TCU   Federal Court of Accounts,
           Tribunal de Contas da União

TRF   Federal Regional Court,
           Tribunal Regional Federal

UNCED   United Nations Conference on Environment and Development

Making Law Matter

1 Environmental Protection and the Rule of Law

THE STORY OF ENVIRONMENTAL LAW in developing countries is often a story of laws that fail to achieve their stated goals. Forestry laws guarantee preservation of rainforests while massive deforestation occurs. Clean water laws set forth rigorous standards as cities and factories dump untreated waste into rivers and streams. Constitutions grandly proclaim that a balanced ecological environment is assured to all citizens while cities grow uncontrollably into unlivable megacities.

Environmental law in developing countries is also often a story of failed regulatory agencies. The regulatory agencies that are charged with implementing and enforcing environmental laws are chronically underfunded and understaffed. Agency salaries tend to be low, and corruption is a constant concern. Regulatory approaches for pollution control and natural resource management that succeed in developed countries seem inadequate or unworkable. Environmental agencies in developing countries often do not have the capacity to implement and enforce the most basic and essential components of environmental law.

The existence of rigorous environmental protection laws and inadequate regulatory agencies, however, creates an opening for a new type of player in environmental protection: legal actors. Courts may be called upon to enforce laws in legal actions against entities that cause environmental harm, and possibly even against the governmental agencies responsible for regulating them. In countries as diverse as India, Kenya, and Colombia, environmentalists have had their day in court. And in response to environmental claims, courts in many developing countries have become increasingly active in the implementation and enforcement of environmental laws.

1

In the 1980s, Brazil's very independent prosecutors were empowered to file environmental enforcement actions against private actors as well as the government. From the state of São Paulo in the industrialized south to the state of Pará in the Amazonian north, public prosecutors began receiving public complaints about environmental problems, opening investigations, and filing civil and criminal actions for environmental harm. Prosecutors assumed this role based on a widespread perception that environmental laws and environmental agencies were failing. With a growing number of environmental cases in their dockets filed by prosecutors, Brazilian judges also became important actors in environmental protection.

This book tells an atypical story about environmental law in a developing country. It tells the story of how the involvement of legal actors in environmental protection in Brazil made environmental law more effective. It finds that the involvement of legal institutions—particularly prosecutors and courts—helped develop a robust, effective environmental regulatory system in Brazil. Legal institutions brought a degree of legal fidelity and sanctioning power that environmental regulatory agencies lacked, and prosecution of environmental cases worked to dispel the longstanding notion of impunity for environmental harm. Moreover, Brazilian legal actors adapted to their new role in environmental enforcement—they developed knowledge of environmental law and mechanisms to resolve environmental cases efficiently and effectively. Brazil stands as a model of how developing countries can empower their legal institutions to act in ways that make environmental law matter.

Environmental Regulation in Developing Countries

Environmental problems have significant political salience, and reforms to legal and institutional mandates in many countries have reflected this significance. Like Brazil, most Latin American countries have written the right to a healthy environment into their national constitutions. They have also created substantial environmental legal frameworks, with laws requiring the use of environmental impact studies, the establishment of air and water quality standards, the protection of natural areas, and other environmental protection policies. Environmental regulatory agencies now exist in most national and subnational jurisdictions.

Environmental regulation refers to the set of rules developed by regulatory agencies to implement environmental laws.[1] The common wisdom is that environmental regulation in developing countries often does not work.[2] As documented by the World Bank (2000: 1–2), regulators are often unable to enforce pollution standards at factories and there is "widespread recognition that traditional pollution regulation is inappropriate for many developing countries." Relatively little empirical research, however, has been done about the operation of environmental regulation in developing countries. Why are regulatory institutions in developing countries unable to enforce discharge standards at factories? What is it about developing countries that makes traditional pollution regulation inappropriate?

Environmental regulation fails in developing countries for many reasons. Often, the proximate cause involves the limited capacity of regulatory agencies (see Nef 1995; Mumme 1998).[3] Regulatory agencies may lack staff, or the staff may be inadequately trained or equipped. They may not have the technical expertise to develop appropriate standards and conduct effective inspections. Agency staff may also be poorly paid, creating conditions for corruption. Often, environmental agencies are the poor relations among governmental agencies, and they are subject to interference by elected officials and more powerful agencies, particularly agencies responsible for economic development. As Brazilians say, environmental agencies frequently lack the "political will" to implement and enforce environmental laws (Findley 1988: 5).

More fundamentally, environmental regulation fails because of the mismatch in political strength between interests that oppose environmental regulation and interests that favor it. The targets of regulation tend to be organized and powerful while the societal beneficiaries of regulation tend to be diffuse and weak. Regulated entities may simply ignore their legal obligations, or they may develop strategic behaviors that enable them to avoid regulation, such as using their political connections to influence particular agency decisions or prevent environmental agencies from growing stronger (see Mueller 2006: 2).

The beneficiaries of environmental law—individual citizens and society as a whole—are often not knowledgeable about the law and their legal rights. They do not expect the law to be enforced and have little ability to affect the regulatory enforcement process. They are also likely to be more willing to trade off environmental quality for economic growth than their counterparts in developed countries (ibid.: 3). In most developing countries, environmentalists are not numerous or organized enough to form a political constituency sufficient to make environmental regulation a priority.

While sometimes blamed, the inadequacy or incompleteness of legal texts is usually a symptom rather than a cause of environmental regulatory failure. In

Brazil and in most other developing countries, the characteristics of legal texts offer only a superficial explanation for the ineffectiveness of environmental regulation. Indeed, quite often, environmental laws in developing countries look very good on paper. Such environmental laws may be merely symbolic, passed to satisfy some political interests but never truly intended to be implemented and enforced (Edelman 1964; Dwyer 1990). As Brazilian experts frequently noted, Brazil's laws were among the most rigorous and complete in the world, but they lacked compliance (see Guimarães, MacDowell, and Demajorovic 1996). Where effective regulatory agencies and political support for environmental protection are present, textual deficiencies are likely to be corrected or rendered unimportant.

It is easy for a developing country to enact environmental legislation that looks a lot like the law of rich countries. The hard part is making those laws work, and often it does not happen. Promising routes toward enforcement that succeed in the difficult context of a developing country are needed. This book shows how the involvement of prosecutors and courts in environmental enforcement may supplement and reinforce weak environmental agencies and societal organizations in ways that lead to greater environmental protection in the challenging context of a developing country.

Prosecutorial Enforcement in Brazil

Brazilian public prosecutors became significant actors in the enforcement of environmental laws and regulations in the 1980s. Brazilian prosecutors are members of the Ministério Público, literally translated as the Public Ministry, but more usefully translated as the "public prosecution service," or simply the "procuracy" (see Voigt 2006: 4).[4] The Brazilian procuracy consists of a state Ministério Público in each of Brazil's twenty-six states as well as representatives of the Federal Ministério Público in each state. Under the 1988 Federal Constitution, the Ministério Público is an independent branch of government empowered to defend environmental interests and other "diffuse and collective interests" (*interesses difusos e coletivos*) as well as carry out its more traditional prosecutorial activities in the area of criminal law.[5] State and federal prosecutors fulfill their environmental mandate by conducting investigations and filing lawsuits to impose liability for environmental harm. This work of the Brazilian Ministério Público, herein called "prosecutorial enforcement," emerged as a new mode of enforcing environmental law—an alternative to the administrative enforcement conducted by environmental agencies.[6]

Throughout Brazil, most significant environmental cases are brought to the courts by public prosecutors. One of the earliest environmental cases filed by prosecutors concerned the twenty-four petrochemical and steel companies that constituted Brazil's largest industrial district, Cubatão. In 1986, São Paulo state prosecutors sued them for $800 million dollars' worth of harm to nearby forests, soils, and waters. In 2001, São Paulo prosecutors sued to force the Shell Company of Brazil to evacuate residents and purchase the properties neighboring a facility where improperly disposed industrial wastes had contaminated soils and groundwater. These are just a couple of examples; between 1986 and 2001, São Paulo state prosecutors filed over three thousand civil lawsuits alleging environmental harm.

While prosecutors first became involved in environmental enforcement in the state of São Paulo in the 1980s, prosecutorial activity diffused to other states in the 1990s and became the dominant mode of environmental enforcement throughout the country. In the Amazonian state of Pará, lawsuits brought by federal and state prosecutors halted the construction of an interstate shipping canal and a major hydroelectric plant, both of which were priority infrastructure projects for the state government. Between 1998 and 2002, federal prosecutors in Pará also filed a series of criminal and civil suits against loggers as well as federal environmental agency officials that exposed corruption and fraud in the harvest and sale of mahogany. The caseload of federal prosecutors in Pará is indicative of the priority placed on environmental prosecution: in 2001, over half of civil cases and about one-third of criminal cases concerned environmental harm.

There are over ten thousand federal and state prosecutors in Brazil, and the majority are empowered to civilly or criminally enforce environmental laws. Of these prosecutors, a handful in each of Brazil's twenty-six states—perhaps a hundred in total—work exclusively in the area of environmental protection. These specialized prosecutors are generally stationed in the capital cities of their state. Some of them work directly on environmental enforcement cases while others staff an office that assists unspecialized prosecutors throughout the state with investigating and filing environmental claims. Brazilian prosecutors are often graduates of the country's best law schools, selected through competitive civil service exams. They have a reputation for being smart and idealistic. Environmental prosecutors often view themselves as public advocates waging battle against greedy or careless businesses and corrupt governmental officials.

The involvement of prosecutors in investigating and filing environmental claims, in combination with the decisions of the judges who hear these cases, has propelled environmental law to a high level of visibility and significance in Brazil. This book shows how, with the active involvement of Brazilian prosecutors, both private and public actors relevant to environmental enforcement began to take environmental law more seriously. Individuals and private organizations, including those that seemed immune to administrative sanctions, began to worry about their compliance. Environmental agency officials became more attentive to the law and more resistant to corruption. Citizens concerned about environmental problems started using the law to challenge the actions of others, including the government itself. In these ways, prosecutorial enforcement contributed to the construction of a legal culture that supports and strengthens environmental law. Environmental law became law that mattered, law that people considered in their everyday decisions and actions.

The Procuracy in Comparative Perspective

Procuracies in developing countries have been the focus of little scholarly attention. Much has been written about the wave of judicial reform that has swept through Latin America, but very little about parallel reforms of prosecutorial institutions (Kapiszewski and Taylor 2006). Many have talked about the increase in judicial power in the region, but few about the growing power of public prosecutors. While the powers of Brazil's procuracy have perhaps expanded most dramatically, the procuracies of many other Latin American countries have also grown in their responsibilities and public profile (Duce and Riego 2006).

The substantial literature about public prosecutors in the United States provides a useful starting point for comparing procuracies across national contexts. A persistent theme in this literature regards the "largely uncontrolled" and "essentially unreviewable" discretionary power exercised by U.S. prosecutors (LaFave 1970: 532; Vorenberg 1981: 1523). The prevalence of plea bargaining in the United States raises particular concerns about the lack of prosecutorial accountability (see Lynch 1997; Remington 1993). Some reformers have promoted the development of internal policy that would make prosecutorial screening and decision making more transparent and consistent (Abrams 1971; Wright and Miller 2002). Others have advocated the external control of prosecutors by, for example, making the rules of administrative law applicable to prosecutorial actions (Davis 1969; Vorenberg 1981; Lynch 1997).

While calls for reform that would reduce discretionary power have generally not been heeded, recent research on U.S. prosecutors has revealed broad changes in how prosecutors approach their work. In the traditional model, the prosecutor's main goal was "to ensure the efficient and effective prosecution of cases presented to them," generally felony cases investigated and presented by the police (Coles and Kelling 1998: 32). In the new "community prosecution" model, the prosecutor's goals include reducing and preventing all types of crime, including low-level disorder and misdemeanor offenses that affect the quality of life in their communities. Prosecutors adopt a problem-solving approach and collaborate to a greater extent with civic groups and other governmental agencies (ibid.: 5; Levine 2005: 1127).

While U.S. prosecutors have long been regarded as powerful social actors, the same is not true of their Latin American counterparts. Traditionally, the Ministério Público in Latin American countries played relatively marginal roles in both criminal prosecution and civil litigation (see Duce and Riego 2006: 17–18). In criminal prosecution, prosecutors may have been formally responsible for charging an offender, but the act of charging was not a discretionary decision, and the police and judges were tasked with most of the important decisions involving investigation and case disposition.[7] In civil litigation, prosecutorial duties included representing weak parties such as minors and incompetents and drafting nonbinding legal opinions for judges to consider in their decisions. In some countries, the Ministério Público was abolished because of its lack of importance (Hammergren 1998: 35; Duce and Riego 2006: 18).

In the past two decades, however, almost all Latin American procuracies have undergone reforms as their criminal justice systems have adopted features of the accusatory (or adversary) model. Across the continent, prosecutors gained new powers in the investigation and processing of criminal cases (Duce and Riego 2006: 20). In Brazil, prosecutors also became extremely active in civil litigation involving public interests such as consumer defense, children's rights, disability rights, and worker health and safety as well as environmental protection.[8] This work has made them important political actors in policy areas formerly dealt with exclusively by the legislative and executive branches. Prosecutors, in turn, activate the judiciary, which may become a political actor in its own right.

In many countries, the opportunities for legal institutions to play a role in environmental protection are growing. Like Brazil, many Latin American countries have written new constitutions that guarantee the right to a healthy environment.[9] Colombia and Paraguay have also constitutionally charged their

Ministério Público with defending environmental interests.[10] Ombudsman offices in Argentina (Defensoría del Pueblo) and Costa Rica (Defensoría de los Habitantes) have powers to protect citizen rights, including environmental rights, against unlawful governmental acts (Correa et al. 1995: 41–42; Agatiello 1995: 73, 69). The United Nations Environment Program (UNEP) has identified the judiciary and other legal stakeholders as key target groups for capacity-building activities in environmental law (Bankobeza 2003: 67).

The increase in prosecutorial powers and activities in Brazil and other countries may be viewed as part of a larger trend of the judicialization of politics (Tate and Vallinder 1995; Arantes 2005: 231). The judicialization of politics refers to the "increased presence of judicial processes and court rulings in political and social life, and the increasing resolution of political, social, or state-society conflicts in the courts" (Sieder, Schjolden, and Angell 2005: 3).[11] Important lines of inquiry about Brazilian prosecutors parallel those about the judiciary (see Taylor 2006; Rios-Figueroa and Taylor 2006; Santiso 2003): the origins of prosecutorial power; the role of prosecutors in public policy; and prosecutorial governance and its reform.

Ultimately, the new responsibilities and powers of Latin American prosecutors raise empirical and normative issues similar to those discussed in the literature on U.S. prosecutors. How much discretion do and should prosecutors have, and how are they held accountable? How often do and should prosecutors use plea bargains and other extrajudicial mechanisms to resolve cases? In what ways do and should prosecutors interact with and be responsive to the concerns of citizen groups and communities? As described in these pages, all these questions arise in the environmental protection work of Brazilian prosecutors.

Variations of Prosecutorial Enforcement Within Brazil

This book examines the operation of prosecutorial environmental enforcement in two very different Brazilian states, São Paulo and Pará. Located in the southeast, the state of São Paulo is the industrial powerhouse of the country (see Map 1.1).[12] The capital of São Paulo state, São Paulo city, is one of the world's megacities. Its metropolitan area is home to about 20 million people, almost half of the population of the state of São Paulo and over 10 percent of all Brazilians. São Paulo's environmental problems are formidable, ranging from the deforestation of the Atlantic Rainforest to industrial pollution from the country's largest factories.

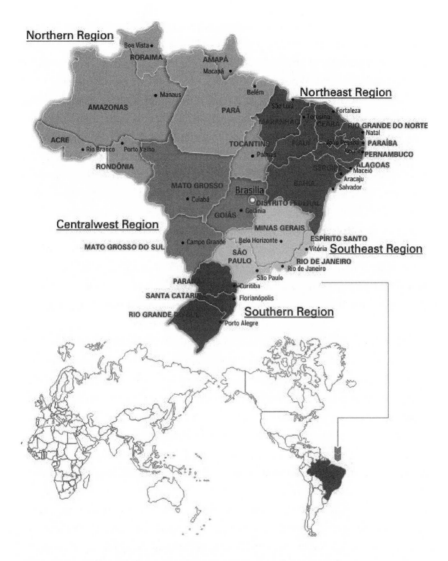

Map 1.1 Map of Brazil Showing Regions, States, Capital Cities, and Country Location
SOURCE: Map reproduced with permission of the Dutch-Brazilian Chamber of Commerce.

Located in the Amazonian northern region of Brazil, the state of Pará is the most populated Amazonian state; its capital city, Belém, is the region's largest port and its economic and cultural center. Pará is the second-largest state in Brazil, accounting for almost 15 percent of the Brazilian national territory but less than 4 percent of its population. Over three-quarters of the state is covered with forests, and it produces almost half of all the wood extracted from the Amazon.[13] Pará's most significant environmental issues involve uncontrolled deforestation and other natural resource exploitation. In 2004, Pará was first among Brazil's states in terms of the total value of fines issued by the federal environmental agency and second in terms of the area that was deforested (Brito and Barreto 2006: 38).

The states of São Paulo and Pará differ significantly in the strength of their environmental institutions. São Paulo has the country's largest concentration of environmental nongovernmental organizations. Its environmental agency is among the oldest in the country, and it is viewed as a model agency for other Brazilian states. Pará is notable for its relative lack of organized environmental interests. Its environmental agency is weak and vulnerable to criticisms of political manipulation and corruption. Indeed, Pará has been the locus of a great deal of environment-related conflict and violence.[14] A "politics of state absence," wherein local governments are headed by regional elites that form part of criminal networks, has predominated in Pará and other Amazonian states (Hochstetler and Keck 2007: 151).

This book examines how prosecutorial involvement in environmental protection has differed in the diverse states of São Paulo and Pará. Brazil's diversity of environmental, social, and political contexts makes it a microcosm of the developing world, and this comparison lends insight into how prosecutorial enforcement might work in many developing country contexts. Importantly, the research concludes that in both São Paulo and Pará, the involvement of legal actors has reduced impunity, enhanced the accountability of environmental agencies, and expanded access to justice. In these ways, prosecutorial environmental enforcement helps construct the rule of law in environmental protection.

The Rule of Law

The lack of compliance with environmental law in developing countries is part of a larger problem involving deficiencies in the "rule of law." This book argues that the involvement of legal actors in environmental protection in Brazil responds to this problem and makes environmental law more effective. Environmental regulatory agencies have become legally accountable for their decisions and actions, and courts have become more accessible to environmental claims. More broadly, the involvement of legal actors in environmental protection helps construct a legal culture in which people take environmental law seriously and generally believe that complying is an obligation.

While it has been used in many senses and for many purposes, the rule of law is generally understood to comprise a set of characteristics of laws and legal institutions that constrain the arbitrary exercise of governmental power. The legal philosopher Joseph Raz (1979: 214–19) theorized that laws in a rule of law system must be prospective, open, and clear; relatively stable; and made under open, stable, clear, and general rules. His conception of the rule of law also included an independent judiciary; open and fair hearings; judicial power to review legislative and executive branch decisions for legal conformity; an accessible judiciary; and legally accountable police.[15]

Definitions of the rule of law like Raz's tend to focus on how laws get promulgated and enforced by the state. Commentators on the rule of law in developing countries look to a greater extent at the characteristics of society and its attitudes toward law. As discussed by Martin Krygier (2002: 13405), the rule of law depends on a "more or less widespread belief in society that laws do and should count." He explains that in postcommunist Russia, establishing rule of law is not just a matter of well-drafted and well-constructed laws but of making people "listen" to what the law is saying Krygier (1997: 50). In other words, the rule of law involves not only having laws and legal institutions that conform to certain rules but also a legal culture that takes laws and legal institutions seriously: a "rule of law" legal culture.[16]

This cultural understanding of the rule of law requires that most members of a society believe that law should, and actually does, guide their behavior. Where these conditions exist, the law penetrates society and becomes part of people's identity. It is not just imposed from above, but constituted from within. People expect the law to apply to them, and they view complying with the law as a societal and personal obligation. According to Krygier, the rule of law depends on a cultural support system in which people are socialized into the values of the rule of law. Signs of such socialization include people's willingness to use law to protect and advance their interests and the levels of "unreflective but routine law abidingness" (Krygier 2002: 13405). While routine enforcement of the law is part of making people listen, it is not the whole answer: legal rules must "enter into the psychological economy of everyday life," becoming a relevant factor not only when conduct is subject to an official response but rather more generally (Krygier 1997: 51).

In Latin America, the "(un)rule of law" has predominated, wherein formal legal rights and institutions are established but fundamental conditions for their effectiveness are lacking (O'Donnell 1999b: 307). According to O'Donnell, the rule of law involves how laws are followed as well as how they are made and applied: the rule of law "is supposed to texture, stabilize and order manifold social relations." When the law is violated with impunity by state or private actors, the rule of law is truncated. A rule of law legal system must establish "networks of responsibility and accountability" that control the lawfulness of both public and private actions (ibid.: 318).

Defined to incorporate its legal-cultural aspect, the rule of law means that people consider and rely on the law when they make decisions and take actions. Rule of law requires that the law "exist, that it be knowable, that its implications be relatively determinate, and that it can be reliably expected to set the bounds within which all major actors, including government, will act" (Krygier 1997: 47). Unlike the more traditional formulations, this definition incorporates people's ideas and attitudes toward law. Like legal culture itself, the rule of law is variable among and within societies. It is a "practical ideal"; while never fully met, the rule of law may be present to a greater degree in some societies than in others (Selznick 1999: 21; Krygier 1997: 48–49). An empirical research agenda arises from the recognition of the cultural dimension of the rule of law. The central questions are "who listens, why and how, and with what effects" (Krygier 2002: 13405).

Studies of Brazilian legal culture reveal the extent to which the cultural dimension of the rule of law has been lacking. Brazilians often quip that some laws simply "stay on paper" (*ficar no papel*) and that "some laws catch on, and others don't" (*há lei que pega, e lei que não pega*). Moreover, Brazil is the land of the *jeito*, by which those with political and social connections have ways to get around or "bend the law" (Rosenn 1971: 514–23). The *jeito*, which includes not only conventional corruption but also situations in which a public servant deviates from the law because it is unrealistic or unjust, has been the norm rather than the exception in many areas of law (ibid.: 515–16). A 1996 survey of law students in the Brazilian state of Rio de Janeiro revealed that only 6 percent believed that conflicts in Brazil were principally resolved through the law and legal institutions; 94 percent considered the *jeito* or the "law of the strongest" to be predominant (Junqueira 2003: 93–95). In a Brazilian public opinion survey, 82 percent agreed that Brazilians disobey most laws, and 80 percent agreed that only the poor have to obey the law (Castro 1997a: 245). The application of law in Brazil is perceived as highly socially contingent.

This book contends that the involvement of legal actors may provide an answer to the rule of law problem of environmental law in developing countries (see Zaelke, Stilwell, and Young 2005). In Brazil, prosecutorial enforcement contributes to a change in the sense of impunity that many Brazilians have about environmental offenses, particularly those committed by powerful economic actors. Prosecutors are placed in a position of oversight of environmental agencies, enhancing agency accountability. Prosecutors also open their doors to public complaints, expanding the public's access to justice for environmental problems. In these ways, the involvement of legal institutions creates the conditions for environmental rule of law in Brazil.[17]

Of course, giving prosecutors and courts a larger role in environmental enforcement does not necessarily lead to more environmental rule of law. The relationship between a rise in the "public prominence" of the judiciary and other legal actors and the construction of the rule of law "is far from straightforward" (Domingo 2005: 23). Domingo finds that the growing power of the Mexican Supreme Court contributed to the construction of the rule of law, but that this positive relationship depends on "the form that the judicialization of politics takes and the specific characteristics in particular political, institutional, and social contexts." In Brazil, bringing environmental law into the ambit of procuracies and courts has strengthened its implementation because legal institutions have strong reputations for integrity, political independence, and public responsiveness and because they have developed specialized knowledge and case management tools that are conducive to resolving environmental problems. In contexts where the characteristics of legal institutions differ in these crucial respects, their involvement may not provide similar rule of law benefits.

Legalism in Environmental Enforcement

Brazil's environmental laws became more effective in changing relevant behavior because a legal institution, the procuracy, was empowered to enforce them through the courts. Yet, many studies of environmental regulation in the United States and other industrialized countries have emphasized the problems associated with having courts, prosecutors, and other legal actors highly involved in regulatory enforcement. These studies have concluded that approaches to environmental enforcement in which regulators seek to cooperate and build consensus with regulated parties without the involvement of legal actors are as effective and more efficient. In short, legal institutions have been viewed as problematic actors in environmental policy.

Studies comparing regulatory enforcement in the United States to that in other advanced industrialized countries have found it to be more legalistic, meaning that it is controlled to a greater extent by formal legal rules and procedures (Kagan 2001: 9).[18] In the United States, regulatory laws are more detailed, prescriptive, and complex; regulators are more likely to issue formal legal sanctions with harsher penalties; relationships between regulators and regulated entities are more adversarial; and regulatory rules are more frequently enmeshed in legal conflict (ibid.: 187; Kagan 1999). Regulatory systems in other advanced industrialized countries are characterized by a greater degree of cooperation between government and industry, lower citizen participation, and little involvement of the courts (Kagan 1997: 168; Badaracco 1985; Vogel 1986; Braithwaite 1985).

Based on their empirical findings, scholars have identified two ideal-typical styles of regulatory enforcement: the legalistic style and the cooperative style. The legalistic style is based on "coercion and compulsion" and is concerned primarily with "the application of punishment for breaking a rule and doing harm" (Hawkins and Thomas 1984: 4; Bardach and Kagan 1982: 71–77). Regulators employ a legalistic style when they are rule bound in their interpretation of the law and threatening in their interactions with regulated parties (May and Winter 2000: 147). The cooperative or conciliatory style, in contrast, relies primarily on techniques of education, advice, persuasion, and negotiation (Hawkins 1984; Hutter 1988). Regulators use communication and compromise rather than punishment to move offenders toward regulatory compliance.[19]

Scholars have sought to assess differences in the outcomes of regulatory styles in terms of effectiveness and efficiency. A regulatory style is effective if it contributes to improving the environment, and it is efficient if it does so at minimum cost (Gunningham, Grabosky, and Sinclair 1998: 26). In contexts where compliance is widespread, much research has shown that a legalistic style tends to increase the costs of regulation without corresponding gains in effectiveness (see Rosenberg 1991; Gunningham, Grabosky, and Sinclair 1998; Kagan and Axelrad 2000; Melnick 1995; DiMento 1986). The greater involvement of lawyers and the judiciary in the United States increases the time, cost, and adversarial character of the regulatory process, but it has not been consistently shown to lead to higher levels of compliance or more environmental improvement (Kagan and Axelrad 2000; Badaracco 1985; Braithwaite 1985).

Yet, in some settings, a legalistic style may be more effective. "Tough" enforcement as employed in the 1970s in the United States produced tangible increases in environmental quality as well as improvements in a variety of other areas of protective regulation (Bardach and Kagan 1982). In a comparative study of pulp mill regulation in the United States and Canada, the legalistic style that prevailed in the United States was shown to be more effective than the cooperative style that prevailed in Canada (Harrison 1995). Canadian regulators lowered their expectations and bent the rules when confronted with noncompliant pulp mills. Similarly, Gunningham (1987) found that the lack of prosecution in the regulation of Australian asbestos mines led to "negotiated noncompliance" with ultimately fatal results.

With prosecutors who have become deeply involved in environmental enforcement since 1985, Brazil permits analysis of whether the involvement of legal actors contributes to greater regulatory effectiveness. Composed of lawyers and often advocating a strict interpretation of the law, the Ministério Público introduces a formal legal dimension into the Brazilian regulatory enforcement process. By describing and analyzing the consequences of prosecutorial enforcement in Brazil, this book empirically analyzes an approach to environmental enforcement that has the potential to make environmental law more effective in the social and legal contexts of developing countries.

The Brazilian case shows that legalistic enforcement is likely to enhance regulatory effectiveness when introduced into a context where regulatory authority is historically weak. As described above, Brazilian environmental enforcement has been plagued by weakness in the rule of law. The long-standing absence of legalism—the lack of control by formal legal rules and procedures—made environmental enforcement susceptible to impunity and corruption. The involvement of Brazilian prosecutors and courts that view the law as their primary reference point for decisions and actions contributes significantly toward the effectiveness of environmental law.

A comparative study of environmental politics in Argentina and Brazil provides further support. Hochstetler (2002a: 53) studied differences in the ability of environmental movements in each country to influence plans to build a large international shipping canal through environmentally sensitive wetlands in the interior of the continent. Brazil's environmentalists were able to block the project while Argentina's environmentalists were not. The most important difference was found to be legal capacity. In Brazil, prosecutors worked with environmentalists in filing a series of legal cases through which courts required the government to prepare more complete environmental impact studies. Hochstetler notes the importance of such court-imposed mandates in "settings where national elites do not fully embrace environmental values" (ibid.).

Clearly, there may be weaknesses and counterproductive consequences of entrusting environmental law enforcement to prosecutors trained in the legalistic traditions of criminal law rather than the problem-solving traditions of regulatory agencies. As shown in this study, however, the Brazilian Ministério Público resolves most of its environmental cases through investigation and the threat of prosecution, using its leverage to negotiate remedial measures. As such, its approach is not entirely legalistic but resembles "flexible enforcement," in which agencies use elements of both the cooperative and legalistic styles to respond in a calibrated way to the behavior of the regulated entity (see Bardach and Kagan 1982; Scholz 1984; Ayres and Braithwaite 1992).[20] The effectiveness of the Brazilian Ministério Público in enforcing environmental laws derives from its flexible use of strong legal powers.

This book thus contends that something is different in the relationship between environment, law, and society in developing countries. Different outcomes result from the involvement of legal actors in the regulatory process in countries that have the political and economic profile commonly referred to as "developing." Where compliance is not widespread and governmental environmental agencies are chronically weak, public prosecutors and courts may bring an essential degree of legal and political heft to environmental law implementation. With a reputation for integrity and professionalism, and sheltered from politics by their judicial branch associations, prosecutorial institutions are potentially much less prone to the types of corruption and political interference faced by environmental agencies. In developing countries, the benefits of having legal actors involved in environmental enforcement may far outweigh any drawbacks associated with a more legalistic approach.

Plan of the Book

Under a new legal framework in which they were charged with defending the "diffuse and collective interests" of society, Brazilian prosecutors became central actors in environmental enforcement. Their involvement challenged the prevailing notions of impunity for environmental violations; established a means of oversight of environmental agencies; and provided citizens with more accessible legal recourse for environmental claims. Prosecutorial enforcement emerged as an alternative, more effective mode of enforcement than the administrative enforcement conducted by Brazilian environmental agencies. The involvement of legal actors in environmental protection significantly enhanced environmental rule of law and made environmental law more effective.

As discussed in Chapter 2, Brazil illustrates the common paradox of environmental law in developing countries: environmental laws may be strong, but environmental agencies are weak. The chapter shows that while Brazilian environmental laws could be considered to be among the most complete and rigorous in the world, they suffered from inadequate implementation and enforcement because environmental agencies were limited by resource constraints and political pressure. To illustrate these dynamics, the chapter describes the trajectory of Brazil's environmental laws and agencies at the federal and state levels with a focus on two contrasting Brazilian states, the industrialized state of São Paulo and the Amazonian state of Pará.

The story of how Brazilian prosecutors and courts became heavily involved in environmental enforcement beginning in the mid-1980s is told in Chapter 3. A series of legal and institutional changes enabled the establishment of a corps of environmental prosecutors, empowered to seek civil and criminal damages for environmental harm in court. With these powers, they took on a new role as the legal advocates of citizens concerned about environmental problems and began acting as watchdogs over the decisions and actions of environmental agencies. By explaining how the prosecutorial mode of enforcement developed in Brazil, this chapter provides insight into the conditions that could lead toward an effective legalistic approach to enforcement in other countries.

Chapter 4 analyzes how the involvement of prosecutors in environmental enforcement helped change the prevailing notion that powerful actors could violate environmental laws with impunity. Many prosecutors were serious and active in their environmental enforcement work—they used strong civil and criminal enforcement instruments to pursue a wide variety of types of environmental harm against a wide variety of defendants. Largely independent of the political branches, the Ministério Público often conducted well-publicized cases against large political and economic actors that environmental agencies lacked power to confront. Yet, while their independence contributes significantly to prosecutors' ability to enforce the law, it also prevents prosecutors from coordinating with each other to enable more consistency in the handling of enforcement cases.

Chapter 5 shows that prosecutorial enforcement also makes environmental law matter by making environmental agencies accountable. Prosecutors are legally able and often willing to challenge the legality of the decisions and actions of environmental agencies and their officials. As prosecutors investigate environmental harm, they become aware of agency responses to particular problems, and they call upon agency officials to account for those responses. Prosecutors have become agency watchdogs, and they have civilly and criminally prosecuted environmental agency officials for corruption and other illegal behavior. The chapter also addresses the tension between accountability and governmental effectiveness, wherein fidelity to legal rules may hinder the types of practical problem-solving techniques that effective environmental agencies utilize.

As discussed in Chapter 6, the involvement of prosecutors in environmental enforcement enabled citizens to mobilize environmental law to advance their interests. Prosecutors established themselves as the legal representatives of society's environmental interests, and citizen groups concerned with environmental problems came to view prosecutors as their partners and allies. The offices of prosecutors and the courts became accessible forums for resolving environmental conflicts. In this way, citizens were empowered to use the law to challenge the environmentally harmful actions of others, including those of the government itself. The chapter also discusses drawbacks of the prosecutorial approach's reliance on the judicial system to impose penalties and how Brazilian prosecutors use extrajudicial settlement agreements to work around the problems of judicial bias and delay.

As shown by comparisons between São Paulo and Pará throughout the book, prosecutorial enforcement is not uniform in its development and effectiveness across Brazil. The procuracies of some Brazilian states prioritize environmental enforcement to a greater degree than others, with notable differences in the extent to which their prosecutors actively investigate and file actions, oversee environmental agencies, and interact with civil society organizations. The concluding Chapter 7 suggests that the level of environmental enforcement activity varies with the degree of prosecutorial independence. Where prosecutors expressed that they and their institutions were protected from the influence of the executive branch, as in the cases of the State Ministério Público of São Paulo and the Federal Ministério Público in Pará, they were more active in environmental enforcement.

Yet, as discussed in Chapter 7, the independence of prosecutors also presented challenges for the effectiveness of prosecutorial enforcement. The São Paulo

Ministério Público was the largest prosecutorial institution in the country and the most active in environmental enforcement, but it lacked mechanisms to coordinate the enforcement activities of prosecutors. Prosecutors burdened environmental agencies with requests for technical information about enforcement cases that were not agency priorities, and they did not adequately coordinate their actions with the agencies or other prosecutors. Prosecutorial independence also raised the important issue of prosecutorial accountability, or the classic question of "who guards the guardians?" (Shapiro 1988). The Brazilian mode of prosecutorial enforcement lacks adequate mechanisms of accountability that would enable oversight of the work of prosecutors themselves.

Finally, the concluding chapter explores the potential for the diffusion of prosecutorial enforcement to other countries. As the involvement of legal actors in environmental enforcement made environmental law more effective in Brazil, similar benefits might be attained by the involvement of legal actors in other developing countries that lack effective environmental law. The particularities of how prosecutorial enforcement developed and diffused within Brazil provides insight into how it might be diffused to other countries, particularly those with similar legal cultures and political characteristics.

2 Strong Laws, Weak Agencies

Currently, FEEMA is trapped in a cycle of decline and cannot fulfill some of the basic functions of an environmental agency such as systematic monitoring of emissions and ambient quality, as well as spot checks and site visits with polluters. Since FEEMA has had to drastically reduce its monitoring and enforcement activities, the definition of management priorities is more difficult, credibility with polluters and the public is reduced, and assertion of the powers required to meet FEEMA's responsibilities is even more difficult. In turn, as a less effective agency, FEEMA has problems in justifying its budgets and asserting its responsibilities toward other agencies.
(World Bank, 1996a: 6)

THE PARADOX OF ENVIRONMENTAL ENFORCEMENT in Brazil is that environmental laws are strong but environmental agencies are weak.[1] Many Brazilian scholars of environmental law and foreign commentators consider Brazil's legal framework to be thorough and sophisticated. The law provides for the use of environmental impact studies and environmental permits; sharing of regulatory power among the various levels of government with a tendency toward decentralization; strict liability for environmental harm; and a uniform system of environmental crimes and administrative penalties. Moreover, comprehensive municipal, state, and federal legislation is bolstered by a constitution that devotes an entire chapter to environmental protection. As stated by one Brazilian commentator, "It can be said that Brazil today has one of the most advanced systems of legal protection for the environment" (Benjamin 1999a).

While Brazilian environmental laws are strong on the books, environmental enforcement has been limited in its effectiveness. Environmental agencies tend to be weak both in terms of their resources and their power to coerce compliance. As stated in a 1998 *New York Times* editorial in support of the proposed

Brazilian Environmental Crimes Law: "Brazil has good laws on the books protecting the Amazon but no legal power to enforce them. The environmental agency can levy only absurdly small fines and collects less than 10 percent of them."[2] While the legal structure is well developed, institutions to enforce the laws have tended to be less so. Indeed, the English term "enforcement" lacks a precise translation in Portuguese.[3]

The weakness of environmental agencies is, of course, not unique to Brazil. Most environmental agencies in the world experience budgetary and political constraints. In many countries, environmental laws have been written as symbolic gestures without a corresponding commitment to enforcement. Political willingness to prioritize environmental problems and devote budgetary resources to their solution is likely to be particularly uncommon in poor countries with more significant economic constraints. In these contexts, political leaders are even more likely to privilege development objectives and have fewer resources to devote to environmental protection. In short, the quest for economic development tends to trump environmental protection.

This chapter tells the story of Brazil's environmental agencies and the administrative enforcement of environmental laws in Brazil. In the first part of the chapter, the evolution of environmental laws and administrative agencies at the federal and state levels in Brazil is described. The states of São Paulo and Pará represent two sides of the spectrum in terms of their institutional capacity for environmental enforcement. The relatively wealthy, industrialized São Paulo of southern Brazil has been the country's leader in this regard while Pará and other poorer states in northern Brazil have lagged behind. The second part of the chapter focuses on the problems faced by environmental agencies. In São Paulo and several other southern states, where agencies were once fairly strong institutions, they have experienced decline. In Pará and many other northern states, agencies have remained small and ill-equipped to deal with the extent of the state's environmental problems. The final part of the chapter describes the environmental enforcement instruments and activities of environmental agencies. Using data from São Paulo and Pará, it shows that the weakness of environmental agencies is reflected in their records of environmental enforcement. In sum, this chapter reaffirms the conventional wisdom that, despite the strength of Brazilian environmental laws, environmental agencies are constrained in their capacities to implement and enforce them.

Federal Environmental Law

Brazilian environmental law is a patchwork of federal and state law. The responsibilities of federal, state, and local governments "are carved up quite differently for various areas of activity and regions of the country" (Hochstetler and Keck 2007: 15). Federal environmental law has played a large role in establishing the legal and administrative frameworks for natural resource management, including forestry, mining, and the protection of natural areas. State law has predominated in the area of pollution control. In geographic terms, federal environmental law plays a larger role in Amazonian states, where the major issues involve natural resource protection, than in the states of southern Brazil, where pollution control issues are most prominent. While federal law has served to establish national guidelines that states seek to conform to, it has not succeeded in harmonizing state-level institutions and capacities.[4]

Brazil began passing environmental laws and establishing environmental agencies before many other developing countries (ibid.: 24). The 1972 United Nations Conference on the Human Environment in Stockholm spurred the first efforts of environmental regulation at the federal level in Brazil. In the conference, the Brazilian delegation led the lobby of developing countries in defending their right to economic development despite the environmental costs.[5] The delegation's motto was "the worst form of pollution is poverty" (Shaman 1996). Yet, despite this outward resistance, the delegation suggested the creation of a federal environmental agency upon its return to Brazil, and in 1973, the Special Secretariat for the Environment (Secretaria Especial do Meio Ambiente; SEMA) was created within the Brazilian Ministry of Internal Affairs.[6]

The creation of SEMA in 1973 was a significant institutional advance. At least in part, it represented an attempt by the military dictatorship and Brazilian diplomats to appear responsive and sensitive to the concerns of developed countries about industrial pollution and other environmental problems (Maglio 2000: 17). Modeled on the U.S. Environmental Protection Agency, SEMA became responsible for coordinating federal pollution control activities, developing pollution standards, and providing education and assistance to state agencies (Shaman 1996). SEMA also created and managed various types of conservation units, including thirty-eight "ecological stations" that were "pristine" areas to be used only for scientific research (Drummond and Barros-Platiau 2006: 92).

Another major advance in Brazilian environmental law occurred in 1981 with the passage of a national environmental framework law, the National

Environmental Policy Act (Lei da Política Nacional do Meio Ambiente).[7] A legislative initiative of SEMA, the law has been called the first "holistic" environmental law in Brazil, "in which the environment is protected in an integral manner" (Benjamin 1999a: 78). Setting forth the instruments of environmental protection, the law included environmental standards; environmental zoning; evaluation of environmental impacts; environmental permitting and monitoring; production of environmental information; economic incentives; administrative and criminal sanctions; and strict liability for environmental harm.[8] As explained further in Chapter 3, the law marked the beginning of the Ministério Público's involvement in environmental protection, authorizing it to file civil and criminal enforcement actions.

The new law also advanced and systematized the decentralization of environmental policy and administration in Brazil. The law established the concept of a National Environmental System (Sistema Nacional do Meio Ambiente; SISNAMA) structured to include: (1) a "paramount authority," namely the National Environmental Council (Conselho Nacional do Meio Ambiente; CONAMA), responsible for making national environmental policy; (2) a "central authority," the federal agency responsible for implementing national environmental policy; (3) "state authorities," the state agencies responsible for implementation and enforcement at the state level; and (4) "local authorities," the municipal agencies responsible for implementation and enforcement at the local level.[9] SISNAMA embodied the idea that agencies at all levels of government would operate as a coordinated system, each performing its function within its jurisdiction.

CONAMA is a body of state and nonstate actors charged with establishing standards and guidelines to orient environmental policy making and implementation (Hochstetler and Keck 2007: 34). It is presided over by the administrator of the federal environmental agency and includes representatives of other governmental agencies, industry, professional societies, and civil society organizations.[10] CONAMA began to function in 1984, and its first significant resolution in 1985 determined that large dams would be considered a polluting activity and would require an environmental permit from the state environmental agency.[11] As commented by Maglio (2000: 22), CONAMA resolutions gained increasing authority in the 1980s and 1990s, attaining the force of law and substituting to some extent for legislative activity in the environmental area.[12]

Indeed, two of the most important legal references in the Brazilian environmental permitting system are CONAMA resolutions. A 1986 resolution established that environmental agencies must require an environmental impact study (Estudo de Impacto Ambiental; EIA) as part of the permitting process for a variety of infrastructure and natural resource extraction projects.[13] The resolution also required that the project proponent prepare an environmental impact report (Relatório de Impacto Ambiental; RIMA) summarizing the conclusions of the environmental impact study in a form that is accessible to decision makers and the public. A 1997 resolution clarified the respective responsibilities of federal and state environmental agencies in the environmental permitting process.[14]

In 1985, the Public Civil Action Law (Lei de Ação Civil Pública) was passed, enabling the representation of environmental interests in court by environmental organizations, the Ministério Público, and other governmental entities. Unlike the National Environmental Policy Act, environmental agencies had no involvement in the making of this law. The forces behind its passage included legal scholars and the Ministério Público, and ultimately the Ministry of Justice. While the law is procedural rather than substantive and relates to public interests generally rather than just environmental interests, it merits inclusion in a general chronology of environmental law because of the broad impact it has had on environmental law and practice in Brazil. The law's development and usage are more fully described in Chapter 3 and subsequent chapters.

The Federal Constitution of 1988 was another major step in the development of Brazilian environmental law. Article 225 ensures that "[e]veryone has the right to an ecologically equilibrated environment, a good used in common by all citizens and essential to a healthy quality of life, imposing a duty on the government and the community to defend and preserve it for present and future generations."[15] Article 225 imposes a duty on the government to protect the environment through, inter alia, defining and preserving protected areas, requiring environmental impact studies "for projects or activities that potentially cause significant environmental degradation," and promoting environmental education.[16] It also includes provisions determining that mining operations must recuperate degraded areas; stating that polluters are subject to administrative, civil, and criminal penalties; and declaring the Amazon Rainforest, the Atlantic Rainforest, the Pantanal, and the coastline to be "national patrimony."[17] In other articles relating to the environment, the 1988 Constitution gives all levels of government joint responsibility for protecting the environment and controlling pollution (articles 23 and 24); states one of the functions of the Ministério Público to be the carrying out of investigations and filing of lawsuits to protect the environment (article 129); and provides that economic activities and land use must respect environmental norms (articles 170, 174, 176, and 186).

The Brazilian constitution has been called the most advanced in the world in terms of its environmental provisions (Milaré 2001: 231–32). Its strength can be credited largely to the work of Fabio Feldmann, a São Paulo environmentalist elected as a representative of the state to the National Constituent Assembly (Hochstetler and Keck 2007: 46–48).[18] Feldmann helped organize and coordinate an environmental lobby that proposed constitutional text, attended public hearings, and staged effective demonstrations. Ultimately, 15 percent of the National Constituent Assembly representatives signed up as members of the nonpartisan, multiparty "Green Front," and article 225 passed with almost unanimous support on the Assembly floor (Hochstetler and Keck 2007: 48–50; Fernandes 1996: 276).

IBAMA, the Brazilian Institute of the Environment and Renewable Natural Resources (Instituto Brasileiro do Meio Ambiente e dos Recursos Naturais Renováveis), was created in 1989 to unify the various federal agencies that dealt with environmental and natural resource issues.[19] It brought together SEMA; the Rubber Bureau (Superintendência da Borracha); the Fishing Bureau (Superintendência da Pesca), and the Brazilian Institute of Forestry Development (Instituto Brasileiro de Desenvolvimento Florestal; IBDF). At its creation, IBAMA had a workforce of over six thousand employees.[20] Given its roots in natural resource management and the predominance of state agencies in the permitting of pollution, IBAMA's main emphasis became natural resource management, with a focus on areas of the country that are particularly rich in natural resources such as the Amazonian region (Shaman 1996). In practice, it has tended to play a supplemental role to state agencies. In states where institutional capacity is more fully developed, IBAMA's role is limited. In states where institutional capacity is lacking, particularly states of the Amazon region, IBAMA's role is significant (ibid.; Huber, Ruitenbeek, and Seroa de Motta 1998: 45).

In 1990, IBAMA was linked to a new federal entity, the National Environmental Secretariat (Secretaria Nacional do Meio Ambiente; SEMAM).[21] The United Nations Conference on Environment and Development (UNCED) held in Rio de Janeiro in June 1992 brought increased national and international attention to Brazilian environmental policy, and in November 1992, the government replaced SEMAM with a new ministry, the Ministry of the Environment (Ministério do Meio Ambiente; MMA).[22]

In 1998, another important federal law was passed, the Environmental Crimes Law (Lei das Crimes Ambientais),[23] which consolidated and enhanced existing laws relating to both administrative and criminal penalties for environmental infractions. The law modernized the system of administrative penalties, providing for fines ranging from R$50 to R$50 million.[24] It also defined the elements and penalties of a wide variety of environmental crimes, including mistreatment or illegal killing of animals, deforestation, pollution, and destruction of historical preservation sites.[25] Under the 1998 law, it is also a crime for a public official to state false or incomplete information in the environmental permitting process or to issue an environmental permit that does not comply with environmental regulations.[26] Both individuals and legal entities may incur criminal liability with sanctions including prison, house arrest, community service, disqualification from the receipt of public contracts or subsidies, and monetary fines (Milaré 2001: 455–59).[27]

State Environmental Law

Brazilian states vary considerably in the development of state institutions for environmental protection. At one end of the spectrum is São Paulo, home of Brazil's first environmental agency and first environmental regulations. On the other end of the spectrum are states such as Pará that have lagged behind in the development of environmental law and institutional capacity. Yet, even where environmental agencies have long histories, many experienced significant structural changes into the early 1990s. In São Paulo, the pollution control agency CETESB has roots back to the late 1960s, but the State Secretariat of the Environment to which it now belongs was created in 1986. In states such as Pará, environmental agencies became consolidated only in the mid-1990s.

The State of São Paulo

São Paulo created the first environmental agency in Brazil in the late 1960s. It was also the first state to implement a system of environmental permitting, an idea that was later incorporated into the National Environmental Policy Act of 1981 and eventually spread to all other Brazilian states. The environmental agencies of São Paulo are the strongest state environmental agencies in Brazil, stronger even than the federal environmental agency in pollution control. Among Brazilian states, São Paulo is the most advanced in terms of its institutions and policies for environmental regulation.

The present-day CETESB, the state-owned Environmental Sanitation Technology Company (Companhia de Tecnologia de Saneamento Ambiental), has its roots in the 1968 creation of the Center of Basic Sanitation Technology (Centro Tecnológico de Saneamento Básico), which was part of the Department of Public Works and was responsible for performing lab tests, studies, and staff training in the areas of water pollution and sanitary engineering.[28] CETESB was converted into a state-owned company in 1973, and an air pollution agency that had been part of the State Department of Health became part of CETESB in 1975. The new pollution control agency was consolidated in 1976 with a state law (referred to as CETESB's law) that established its authority and responsibilities.[29]

One of the most significant aspects of CETESB's law was the creation of a permitting system for air, water, and soil pollution sources, called the System of Prevention and Control of Environmental Pollution. In the late 1970s and early 1980s, CETESB grew quickly as it established field offices throughout the state and began issuing permits, monitoring compliance, and imposing administrative penalties for noncompliance.[30] By the early 1990s, CETESB had 9 field offices in the São Paulo metropolitan area and 22 field offices throughout the rest of the state.

CETESB gained respect and recognition for its successes in dealing with the extreme pollution problems of Cubatão in the 1980s. Cubatão is the largest and most important industrial district in the country, home to about twenty-five petrochemical and steel companies. It is located an hour outside the city of São Paulo near the state's principal port of Santos. In 1983, Cubatão generated $1 billion in exports and produced 47 percent of Brazil's nitrogen, 40 percent of its steel, 38 percent of its fertilizers, 32 percent of its phosphoric acid, 30 percent of its polyethylene, 25 percent of its chlorosoda, 18 percent of its bottled gas, and 12 percent of its gasoline (Findley 1988: 52).

In the early 1980s, the area surrounding Cubatão became known as the *vale da morte* (valley of death) because of high levels of industrial pollution suspected of causing serious birth defects and illnesses. As explained by Maglio (2000: 113), CETESB confronted the Cubatão pollution problem through a broad program of innovative environmental enforcement techniques from 1983 to 1990, including the development of technical expertise, financing for pollution control equipment, transparency in governmental communication regarding the causes of the problem, and local community participation. According to the agency, the program resulted in an 89 percent reduction of particulate emissions, an 88 percent reduction of water pollutants, and the incorporation of hazardous waste treatment systems by 90 percent of the Cubatão industries.[31]

Based on its work in Cubatão, CETESB became nationally and internationally recognized for its technical capacity and its pollution prevention and control activities. CETESB was called upon to provide technical assistance to other states and even other countries, and was recognized by the United Nations as one of sixteen centers of reference for environmental issues and by the World Health Organization as one of the five institutions in the world with most expertise on water supply and sanitation (State of São Paulo/SMA 1998: 65). In the 1980s, CETESB developed international technical cooperation agreements with environmental agencies and other institutions in the United States, Germany, Canada, Great Britain, and Japan (State of São Paulo/SMA 1992b: 80). Through these agreements, CETESB scientists and engineers were often provided with opportunities to attend trainings or complete postgraduate studies abroad.

A nationwide survey of state environmental agencies in 1987 by the Brazilian Association of State Environmental Agencies (Associação Brasileira de Entidades Estaduais de Meio Ambiente; ABEMA) revealed that CETESB was by far the largest state environmental agency, with over two thousand employees.[32] Rio de Janeiro's State Environmental Engineering Foundation (Fundação Estadual de Engenharia do Meio Ambiente; FEEMA), founded in 1975, was the second-largest agency with a staff of about one thousand. Together, São Paulo and Rio de Janeiro accounted for over half of the entire number of environmental agency staff in Brazil, more than those in the other twenty-four states and the federal district combined. Moreover, of a total public expenditure of about $61 million on state environmental agencies in Brazil, São Paulo absorbed about 75 percent and Rio de Janeiro about 6 percent (Filho 1993: 59).

The institutional framework for natural resource protection also developed in São Paulo in the 1980s. In 1983, in response to the 1981 National Environmental Policy Act, São Paulo established the State Environmental Council (Conselho Estadual do Meio Ambiente; CONSEMA).[33] The State Department of Natural Resource Protection (Departamento Estadual de Proteção de Recursos Naturais; DEPRN) of the State Secretariat of Agriculture was responsible for enforcing forestry, watershed protection, and fishing laws with the assistance of the state Forestry and Watershed Police (Comando de Policiamento Florestal e de Mananciais) (State of São Paulo/SMA 1992a: 112).

In 1986, the State Secretariat of the Environment (Secretaria de Estado do Meio Ambiente; SMA), was created to bring the various environmentally related state institutions under a single secretariat.[34] SMA was structured to include four main divisions: environmental permitting and natural resource protection; environmental planning; environmental education; and technical information and research.[35] CETESB and a forestry foundation were institutionally linked to the new SMA, though they retained some characteristics of independent institutions, including separate budget authorizations and legal personalities.[36]

In this new institutional structure, CETESB remained responsible for enforcing environmental regulations in industrial pollution settings, and DEPRN (now as part of the SMA) and the Forestry and Watershed Police remained responsible for enforcing environmental regulations regarding natural resource use. To provide coverage throughout the state, both had decentralized enforcement structures. In 2001, CETESB had thirty-four regional offices throughout the state and DEPRN had twenty-four (Dias and Sanchez 2001: 170). In 2001, the name of the Forestry and Watershed Police was changed to the Environmental Police (Comando de Policiamento Ambiental).

Given the capacity of the state environmental institutions, the federal environmental agency IBAMA has played a relatively small role in São Paulo. With a delegation of about 260 staff members in the state, IBAMA's responsibilities are largely limited to administering federal protected areas, running two national research centers, and dealing with issues of international or interstate significance such as the protection of sea turtles, the trafficking of animals, and the construction of dams.[37] However, due to the lack of a clear division of institutional responsibility between the federal and state levels, there has been a history of conflict between SMA and IBAMA in São Paulo as well as in other states. With respect to the remaining areas of rainforest in the state, Maglio (2000: 110) states that this conflict "generates large inconsistencies and has negative repercussions for forest protection in the state of São Paulo."[38]

The legal and administrative framework in São Paulo did not experience significant changes in the 1990s. Indeed, the law governing the activities of CETESB has not been significantly altered since its enactment in 1976. While many scholars and practitioners discussed the need for a new state environmental code or changes to the 1976 law, no advances were made. However, as detailed below, São Paulo environmental agencies—and particularly CETESB—suffered a notable decline in institutional resources and capacity in the 1990s.

The State of Pará

Pará provides a sharp contrast to the state of São Paulo in terms of the development of institutional capacity for environmental protection. While Pará's first environmental department, initially part of the State Secretariat of Health, was established in 1986, its Secretariat of the Environment did not truly begin functioning as an agency until the passage of the state's first environmental law in 1995.

Pará's political and economic profile is much different from that of São Paulo. As explained by a federal environmental prosecutor in Pará, "São Paulo is an industrialized country—with major problems being those of industrial pollution, urbanization, etc. Pará is a frontier state—with major problems of deforestation and a model of development predicated on large infrastructure projects and extractive industry" (personal interview, 2000). Governmental institutions in Pará are generally weak, struggling to cover the state's expansive and sparsely populated territory. Indicative of this weakness, federal environmental agency officials estimated in 2000 that over 80 percent of logging in the state was done illegally.[39]

The 1987 ABEMA survey cited above provided stark evidence of the unequal development of institutional structure for environmental protection among Brazilian states. In addition to showing that environmental protection capacity had advanced principally in the most economically developed and industrialized states of São Paulo and Rio de Janeiro, the study found that three states did not have an environmental agency, four states had agencies with no more than 10 staff members, and three agencies did not have any motor vehicles.[40]

While not among the states lacking institutional capacity in the late 1980s, Pará had a very weak administrative framework for environmental protection. In 1987, the environment department of the Secretariat of Health was responsible for environmental protection and had a total of 20 staff members (Dourado 1993: 123). This number grew to 158 by 1991, spurred by the passage of a new state constitution in October 1989 that, like the 1988 Federal Constitution of the previous year, gave priority treatment to environmental problems and expanded governmental responsibilities in environmental protection. The 158 employees were distributed among the director's office, an information technology office, and six divisions: project analysis, special studies, the laboratory, environmental toxicology, environmental enforcement, and environmental education (ibid.: 124).

In 1988, the state of Pará created a new division, the State Secretariat of Science, Technology and the Environment (Secretaria de Estado de Ciência, Tecnologia e Meio Ambiente; SECTAM), although its institutional structure was defined only in 1993.[41] Moreover, according to internal SECTAM documents, the agency was relatively inactive in permitting and enforcement until 1995, when the State Environmental Code was passed.[42] The code marked an important advance in Pará's legal protection for the environment.[43] The law sets forth the framework for environmental policy in the state, including its institutional organization, areas of activity (such as water pollution, mining, and land use), and legal and policy instruments (such as public participation, permitting, inspections, and sanctions for noncompliance). It also established the State Environmental Council (Conselho Estadual do Meio Ambiente; COEMA).

Owing to the weakness of the state environmental agency SECTAM, the federal environmental agency plays a much larger role in Pará than it does in São Paulo. Most significantly, IBAMA's state office in Pará (IBAMA/PA) is responsible for implementing and enforcing forestry laws in the state.[44] In 2001, IBAMA/PA had 320 employees in Pará—140 employees in Belém and 180 scattered through the rest of the state—compared to only 255 at SECTAM.[45] At the same time, IBAMA/PA staffed a state headquarters in the capital Belém, sixteen field enforcement offices, and eight federal protected areas in the state. In comparison, SECTAM has only its headquarters in Belém, with no permanent presence outside the capital. In terms of enforcement personnel, IBAMA/PA's enforcement division had 70 inspectors while SECTAM's had only 18.[46]

While IBAMA's presence in Pará remained significant, a trend toward the transfer of regulatory authority from the federal to the state government was apparent after 1990. An internal report of SECTAM explains that before 1995, "Large and small environmental problems were almost all treated as a subject of discussion exclusive to environmentalists and representatives of the federal government, especially IBAMA. The state government was able to participate only in a few rare cases, and always in a merely supporting role."[47] In the latter half of the 1990s, the state became more present in environmental policy as state environmental permitting programs and other environmental management activities were expanded. In the early 2000s, the Pará state government sought to upgrade its legal and institutional framework to enable the state environmental agency to assume responsibility for environmental permitting in the forestry sector.[48]

Environmental Agencies in Crisis

Environmental agencies in Brazil experienced crisis in the 1990s.[49] They suffered a trend of institutional decline, as in the case of CETESB of São Paulo and the federal agency IBAMA, or remained too weak to be effective, as in the case of SECTAM of Pará. Decline and weakness are evident through an examination of agency staffing levels, budgets, and salaries as well as in the attitudes of agency personnel. In addition, environmental agencies throughout Brazil suffered from political interference and corruption. Many concerned with environmental problems viewed agencies as lacking the degree of independence from the executive branch necessary to enforce environmental laws, particularly when enforcement would negatively affect an activity or project favored by the executive branch.

Agencies in Decline

In the 1980s, environmental agencies in São Paulo and several other southern states grew in size and capacity. The pollution problems of large cities and industrial areas such as Cubatão, and the attention they drew both nationally and internationally, made environmental protection a political priority. The environmental agencies of São Paulo, particularly CETESB, came to be considered "model agencies" for Brazil and for poor countries generally.

In the 1990s, the political winds shifted. Environmental agencies experienced significant resource shortages as the Brazilian government cut budgets and froze hiring in line with a series of fiscal reform measures (Hochstetler 2002b: 83). An agenda of state reform prevailed, and environmental agencies decreased in terms of both size and political importance. Many CETESB officials expressed their view that CETESB was not what it had been—resource shortages, reduced salaries, loss of expertise, and the absence of new hires weakened the agency. Increasingly, there was a tangible sense among employees that the "glory days" of CETESB were over.

The budget cuts experienced by environmental agencies in São Paulo and other Brazilian states were part of the larger "fiscal crisis" of Brazil. In 1994, the "Real Plan" (named after the new currency) was instituted to stabilize the currency after a period of high inflation. The plan was linked to fiscal reforms, particularly the elimination of deficit spending at all levels of government (Bresser Pereira 1996: 198). The federal government required states to reduce their expenditures and balance their budgets, leading to budget cuts for a wide range of state agencies. An International Monetary Fund "rescue package" in 1997 of $41 billion further obligated the Brazilian government to cut spending (see Albuquerque 2000; Montanye and Welch 1999: 13).

The result of these economic policies was a broad program of state reform with a variety of impacts on the public sector at both the state and federal levels. Maglio (2000: 45) explains that these reform measures had negative consequences for environmental agencies in Brazil. As he concludes, "The state environmental systems were not strengthened in the 1990s and their financial situations worsened. Projects seeking to strengthen institutions came up against the deficiencies and the personnel losses in the state and federal public sectors. State reform is being carried out without a new proposal for environmental regulation" (Maglio 2000).

CETESB typifies the experience of environmental agencies in several Brazilian states, particularly those that developed significant institutional frameworks in the 1980s. After reaching a peak of over three thousand employees in 1992, the number of employees declined through the rest of the decade.[50] Between 1992 and 2001, CETESB lost more than a third of its employees. 80 percent of those who left did so in the three years between 1994 and 1997, and many of them were the most highly paid and qualified professionals in the agency (ibid.: 114). Not including CETESB employees, the State Secretariat of the Environment (SMA) lost a similar percentage of its personnel in the same period, with a staff reduction of 35 percent between 1994 and 2000.[51]

One strategy used by CETESB to replace lost employees was to increase the use of interns. The number of interns almost quadrupled from 101 to 389 between 1993 and 2001.[52] This is considered problematic by many permanent employees, as interns are inexperienced and stay at the agency for only one or two years. One employee remarked that CETESB has turned into an "agency of interns" (personal interview, 2002).

The budgets of CETESB and SMA tended to fall in the second half of the 1990s.[53] CETESB budget data show that the resources it received from the state treasury declined by almost a third (31.5 percent) between 1995 and 2000.[54] In these years, CETESB was able to supplement its budget with revenues from fines collected in a newly instituted vehicle emissions control program. By the year 2000, however, these revenues began to fall off as most vehicles in the state had come into compliance with regulations.[55] The proportion of the state's budget that went to the SMA also declined notably. Between 1992 and 1995, the SMA received an average of 0.69 percent of the state budget. Between 1996 and 2001, this figure averaged 0.53 percent.[56]

Reduced salaries are a further indication of crisis in the state environmental agencies. The average salary at CETESB in 2002 was R$2,300/month (US$814), with a range between an average of R$830/month (US$294) for maintenance personnel and R$4,830/month ($1,710) for agency directors.[57] While historical salary data were not available, CETESB employees frequently complained that their real salaries had decreased significantly since the mid-1990s because of the lack of cost of living adjustments (personal interview, 2002). Most opportunities and funding for foreign study and training also dried up in the 1990s. Moreover, CETESB pensions are considered inadequate at a maximum of ten times the national minimum wage, equaling less than half the salary that an experienced CETESB employee might receive while working. One CETESB manager explained that over half of current CETESB employees were actually retired but continued to work in order to draw their pension as well as their normal salary (personal interview, 2002).

CETESB's budgetary problems led to a notable decline in employee morale. As explained by an inspector: "[CETESB must] clarify priorities and design programs to solve priority problems. It is losing credibility the longer it fails to do this. It is also losing technical capacity, its main source of credibility. People don't feel motivated or inspired to work. We are lacking goals, leadership, resources, training, rewards, and new people" (personal interview, 2002). The managers of field offices complain that they are unable to choose their staffs and their staffs are deficient in terms of both productivity and skill. One field office manager stated that if he could fire and hire freely, he would replace his eight current inspectors with five new, motivated inspectors (personal interview, 2001). When asked about his staff, another field office manager confirmed that the problem was quality rather than quantity and explained that without retraining and other incentives, inspectors lack both the motivation and the ability to recognize and deal with new environmental problems that are arising (personal interview, 2002).

The environmental agencies of other southeastern and southern states such as Rio de Janeiro, Rio Grande do Sul, and Minas Gerais experienced similar declines in the 1990s.[58] A 1996 World Bank study of environmental management in Rio de Janeiro found that over the previous eight years, FEEMA, the state pollution control agency, "underwent drastic decline caused by poor political support, very limited budgets, and weak strategic direction" and was "currently paralyzed by an excessive number of poorly paid and unmotivated staff and serious budget rigidities" (World Bank 1996a: 6). The study described a "cycle of decline" in which budget cuts lead to reduced levels of enforcement activity and loss of agency credibility, which lead in turn to more budget cuts. Real average monthly salaries for professional staff of FEEMA eroded from the equivalent of nearly US$2,500 in 1990 to US$900 in 1996, levels that were not competitive with salaries in the private sector, state enterprises, or even other government agencies (ibid.: 27). Moreover, given budget cuts, funds for needed items such as routine laboratory analyses and inspection vehicle maintenance were often not available.

In the southern state of Rio Grande do Sul, an incentive plan offered to environmental agency employees in the 1990s induced over 30 percent of agency scientists and engineers to leave. Worsening the loss, the most qualified employees most often took advantage of the plan and sought employment in the private sector (Cappelli 2000: 55). Conducting research on three Brazilian states—São Paulo, Minas Gerais, and Sergipe—Maglio (2000) found that in the 1990s, state environmental agencies generally suffered budget losses and became increasingly structurally deficient in terms of technical resources and salary levels. He also finds that they lacked strategic planning, reducing their social importance and ability to influence public policies.

In a 1998 publication, the World Bank determined that the decline of environmental agencies was a general trend in Brazilian states. "Civil service rigidities and budget cuts have led to the deterioration of working conditions and erosion of capacity in environmental agencies of several states. Many agencies lack the skills, incentives, and budgets necessary for systematic collection of ambient environmental data and the speedy processing of license applications. Most agencies lack the political backing for effective enforcement" (World Bank 1998: 19).

Environmental agency decline was not limited to the states, but also occurred at the federal level. At its creation in 1989, IBAMA had a staff of 6,230. Over 90 percent of the new IBAMA employees came from the Forestry Institute (57 percent) and the Fishing Institute (34 percent). Six percent came from the predecessor environmental secretariat (SEMA), and the remaining 3 percent came from the Rubber Institute. IBAMA's workforce reached a peak of 6,544 in 1991 and then slowly declined to 5,266 by the year 2000.

While the four federal agencies that were unified to create IBAMA were all natural resource related, they had different institutional cultures that were difficult to meld. Fewer than three hundred of the new IBAMA employees had direct experience with environmental problems.[59] In its early years, IBAMA also experienced administrative instabilities and changes in agency leadership (twelve leaders, with very different styles, in its first eight years); unresolved tensions from the lack of clear institutional boundaries regarding the role of each level of government in environmental management; and the fiscal crisis affecting public administration generally.[60] As explained by Fernandes (1996: 280),

"IBAMA inherited the problems of the several organizations that it replaced, and, despite its large structure, it has been ineffective and chronically under-funded, as well as understaffed, considering the reach of its jurisdiction and the nature of the problems it has to confront."

An audit of IBAMA conducted by the Federal Court of Accounts (Tribunal de Contas da União; TCU)[61] in the late 1990s found significant weaknesses in the issuance and collection of administrative penalties. The audit showed that IBAMA collected only 14 percent of the administrative fines and permitting fees that it was owed in 1988 and 1999.[62] The TCU observed that errors were made in 80 percent of the citations; deficiencies were found in the information systems used in fine collection; and delays in the agency's consideration of appeals averaged 136 days for review of an appeal in eleven Brazilian states. The collection of administrative fines did not improve thereafter: from 2001 to 2004, only 11.5 percent of administrative fines issued in the Amazonian region were collected.[63]

In 2002, IBAMA was granted a long-awaited authorization to hire a group of six hundred new permanent employees. An IBAMA statement announcing the job openings explained that even after adding these new employees to the existing staff, the institution would still have a personnel deficit.[64] It cited an internal study from 1991 showing that the agency required twelve thousand employees to adequately fulfill its responsibilities. Highlighting the deficit in enforcement, the announcement revealed that IBAMA had only one enforcement official for every 11,000 square kilometers in the Amazon (an area about four times the size of the U.S. state of Rhode Island) and one official for every 6,000 square kilometers in other parts of the country.[65] Importantly, the 2002 round of hiring represented a moment of institutional renewal and growth for IBAMA. As explained in the announcement, the hiring was part of a restructuring of IBAMA aimed at "modernizing, updating information technology, increasing institutional agility, and improving the agency's services to society."[66]

Agencies that Lack Capacity

Pará's environmental agency SECTAM did not suffer decline in the 1990s, but rather it simply remained weak. The number of state employees in Pará dealing with environmental compliance and enforcement remained roughly the same from 1991 to 2002. In 1991, Para's environmental agency had a staff of 158. Of them, 123 worked in the agency's six technical divisions: project analysis (responsible for issuing environmental permits), special studies, the laboratory, environmental toxicology, environmental enforcement, and environmental education (Dourado 1993: 124).

In 2002, SECTAM had a total of 255 employees in offices related to the environmental protection activities of the agency.[67] Of these, however, fewer than half (117) worked in the Environmental Directorate offices that corresponded to the six divisions in which 123 employees worked in 1991. The remainder worked in areas such as the library, communications department, remote sensing lab, and international cooperation office, constituting a much larger and more developed support structure. Between 1991 and 2002, the number of staff in environmental enforcement increased from 8 to 17, and the number of staff in project analysis declined from 56 to 38.[68] Overall, while the number of enforcement officials doubled, staffing levels remained very low in areas critical to implementation and enforcement.

In the "critical evaluation" section of an internal report covering the years 1995 to 2001, SECTAM cites its weaknesses in environmental protection (State of Pará/SECTAM 2002). These weaknesses included the small number of technical employees to conduct routine and external project activities; the inadequacy of the organizational structure for the operational demands of SECTAM; low salaries implying the loss of qualified personnel to the private sector; the need for regulations that implement the laws and instruments of environmental management; the lack of equipment to develop environmental protection activities; and the lack of indicators that allow results to be measured.

SECTAM's staff was less than one-tenth the size of the São Paulo SMA, while the state of Pará is five times as large as São Paulo. Moreover, SECTAM had only a single office in the capital city from which to administer its activities throughout the state. As a result, there were large areas in which the state agency, and the state government more generally, were essentially absent. The size of the state and the difficulty of access to many areas are often cited as reasons for the environmental agency's inability to protect the Amazon forest (see Magalhães Lopes 2000: 22). SECTAM itself acknowledges the problem: "As the second-largest Brazilian state, Pará occupies almost 15 percent of the national territory. The challenge of administering it presents itself, therefore, in the same proportions as its territorial extension" (State of Pará/SECTAM 1999).[69]

Since its inception, SECTAM has advocated for environmental protection responsibility to be decentralized to municipalities rather than building a sufficient structure at the state level. Its internal reports highlight "decentralization of environmental management" as one of the fundamental pillars of state environmental policy. "Of particular importance . . . is the Program for the Decentralization of Environmental Management which has the objective of equipping municipalities to execute environmental management in their jurisdictions, with the goal of sharing environmental control activities in the extensive territory of the state" (ibid.). A 2002 internal report cites progress made toward decentralization, including fourteen planning workshops in municipalities, technical-financial cooperation agreements with twelve municipalities, and decentralized implementation agreements with three municipalities.[70] Despite the progress, however, the report includes among SECTAM's weaknesses "the absence of an effective policy to expand the process of decentralization of environmental management to the municipalities" (State of Pará/SECTAM 2002).

Decentralization of environmental management to the municipalities, a principle embraced in the 1988 Constitution and other environmental legislation, has been difficult to achieve throughout Brazil. Even in states of southern and southeastern Brazil, the development of institutional capacity at the municipal level has been slow and inconsistent.[71] In Pará, the task can be expected to be even more difficult given the weakness of municipal governments generally. Indeed, some municipal governments in the state are led or supported by local residents heavily involved in illegal natural resource extraction.[72]

The deficiencies of SECTAM are in part compensated by the presence and involvement of IBAMA in the state. As mentioned earlier, IBAMA/PA remained responsible for permitting and monitoring logging activities. It is IBAMA's second-largest state delegation in the country, with 320 employees and, in 2002, about seventy-five forestry inspectors and sixteen regional enforcement offices. Yet IBAMA's difficulties in the 1990s had repercussions in Pará. One IBAMA employee estimated that in the 1980s about seven hundred federal employees in Pará worked in the agencies that were later merged to form IBAMA, mostly from the Brazilian Institute of Forestry Development (IBDF). Both the number of staff and the resources available to maintain agency infrastructure and equipment declined in the 1990s (personal interview, 2002).

The weakness of environmental institutions in Pará is not unique to Pará but rather characteristic of states in the Amazonian north and other poor regions of the country. A study conducted in the early 1990s compared environmental staff and vehicles per hectare of land area in the seven Amazonian states.[73] In all the Amazonian states, there was under one employee per 100,000 hectares. Pará and the neighboring state of Tocantins had the worst proportions at almost 800,000 hectares per employee.[74] A 1992 evaluation of Brazilian environmental agencies documented particular weakness in the northern, northeastern, and central western states of Brazil. In these regions, agencies tended to be severely understaffed, offered poor salaries, and lacked capacity in environmental permitting and monitoring compliance with permits (State of São Paulo/SMA 1992a).

Corruption and Political Interference

Corruption and interference by political actors outside the agency are often cited as problems in Brazilian environmental agencies in addition to deficiencies in budgets and staffs (see Hochstetler 2002b; Sadek and Cavalcanti 2003). Unfortunately, the levels and effects of political interference and corruption are very hard to measure. These levels may be relatively minor, with a small effect on regulatory outcomes, or they may be very prevalent and serious. Moreover, while corruption is universally denounced, opinions differ regarding how much political interference is appropriate and desirable in a democratic system. Those most concerned with the democratic legitimacy of an environmental agency may view the influence of outside political actors on agency decisions as appropriate and necessary to ensure democratic control of the agency. Those favoring an environmental agency that makes decisions based primarily or exclusively on technical criteria rather than political criteria may view such influence as inappropriate and even illegitimate.

Corruption occurs when public assets are illegally transferred into private hands (Pérez-Perdomo 1995). It assumes a wide variety of forms and may occur at any level of government, from traffic cops up to the president (see Tulchin and Espach 2000). A public official may receive a bribe for performing a legal duty speedily or for not performing it at all (Rosenn 1971: 515–16). Public funds may be misused, stolen, or misappropriated in a way that results in private enrichment (Fleisher 2002: 14). A public official may sell government property for personal gain, or he may receive a kickback from a contractor as part of the procurement process. Alternatively, a public official may make a biased decision for which he receives a generous contribution for his next political campaign (ibid.). Such behaviors are often deeply rooted in political and social culture, and the exact parameters of what should be identified as corruption varies with the peculiarities of specific countries and regions (Tulchin and Espach 2000: 4).

Corruption in Brazilian environmental agencies is often suspected and complained of, but seldom studied and written about.[75] One of the most comprehensive studies of Brazilian environmental enforcement refers to it only obliquely: "a potential reason for the low efficacy of environmental law enforcement is corruption, involving acts ranging from issuing permits that make illegal logging operations appear legal to perpetrating a fraud that lets violators escape punishment" (Brito and Barreto 2006: 38). In their study of Brazilian environmental policy, Hochstetler and Keck (2007: 151) conceptualize corruption as part of a larger "politics of state absence" in the Amazon. Criminal networks and political networks became intertwined as members of criminal networks co-opted public officials or ran for office themselves, and public officials became active in criminal networks (Hochstetler and Keck 2007: 153).

Stories of corruption among high-level officials in IBAMA began emerging in the late 1990s.[76] In 2003, IBAMA began to seriously attack corruption in its own ranks. Whereas only 10 IBAMA employees were fired for corruption between 1989 and 2002, between 2003 and 2006 around 90 were fired and 300 others were subject to disciplinary actions.[77] Most of these employees were caught through sting operations that IBAMA undertook in cooperation with the Federal Police and the Federal Ministério Público.[78] More than fifteen large operations conducted from 2004 through 2007 aimed at cracking down on environmental crimes, particularly in the forestry sector.[79] In a typical operation, after months of investigations, a team of police and agency inspectors acquired *mandados de busca e apreensão* (search warrants) and *mandados de prisão* (arrest warrants) prior to executing the operation.[80] In total, the operations resulted in the arrests of over 500 people for environmental crimes, among them 116 IBAMA employees.[81] In addition, IBAMA closed 1,500 illegal sawmills and issued over R$2.8 billion in fines.[82]

While corruption in environmental agencies is more commonly complained about in Amazonian states, it also occurs in southern Brazil. Conducted in 2005, Operation Euterpe was reportedly the largest police operation targeting environmental crime outside the Amazon. It focused on illegal resource extraction and permitting of new construction in protected areas in the state of Rio de Janeiro. Of the 32 people arrested, 24 were IBAMA employees, constituting over a quarter of all IBAMA employees in Rio de Janeiro.[83] One São Paulo prosecutor described another arrangement in which the director of the São Paulo state environmental agency maintained a consulting firm on the side whose clients received special treatment in their permit applications (personal interview, 2000).

Environmental agencies in Brazil are also susceptible to interference by outside political actors. As a general rule, Brazilian environmental agencies tend to be among the least powerful agencies in the government. They have difficulty defending policies and administrative actions that run contrary to the priorities of political leaders and other governmental agencies. As stated by one commentator on environmental governance in São Paulo, "In the context of the state governmental structure, environmental agencies have a marginal position, lacking the power sufficient to implement decisive actions . . . we can conclude that environmental issues have little ability to influence government policies, occupying a secondary, limited and subordinated place" (Ferreira 1998: 122). In this context, political leaders outside the agency have ample opportunity to influence the decisions and activities of environmental agency officials.

A measure of the extent to which an agency may be politically influenced is the number of high-level agency positions that the executive fills through an appointment process. Political appointments are referred to as *cargos de confiança* (positions of confidence) or *cargos comissionados* (commissioned positions) and may be held by either permanent agency employees or those without prior agency affiliation with the agency. While a certain number of political appointments may be viewed as necessary in terms of democratic accountability, critics argue that appointments are too numerous and are given as political rewards to unqualified people. Studies have documented that the Brazilian president has the power to fill many more positions through political appointment than his counterparts in the United States or Japan (Hochstetler and Keck 2007: 25–26).

Of employees on CETESB's staff, about 17 percent hold commissioned positions either in CETESB or in the State Secretariat of the Environment.[84] Based on year 2000 data, their salaries were, on average, over twice the average agency salary.[85] Given these salary differentials, employees holding commissioned positions are likely to be anxious to protect their positions. They are likely to fear demotion if they aggressively enforce environmental laws in projects that have the backing of political leaders. As an example, an environmental prosecutor cited a 1990s case involving a new auto assembly plant that the state governor had promoted as key for the state's economic development. State environmental agencies failed to require an environmental impact study even though federal environmental law pointed to the need for such a study. In this case, political influence seemed to make the top agency officials unwilling to enforce the law in a way that would create obstacles to the governor's plans.

In addition, the large percentage of commissioned positions leads to a high degree of internal change and disruption when a new government is elected or a new Secretary of the Environment is appointed.[86] As stated in a 1992 analysis of environmental institutions in São Paulo, "One of the banes of the environmental protection establishment is the almost total turnover in management, policies and guidelines that occurs every time there is a change in government" (State of São Paulo/SMA 1992b: 77). Many CETESB employees complain that the continual turnovers have led to a lack of sustained priorities within the agency. Indeed, reducing the usage of commissioned positions in state agencies was one of the formal objectives of the state reform in the mid-1990s. Personnel cuts were justified, in part, on the basis that elected officials used appointed positions as political rewards (Maglio 2000: 114). Maglio explains, however, that while the "so-called reengineering" severely reduced the number of well-qualified, highly paid technical staff in CETESB, it "failed to achieve its formal objective—the elimination of the use of public sector jobs for political ends."

In states such as Pará, the problems affecting agency personnel are even more fundamental. Due to fiscal crisis in the years of its creation and consolidation, SECTAM was never authorized to hold a competitive civil service exam to fill the new positions. Rather, employees came from other government agencies or were hired through other mechanisms such as short-term contracts. For this reason, most SECTAM employees do not have the job security associated with a typical public sector job. Of the 117 employees who worked in the Environmental Directorate in 2002, only 46 (39 percent) were permanent SECTAM employees with full job security.[87] The majority of employees, even many who have been with the agency since its inception, worked on a temporary or contract basis.[88] This situation is common in states where environmental agencies were created in the 1990s and staffed with personnel from preexisting governmental agencies (ibid.: 46). As a result, many agency employees are in precarious positions that may be easily changed or eliminated. Such employees are presumably more susceptible to inappropriate political influences.

Measuring Administrative Enforcement

Environmental agencies in Brazil conduct three primary activities in the enforcement of environmental laws. They issue environmental permits; they perform inspections; and they impose administrative penalties for noncompliance. This section describes and analyzes the environmental enforcement activities of two state environmental agencies, CETESB in São Paulo and SECTAM in Pará, as well as the IBAMA office in Pará (IBAMA/PA). It shows that in the 1990s, CETESB devolved into a pattern of "negotiated noncompliance," in which persistent violations of permit requirements were tolerated. In Pará, SECTAM's administrative enforcement was almost nonexistent. After an explanation of the instruments used by environmental agencies, enforcement data from the environmental agencies are presented. The data are analyzed with the goal of understanding changes that occurred in the effectiveness of environmental enforcement in the 1990s in each state.

Permits, Inspections, and Sanctions

This section describes the three primary instruments of administrative enforcement in Brazil: permitting, inspections, and sanctions. Environmental permitting, the preventative facet of environmental enforcement, is perhaps the most important tool of Brazilian environmental agencies. While permitting differs somewhat among states, a general model is followed throughout the country that includes the usage of three types of environmental permits: *licença prévia* (preliminary permit), *licença de instalação* (installation permit), and *licença de operação* (operating permit).[89]

The installation and operating permits were first instituted in São Paulo as part of the state's environmental permitting system that began with CETESB's law in 1976.[90] According to this law, installation permits are required for subdivisions; the construction, reconstruction, or remodeling of a building containing a source of pollution; the installation of a source of pollution in an existing building; and the enlargement or alteration of a source of pollution (article 58). The installation permit should be requested and acquired by the developer of the project before the installation of the new pollution source. It sets forth the conditions that the project developer must meet to comply with the law and thus obtain the operating permit. The operating permit, in turn, should be acquired before the activity begins to function. As stated in the law, "The operating permit will not be issued where all the conditions set forth in the installation permit have not been met, or where there is indication or evidence of the emission of pollutants into the water, air, or soil" (article 65).

The preliminary permit came into use in the 1980s with the National Environmental Policy Act of 1981 and subsequent CONAMA resolutions that made the environmental impact study a legal requirement for certain types of projects. A 1986 CONAMA resolution determined that environmental impact studies would be required for about 15 specific types of projects, including oil and gas pipelines; energy transmission lines carrying more than 230 kilovolts; fossil fuel and mineral extraction; landfills; electricity generation plants of more than 10 megawatts; and industrial districts.[91] The 1988 Constitution declared that a permit shall be required for "projects or activities potentially causing significant environmental degradation."[92] A 1997 CONAMA resolution provided a longer and more detailed list of such activities, including activities of mining, industry, infrastructure building, agriculture, and natural resource use.[93]

In São Paulo, the responsibility for environmental permitting is shared by CETESB and the SMA's Department of Environmental Impact Evaluation (Departamento de Avaliação dos Impactos Ambientais; DAIA). When the project is of a type that may cause "significant environmental degradation," as governed by the Constitution and the CONAMA resolutions, the project must first get a preliminary permit from DAIA. In order to acquire this preliminary permit, an environmental impact study or other analytical report is generally required.[94] The project's installation and operating permits are then issued by CETESB or DAIA, depending on the nature of the project. When the project is an industrial activity that may cause water, air, or soil pollution, the installation and operating permits are acquired from CETESB. When the activity does not involve industrial pollution, DAIA issues the installation and operating permits. In Pará, SECTAM is responsible for issuing the preliminary permit as well as the installation and operating permits.

A second enforcement activity performed by environmental agencies is conducting inspections. Inspections are usually conducted in response to a public complaint, to gather information for the issuance of an environmental permit, or as scheduled monitoring of a priority pollution source. CETESB is one of the few environmental agencies in Brazil that has the resources to conduct routine inspections outside of those made necessary by public complaints. A 1996 World Bank report focusing on the management of environmental pollution in the state of Rio de Janeiro found that "most inspections and enforcement actions in the state of Rio are driven by complaints—if they are undertaken at all—or follow requests by the judicial branch to which FEEMA must respond" (World Bank 1996b: 91). In CETESB's Cubatão field office, where minimal new permitting takes place, three out of four inspections are scheduled enforcement inspections rather than inspections made in response to public complaints. In a CETESB field office located in the São Paulo metropolitan area, half of all inspections are made for the processing of environmental permits, and most others are made in response to complaints. Only one of every eight inspections is part of a scheduled monitoring program of priority pollution sources.[95] Pará's SECTAM exemplifies the plight of many environmental agencies in Brazil. With only 17 enforcement officials, SECTAM makes inspections only in response to public complaints.

The third primary enforcement activity performed by environmental agencies in Brazil is the imposition of penalties for noncompliance. Administrative sanctions include warnings, fines, and facility closures. The issuance of warnings and fines is similar across Brazilian states. Upon discovering a violation of the law, the inspector usually issues a warning. If a follow-up inspection shows that the situation is not corrected, the inspector then issues a fine. The inspector continues to monitor the situation, imposing up to three fines of increasing severity. If the situation remains uncorrected, the inspector may then issue a daily fine. If the warning and fines are unsuccessful in changing the offending activity, the agency may take action to close down the activity.

In the case of São Paulo, warning and fines are directly imposed by the inspectors. Closures require the approval of the Secretariat of the Environment. In the case of a proposed closure, CETESB presents the evidence to the state secretary of the Environment, who then chooses whether or not to order a closure of the activity. If the Secretary authorizes the closure, CETESB officials accompanied by police construct physical barriers such as chaining the gates of a factory or blocking a driveway to prevent the activity from continuing. SECTAM inspectors may issue a warning but they do not have the authority to issue a fine. Rather, they must recommend the issuance of a fine to the director of the Environmental Division, who then must recommend it to the Secretary of SECTAM, who may then issue the fine.

Enforcement by CETESB

The record of enforcement at CETESB is mixed. While the enforcement division lost personnel in the 1990s, it did not suffer as great a loss as the rest of the agency. Moreover, the number of permits, inspections, and warnings tended to increase over the decade, while the number of fines stayed roughly the same. This section shows that while the data do not reveal a marked decrease in enforcement capacity or activity in the 1990s, the agency allowed a high degree of noncompliance in its permitting requirements and suffered weaknesses in its sanctioning powers.

In the 1990s, CETESB's enforcement section, the pollution control division, lost personnel, albeit at a lower rate than the environmental agency as a whole.

Whereas the agency lost about 36 percent of its employees from its 1992 peak to 2001, the pollution control division lost only about 20 percent.[96] To reduce the pollution control division's losses, employees from other parts of CETESB were brought into the division and trained as inspectors. This opportunity was enticing to employees in other parts of the agency because inspectors receive a 30 percent increment in their salaries as a benefit for encountering hazardous conditions on the job. Notably, CETESB also managed to increase the number of local enforcement offices in the state in the 1990s. In the early 1990s, CETESB had nine enforcement offices in the São Paulo metropolitan region and twenty-two in the rest of the state. By 2000, three more had been added outside the metropolitan area, for a total of thirty-four enforcement offices throughout the state.

Table 2.1 shows the number of installation and operating permits issued by CETESB from 1990 to 2003.[97] The number of permits issued by CETESB increased significantly in the late 1990s, particularly after 1998. While the increases in the number of permits issued each year might be interpreted as evidence of an increasingly active and effective environmental agency, the trend is more accurately interpreted as a reflection of the earlier failures in the agency's permitting system. Indeed, there seems to have been a widespread practice of "negotiated noncompliance" in which companies were allowed to continue operating without the necessary permits (Gunningham 1987).

Although CETESB's law required that all pollution sources hold an operating permit in order to function, many were functioning without one at the time the 1998 Environmental Crimes Law was passed.[98] Often, such facilities had applied for and received an installation permit, but had not fulfilled the requirements imposed by the agency to receive their operating permit. As explained by one former agency official, "Many companies had been functioning illegally [without the required permit] for ten or fifteen years. The agency kept imposing small fines and extensions, and it didn't change anything." As stated by another agency official, "if the guy didn't comply with the requirements of his installation permit, we gave him more time to comply, and sometimes that time period ended, and he still had not complied. So we would fine him and give him more time. And when he didn't pay again, we would fine him and give him more time. And this happened over and over. With some companies, this continued for sixteen or seventeen years."

With the passage of the Environmental Crimes Law, the absence of a required permit was transformed from an administrative infraction to a criminal violation. Moreover, under the 1998 law, environmental agencies and their directors could be held jointly liable for the criminal violation.[99] In the years following the passage of the law, the number of permits issued by CETESB rose markedly (see Figure 2.1). Between 1990 and 1997, the number of permits issued per year remained relatively flat with an average of about 6,700. In 1998, the number of permits issued rose to 9,682, a greater than 30 percent rise over the number of permits issued in 1997. In 1999, the number of permits issued (15,147) was more than double the number issued in 1997 (7,387), and the number of permits issued remained high from 2000 through 2003, exceeding 16,000 per year.

Table 2.1 Environmental Permits Issued by CETESB, 1990–2003

Type of Permit	1990	1991	1992	1993	1994	1995	1996
Installation	3,688	3,747	3,418	3,215	3,180	3,548	3,821
Operating	2,766	2,823	3,077	3,067	2,938	3,267	3,577
TOTAL	6,454	6,570	6,495	6,282	6,118	6,815	7,398

Type of Permit	1997	1998	1999	2000	2001	2002	2003
Installation	3,763	5,457	7,722	8,043	8,034	7,976	7,523
Operating	3,624	4,225	7,425	8,199	8,432	8,826	8,497
TOTAL	7,387	9,682	15,147	16,242	16,466	16,802	16,020

SOURCE: "SIPOL Total Documents per Year," March 2007, pers. comm., CETESB Pollution Control Division.

Figure 2.1 Environmental Permits Issued by CETESB, 1990–2003

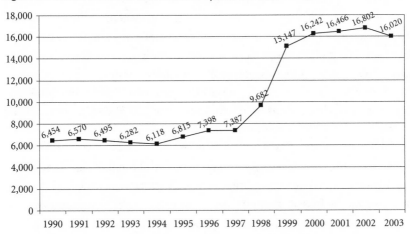

SOURCE: "SIPOL Total Documents per Year," March 2007, pers. comm., CETESB Pollution Control Division.

CETESB officials acknowledge that the Environmental Crimes Law changed a culture of leniency that had developed over time. As stated by one, "CETESB created a culture of letting the violator get away with not having all the necessary permits. We would talk to him, pressure him, inspect him, fine him—but we wouldn't recommend closure quickly. . . . This had become the norm" (personal interview, 2002). Another states, "I think the law was very important for the environmental agency, for CETESB. It changed the way things worked—it became clear that a company would not continue getting time extensions indefinitely" (personal interview, 2001). In other words, the 1998 law helped to end the prevailing practice of negotiated noncompliance.

The number of CETESB inspections tended to increase between 1990 and 2003, from about 37,000 to 47,000 per year (see Table 2.2).[100] Most notably, between 1997 and 1998, the number of inspections jumped over 15 percent from under 41,000 to over 47,000 per year. This increase is linked to the increase in the number of permits issued in 1998 and thereafter, as inspections are often required by CETESB for final permit approval. Given that CETESB receives on average about 18,000 public complaints per year, it is likely that about a third to half of CETESB inspections in these years were conducted to follow up on a complaint.[101] In 2001, each of CETESB's 470 inspectors conducted about one hundred inspections per year, or about two per week (personal interview, 2002).

The annual numbers of CETESB warnings and fines were roughly constant in the 1990s, with the exception of an upsurge in the number of fines during the years of 1993 to 1995 (see Table 2.2 and Figure 2.2).[102] Data on the number of facility closures, available from 1995 to 2001, show that there were on average fourteen closures imposed by the agency per year. As evidenced by the low number, facility closure is rarely used in administrative enforcement. In the years 2001 to 2003, the data evidence a significant increase in the annual number of warnings, with a less significant increase in the annual number of fines.

A comparison of the number of warnings and fines with the number of permits issued and inspections conducted shows that CETESB reduced its reliance on sanctions over the course of the 1990s (see Table 2.2). Even as more facilities entered the permitting system and more inspections were conducted in the 1990s, the number of warnings and fines remained about the same. In 1990, one warning was issued for every 8.4 inspections, and one fine was issued for every 15.6 inspections. In 1999, one warning was issued for every 10.6 inspections, and one fine was issued for every 22.5 inspections.

Table 2.2 Inspections, Warnings, Fines, and Closures by CETESB, with Ratios of Inspections to Warnings and Fines, 1990–2003

Year	Inspections	Warnings	Inspections/ Warnings Ratio	Fines	Inspections/ Fines Ratio	Closures
1990	37,370	4,448	8.4	2,389	15.6	n/a
1991	35,724	4,744	7.5	2,062	17.3	n/a
1992	36,641	4,230	8.7	2,590	14.1	n/a
1993	43,842	4,960	8.8	4,312	10.2	n/a
1994	41,162	3,854	10.7	4,157	9.9	n/a
1995	41,027	4,815	8.5	3,484	11.8	20
1996	40,257	3,895	10.3	2,391	16.8	8
1997	40,690	4,542	9.0	2,169	18.8	9
1998	47,271	5,155	9.2	2,499	18.9	25
1999	49,174	4,646	10.6	2,187	22.5	15
2000	45,653	4,460	10.2	2,089	21.9	2
2001	46,698	5,882	7.9	2,401	19.4	18
2002	48,349	5,801	8.3	2,969	16.3	n/a
2003	46,023	6,207	7.4	2,546	18.1	n/a

SOURCE: 1990–1994 data from "SIPOL Total Documents per Year," pers. comm., CETESB Pollution Control Division (November 2001 and March 2007); 1995–2003 data from "Resumo das Atividades Desenvolvidos," pers. comm., CETESB Pollution Control Division (January 2002 and April 2007).

Figure 2.2 Warnings and Fines Issued by CETESB, 1990–2003

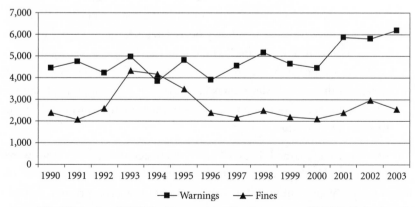

SOURCE: 1990–1994 data from "SIPOL Total Documents per Year," pers. comm., CETESB Pollution Control Division (November 2001 and March 2007); 1995–2003 data from "Resumo das Atividades Desenvolvidos," pers. comm., CETESB Pollution Control Division (January 2002 and April 2007).

The relative decline in the number of sanctions issued by CETESB in the 1990s may have indicated a trend toward weaker enforcement. Inspectors may fail to detect violations or issue sanctions due to lack of knowledge, lack of time, or lack of incentive. Indeed, several CETESB supervisors emphasized the declining quality and motivation of their inspectors. As stated by one, "We have had a large loss of people, a flattening of salaries, and a series of other problems. And unfortunately this causes a certain change in the rhythm of things; people's rhythm gets a little bit slower . . . the attitude is often, well, I'm going to continue, but I'll just do things a little more slowly" (personal interview, 2002). This supervisor also noted the lack of and need for continuing technical training for inspectors. Another supervisor stated, "If I had the power to fire and hire, I would fire eight out of nine of them, hire five new ones, and I would be better off than I am now" (personal interview, 2001). He explained that most of his inspectors were doing the minimum necessary to remain employed until they retire.

Yet, less usage of sanctions does not necessarily indicate weaker enforcement. The need for sanctions may decrease due to greater compliance, greater use of non-sanction-based approaches, or the adoption of more powerful sanctions. The relative decline in sanctions issued by CETESB in the 1990s occurred over the same period that the Ministério Público became more active, perhaps replacing some of the need for CETESB sanctions. Moreover, some CETESB officials point out that companies fear negative publicity so much that they avoid behavior that may result in a fine. As explained by one CETESB official:

> Today, we are in a latter period of environmental enforcement where the game is not just about fines—the industry doesn't want to be fined, not only for the financial burden but for the harm to its image. They fear being publicized for receiving a fine from the environmental agency. So, the fine is a stronger instrument than it was when it was just feared for its financial implications. Now it is not necessary to use the fines as much as we used them in the past. (Personal interview, 2001)

The official also explained that CETESB fines issued in the latter 1990s were more punitive. The high inflation rates of the early 1990s made the value of fines extremely low, but with the stabilization of the new currency in 1994, the values of fines became "reasonable" (personal interview, 2001). Whatever the reason for the decline in the 1990s, it is worth noting that in the 2000s, CETESB's rate of sanctioning generally rose again. In 2003, one warning was issued for every 7.4 inspections, and one fine was issued for every 18.1 inspections.

CETESB's administrative fines were reasonably high by the late 1990s, but they were often never collected. In the 1970s and 1980s, the state's Department of Water and Sewage (Departamento de Aguas e Esgotos; DAE) collected fines on behalf of CETESB.[103] It stopped doing so in the late 1990s, and no alternative arrangement for the collection of fines was established (personal interview, 2002).[104] An official in the CETESB legal department admitted in 2001 that the collection of fines had been in disarray for several years, and that many of the fines were never collected. In addition to the collection problems, fines were often held up in legal challenges for many years. In 2001, CETESB's legal department had a caseload of over 4,400 legal and administrative cases, the large majority of which were filed to contest agency fines or the agency's authority to impose fines (personal interview, 2002).[105] As such, CETESB's lawyers were primarily occupied with defending the agency against legal claims rather than using legal instruments to enforce environmental laws.

While the data on enforcement at CETESB are not complete or conclusive, they do indicate weaknesses. The likelihood of receiving a fine decreased over the course of the 1990s, and the agency's system for collecting fines broke down. And while the permitting system grew markedly in the late 1990s, the question could be raised of whether the agency would have the personnel and resources to ensure actual compliance with permit requirements.

Enforcement by SECTAM

Enforcement data from the Pará state environmental agency, SECTAM, show a generally low level of activity, particularly in issuing warnings and fines. In particular, the data show that while the agency succeeded in expanding its permitting programs in the late 1990s, its enforcement capacity and actions remained very limited.

Table 2.3 shows the number of permits issued by SECTAM in Pará, with a notable increase beginning in 1997. As in São Paulo, the Environmental Crimes Law likely contributed to the increases in the number of permits, but observers also credited SECTAM's institutional consolidation in the mid-1990s.[106] Prior to that, SECTAM was simply not adequately functional to impose a mandatory permitting system.

The data also reveal that SECTAM does not use the installation permit very frequently, but rather appears to directly issue the operating permit. Between

Table 2.3 Environmental Permits Issued by SECTAM, 1986–2001

Type of Permit	1986	1987	1988	1989	1990	1991	1992	1993
Preliminary	2	9	7	179	61	10	n/a	n/a
Installation	1	2	7	6	152	130	n/a	n/a
Operating	0	5	9	15	28	189	n/a	n/a
TOTAL	3	16	23	200	241	329	n/a	n/a

Type of Permit	1994	1995	1996	1997	1998	1999	2000	2001
Preliminary	12	13	16	38	39	91	106	57
Installation	39	29	92	54	107	144	133	252
Operating	123	161	343	960	1,009	1,257	1,258	1,344
TOTAL	174	203	451	1,052	1,155	1,492	1,497	1,653

SOURCE: State of Pará/SECTAM (2002).

1994 and 2001, a total of 6,455 operating permits were issued, compared to only 850 installation permits. As the operating permit is generally only issued after project-specific conditions set forth in the installation permit have been complied with, the lack of usage of the installation permit may signal that the Pará environmental agency imposes few such conditions for the acquisition of the operating permit and/or does not verify that such conditions are met before issuing the operating permit.[107]

The number of inspections conducted by SECTAM tended to increase between 1994 and 2001, but it still remained very low.[108] On average, SECTAM conducted 250 inspections annually from 1994 to 1997, and about 450 inspections annually from 1998 to 2001. Considering the number of inspections conducted in 2001 (654), the year in which the most inspections were conducted among all years for which data are available, SECTAM's seventeen inspectors each conducted fewer than 40 inspections per year, or less than one per week. Moreover, the number of SECTAM inspections in 2001 is only 40 percent of the number of permits issued in the same year (1,653). In São Paulo, in contrast, three times more inspections were conducted than permits issued. SECTAM's inspections appear to be driven largely by public complaints, and the agency generally does not make an inspection before issuing an environmental permit.

The numbers of warnings, fines, and closures by SECTAM are presented in Table 2.4. The agency grouped warnings and fines together, rather than providing separate data for each. The number of warnings and fines rose over the decade, with the most significant increase occurring between 1994 and 1995 at the time of the agency's consolidation and passage of the state environmental law. The number of closures imposed by SECTAM varied through the decade, averaging 8 per year for the years in which data are available. The number of warnings and fines relative to the number of inspections was much higher for SECTAM than for CETESB. SECTAM issued a warning or fine, on average, for every two inspections it conducted. This high rate of sanction is likely to be indicative of a high rate of noncompliance.

While data were not available, it is likely that warnings rather than fines account for the large majority of the enforcement actions. As described above, the secretary of SECTAM is the only one in the agency with the authority to issue a fine. As a direct political appointee of the governor, replaceable at will, the secretary is likely to be very cautious in imposing fines, particularly on individuals and companies of political importance. Given this situation, the number of fines can be expected to be quite low.

A 1999 study of SECTAM's enforcement work in the years of 1992 to 1994 highlighted its ineffectiveness (Lopes 1999). It found that inspections occurred only in reaction to complaints or because of a failure to submit required paperwork, and that only 5 percent of all permitted sawmills and 1 percent of all permitted agricultural facilities were inspected in a given year. Indicative of the small geographic reach of the state agency, all the inspections occurred in 20 municipalities out of a total of 143 municipalities in the state. Of the 154

Table 2.4 Warnings, Fines, and Closures Issued by SECTAM, 1994–2001

Year	Warnings and Fines	Closures
1994	40	7
1995	155	1
1996	121	1
1997	141	3
1998	189	n/a
1999	297	27
2000	169	13
2001	185	4

SOURCE: State of Pará/SECTAM (2002).

sanctions that were issued by the agency in these years, only 54 (35 percent) were fines, all of which were classified as "not serious" as opposed to "serious" or "very serious." While state environmental law authorized fines of up to US$114,200, the average value of the fines was US$870. Significantly, the study found that none of the fines issued in these years was actually paid.

Enforcement by IBAMA in Pará

IBAMA plays a critical role in environmental enforcement in the state of Pará because it is responsible for implementing and enforcing forestry laws.[109] A 2005 study of fifty-five forestry-related enforcement cases initiated between 1999 and 2002 revealed several deficiencies (Brito and Barreto 2006). Of the cases studied, only 8 percent directly alleged deforestation or other illegal activities taking place at the forestry site, while almost three-quarters (72 percent) of the cases alleged unauthorized storage or transport of forest products. This finding reflects the fact that most of IBAMA's monitoring takes place on roads and other transportation corridors rather than in the field at the site of illegal deforestation.

A low collection rate of administrative fines was also evidenced. At the time of the study, fines had been paid in only 15 percent of the cases, summing to only 3 percent of the total amount of fines levied in the fifty-five cases.[110] In 58 percent of the cases, fines were overdue and IBAMA had taken some sort of action toward their collection, such as initiating a judicial action to collect payment or including the fine as a debt in the government's registry of *dívida ativa* (accounts receivable).[111] In 13 percent of the cases, fine collection was unable to proceed because of either inadequate identification of the violator or other procedural problems with the case. The other 14 percent of the cases were still in the process of being administratively or judicially appealed by the violator, including a small number of cases that had already been dismissed. Long delays in the collection of fines were apparent: the median age of the cases in which fines were already due was about three years.[112]

The study faulted various factors for the slow processing and lack of effectiveness of IBAMA's administrative fines. It found a relatively high rate of appeals, particularly in cases where fines were high. Violators appealed the citations in about a third of the cases (31 percent), representing over half of the total value of the fines (52 percent). Processing an administrative appeal took about six months. The study also observed that only 11 percent of the cases had been judicially enforced by IBAMA, and suggested that IBAMA should do so more often.[113] The study concluded that IBAMA/PA had an inadequate number of lawyers on staff to handle enforcement cases, and it strongly recommended that IBAMA focus its enforcement resources by prioritizing cases that involve the largest fines and environmental harm.

While deficiencies remained, IBAMA's effectiveness improved as corruption was exposed and enforcement activity increased in the 2000s. For example, a series of police raids in an area in southern Pará infamous for deforestation, the "Terra do Meio," reportedly led to a 60 percent drop in the area deforested between 2005 and 2006.[114] Over the course of several months, 121 citations were issued, 68 vehicles were impounded, and R$60 million in fines were issued. Between 2001 and 2004, the total value of fines issued annually in the Amazon region by IBAMA increased from R$217.5 million to R$611.5 million (Brito and Barreto 2006: 43).[115]

Conclusion

This chapter has sketched the strength of Brazilian environmental laws and the weakness of Brazilian environmental agencies. The legal framework for environmental law in Brazil is widely considered to be quite sophisticated. At the federal level, highlights include an environmental policy framework law, a constitutional chapter dedicated to the environment, and an environmental crimes law. State law is dominant in the area of pollution control, with the environmental permitting systems of states such as São Paulo and Rio de Janeiro dating from the 1970s.

Brazilian environmental agencies, while varying widely in their capacities, have not lived up to the promise of Brazilian environmental law. São Paulo's CETESB is the largest and most well-regarded environmental agency in Brazil. But along with other relatively capable state and federal environmental agencies, it has suffered institutional decline in the 1990s. In other states such as Pará, environmental agencies were just being consolidated in the 1990s and remained weak and relatively inactive. Data on environmental enforcement in the states of São Paulo and Pará reflect the problems experienced by their environmental agencies. In CETESB, major weaknesses included a pattern of negotiated noncompliance, in which companies were allowed to continue operating over many years without the required legal permits, and a breakdown in the system for collecting administrative fines. SECTAM enforcement data show a generally low level of activity, with very few inspectors and inspections, and very little use of administrative fines.

Brazilian environmental agencies tend to be "poor relations" in the governmental family. In many cases, environmental agencies may simply be denied the resources to develop technical capacity to implement the law. Even where agencies have sufficient technical capacity, environmental enforcement is not treated as a governmental priority. The result is a profound disconnect between environmental law "on the books" and environmental law as it operates in practice. Brazil is not alone in this regard—these are common problems of environmental agencies throughout the world, particularly in developing countries.

3 Becoming Environmental Prosecutors

With the chapter on the Ministério Público, I have the impression that we are taking—if it is accepted by the Assembly—a historic step. It is a historic step, and one with very important theoretical repercussions, because we are creating an organ outside the scheme of the three powers. It is an organ of enforcement that does not fit in any of the branches of Montesquieu's scheme. Why are we proposing financial, political, and administrative autonomy for this organ? Because we want a strong agent of legal enforcement.

Plínio de Arruda Sampaio, member of the Constitutional Assembly of 1988 (cited in Kerche 1999: 61)

BEFORE THE 1980S, the Ministério Público was not a significant actor in environmental protection. This chapter explains the legal and institutional transformation through which the Ministério Público became involved in defending environmental and other public interests. Whereas the Ministério Público had traditionally been dedicated primarily to criminal prosecution, defending public interests through civil litigation became an equally important part of its work.

Historically, the Brazilian Ministério Público was formally linked to the judicial branch but politically controlled by the executive branch. In the 1980s, it gained independence from both and arguably became a "fourth branch" of government. Prosecutors became critical actors in environmental enforcement, constituting an alternative enforcement institution independent of environmental agencies and the executive branch. Their work may be referred to as "prosecutorial enforcement," differentiating it from the administrative enforcement carried out by environmental agencies.

In many ways, the rise of prosecutorial enforcement—a more legalistic approach to environmental enforcement—may be viewed as a response to the problems of administrative enforcement in Brazil, which were examined in Chapter 2. Brazilian prosecutors, historically responsible for the legal defense of weak and underprotected interests, were able to extend their mandate to the legal defense of environmental interests in part because the state was perceived as deficient in this area. As stated in the declaration of a meeting of Brazilian environmental prosecutors in 1992, "Legislative changes in the 1980s and the incapacity of the state to respond [to the environmentalists' demands] with stronger environmental agencies transferred the most crucial part of the enforcement of environmental laws to the judicial sphere. And it was precisely in this process that the Ministério Público came to play a decisive role" (Milaré 1992: 244). By explaining how prosecutorial enforcement developed in Brazil, this chapter provides insight into the conditions that could lead toward a more legalistic approach to enforcement in other developing countries.

The first part of this chapter focuses on the building of the legal framework that enabled the Ministério Público's environmental prosecution work. It describes the legal changes of the 1980s and explains how they occurred. The second part of this chapter shows how the institution expanded and reconstructed itself based on its new legal framework. The institution-building process included diffusing the new institutional role throughout the country, institutional growth and restructuring, more selective recruitment, and the development of an esprit-de-corps around environmental and other public interest work.

Legal Reform

A series of changes in Brazilian law, culminating in the 1988 Constitution, redefined the institutional mission and profile of the Brazilian Ministério Público. Whereas it had been an arm of the executive branch, it became a largely autonomous institution positioned outside the three traditional branches of government. Whereas criminal prosecution had been primary, civil litigation to defend "diffuse and collective interests" acquired an importance within the institution that was equal or greater than criminal prosecution.[1] Brazilian political scientists have identified the changes in the powers and role of the Ministério Público as the most significant institutional reform in the 1988 Constitution (Kerche 1999: 61; Sadek and Cavalcanti 2003: 207).

The first part of this section is a brief discussion of the historical evolution of the Ministério Público. The second section reviews the legal changes that altered the Brazilian Ministério Público and led to its importance in environmental protection. The third section shows how this remarkable institutional transformation may be explained by looking at both the political skill of the

Ministério Público and the political context during the country's redemocratization in the wake of the military dictatorship.

The Ministério Público in Historical Perspective

The Brazilian Ministério Público is a descendent of the French *Ministère Public*, which traces its roots to the group of lawyers employed by the French crown in the thirteenth and fourteenth centuries (Cappelletti 1978: 776–77). Over time, these lawyers became "permanent public officers attached to the courts," where they served as the king's representatives (ibid.: 777). From France, the institution spread to other countries with civil law systems, and it was incorporated into Portuguese law by the fifteenth century and transplanted to the Brazilian colonies in the seventeenth century (Macedo Júnior 1995: 39). In its general functions, the *Ministère Public* in civil law countries constitutes an analogue to the attorney general in common law countries. It is the corps of governmental attorneys responsible for criminal prosecution, the institution that exercises the state's monopoly on accusing and prosecuting criminals.[2] Both institutions have also historically held the power to intervene in and, in some cases, initiate civil litigation that involves the interests of the general public (Langer 1988: 293).[3]

While clear similarities exist between the *Ministère Public* and the attorney general, important distinctions derive from broad differences between civil and common law systems. As explained by Merryman (1985: 34–38), the civil law judge is a very different figure than the common law judge. Rather than a "culture hero" or an "important person," civil law judges are civil servants, functionaries of the government, government bureaucrats. The same essential difference exists between civil and common law prosecutors. Indeed, as described below, the careers of judges and prosecutors are more closely related in civil law systems than in common law systems. In line with their more bureaucratic roles, civil law prosecutors also assumed a greater role in private civil litigation than common law prosecutors. Civil law prosecutors were traditionally called upon to assist judges by rendering legal opinions in certain types of cases, particularly cases involving personal status and family relationships. The following sections describe the *Ministère Public*'s association with the judicial branch and its historical role in civil litigation.

The Ministère Public and the Judicial Branch

Civil law prosecutors of the *Ministère Public* have traditionally been more associated with the judicial branch than common law prosecutors. As described by Cappelletti (1978: 777), their status was halfway between that of the judiciary and the executive. While historically appointed by the executive, they were often formally and organizationally related to the judiciary. They became known as the "Parquet" or "standing judges," judges who made their arguments while standing on the *parquet*, or floor, in front of the seated judges.

Reflecting this background, the Brazilian Ministério Público has been formally associated with the judicial branch or positioned outside the three traditional branches of government for most of its history. Brazil's first federal constitution in 1891 provided for a federal attorney general in the chapter on the judiciary (Mazzilli 1997: 4; Macedo Júnior 1995: 42). The short-lived Constitution of 1934 located the institution in a chapter outside those dedicated to the other branches, while the 1937 Constitution, written under the dictatorship of Getulio Vargas (Estado Novo), essentially collapsed all three branches of government into the executive. The postdictatorship Constitution of 1946 reinstated the formal independence of the Ministério Público contained in the Constitution of 1934. In the more recent military dictatorship, which lasted from 1965 to 1985, the Ministério Público was first made part of the judicial branch in the Constitution of 1967 and then, with a hardening of the dictatorship in 1969, it was made part of the executive branch (Macedo Júnior 1995: 42–43). As would be expected, the Ministério Público generally had less formal independence from the executive branch in periods of dictatorship.

The Brazilian Ministério Público's relationship to the judiciary is also apparent in its recruitment and organization. Entrance to both the Ministério Público and the judiciary is by competitive *concurso público* (civil service exam), and new entrants are generally young, recent law graduates. After a period of training, Brazilian judges and prosecutors begin their careers by being assigned to work in a less populated judicial district, often in a rural area where they serve as the only representative of their respective institutions. At this level, the prosecutor generally works closely with the judge, often with an office in the local courthouse. Both judges and prosecutors advance through promotions to work in more populated areas, and ultimately, in the appellate courts.

Despite its formal associations and resemblance with the judicial branch, the Brazilian Ministério Público often acted like an arm of the Brazilian executive branch (Kerche 1999).[4] Federal prosecutors, unlike state prosecutors, directly served the executive branch as its legal defense in civil litigation.[5] At both the federal and state levels, the executive branch had political control of the institution through its ability to replace the attorney general at will and its allocation of budgetary resources. Moreover, Brazilian prosecutors did not generally enjoy the same status as Brazilian judges in terms of job security and benefits (Sadek and Cavalcanti 2003: 205).[6]

The Role of the *Ministère Public* in Civil Litigation

In the case of both the civil law *Ministère Public* and the common law attorney general, the primary activity of the institution was criminal prosecution. However, the *Ministère Public* in civil law countries tended to play a larger role in protecting the public interest in private civil litigation than the attorney general in common law countries. In Brazil and other civil law countries, prosecutors represent the "interests of society and the law" in ordinary judicial proceedings between private individuals, acting as a *fiscal da lei*, or overseer of the application of the law (Merryman 1985: 103; David 1978: 498). As explained by Merryman, the theory behind this "public interest" function is that parties could not be expected to present all arguments in a given dispute and, thus, the representative of the *Ministère Public* was necessary "to assure that an impartial view, in the interest of the law, is presented." Most commonly, civil law prosecutors intervened in private litigation that involved weak individual parties such as "minors, widows, absentees, and incompetents," often in cases involving marital and paternity disputes (Cappelletti 1978: 778). In their role of *fiscal da lei*, prosecutors generally intervened in cases by submitting nonbinding *pareceres* (legal opinions) for the judge to consider in making his final decision. In some countries, the institution also gained the power to initiate civil suits to protect certain types of public interests.[7]

This role as *fiscal de lei* is exemplified in Brazilian law. The Brazilian Civil Code of 1917 gave the Ministério Público the role of intervening in litigation involving foundations, nullification of marriages, juveniles, absent parties, and several other types of cases. The Civil Procedure Code of 1939 required the Ministério Público to intervene as a *fiscal da lei* in these situations and others involving "central values of the predominantly rural and agrarian bourgeois social and economic order" (Macedo Júnior 1995: 42–43). Other laws, such as the Bankruptcy Law of 1945, the Law of Work Accidents of 1970, and the Law of Public Records of 1973 also specifically reserved the function of *fiscal da lei* to the Ministério Público (ibid.: 44).

The 1973 Civil Procedure Code expanded the potential for the Ministério Público to intervene in civil litigation by including "any case in which there is a public interest, as evidenced by the nature of the controversy or the party."[8]

As argued by Arantes (2002: 31–38), this generic and broad mandate to represent the public interest set the stage for the reforms of the 1980s. After the passage of the 1973 Civil Procedure Code, Brazilian law assigned responsibilities in civil litigation to the Ministério Público to a much greater extent than other civil law countries such as Germany, Italy, France, or Spain (ibid.: 37–38; Ferraz and Guimaraes Júnior 1999: 25).

Expansion of the Ministério Público's Role

Before the 1980s, the Brazilian Ministério Público may be considered quite typical of the *Ministère Public* in civil law countries in terms of its political position and institutional functions. In the 1980s, however, the Brazilian Ministério Público began forging a different path in two significant ways. First, its role in civil litigation was dramatically expanded as it was empowered to initiate lawsuits in the name of the "diffuse interests" of society, a newly defined set of interests that previously had no legal validity or representation.[9] Second, it attained a substantial degree of institutional independence as the 1988 Constitution limited the executive branch's control over the institution and the activities of individual prosecutors.

New Powers in Civil Litigation

With the 1981 National Environmental Policy Act (Lei da Política Nacional do Meio Ambiente), the Ministério Público's legal authority to act in civil litigation reached a new dimension. The law authorized the Ministério Público not just to intervene but also to initiate civil litigation on behalf of environmental interests. And unlike previous interests that the Ministério Público had been authorized to represent, the environment was not simply an underrepresented individual interest but rather a "diffuse interest," an interest of society generally. The law stated, in relevant part, "the Federal and the State Ministério Público may bring civil and criminal liability actions for damages caused to the environment."[10]

The role of the institution in defending diffuse interests was made explicit in the Public Civil Action Law of 1985 (Lei de Ação Civil Pública). This federal law authorized the Ministério Público, as well as other governmental entities and civil society organizations, to bring an *ação civil pública* (public civil action) to assign civil liability for harm to environmental and consumer interests as well as to artistic, aesthetic, historical, and scenic values.[11] According to one prosecutor "the law represented, without doubt, a revolution in the Brazilian legal order, as the judicial process stopped being seen as an instrument merely for the defense of individual interests and became seen as an effective mechanism for the participation of society in . . . those conflicts that involve supraindividual interests" (Milaré 2001: 510). Yet another prosecutor states that the Public Civil Action Law "inaugurated a new phase of Brazilian law and opened a new horizon for the activities of the Ministério Público in the civil sphere. . . . In this new phase, the prosecutor assumes the role of a true lawyer of the collective and diffuse interests of society" (Macedo Júnior 1995: 42).

The passage of the 1988 Constitution consolidated the Ministério Público's new role as a defender of societal interests. Three articles—nos. 127, 128, and 129—were dedicated to the Ministério Público. Article 127 refers specifically to societal interests, proclaiming the Ministério Público to be "a permanent institution, essential to the judicial function of the State, responsible for the defense of the legal order, the democratic regime, and inalienable societal and individual interests."[12] Article 129 lists nine institutional functions of the Ministério Público. Aside from retaining exclusive authority to prosecute criminal cases, prosecutors are constitutionally charged with "zealously advocating to ensure that the government and publicly relevant services respect constitutional rights" and "using civil investigations and public civil actions to protect the public and social patrimony, the environment, and other diffuse and collective interests."[13] Other relevant functions listed in article 129 include defending the rights of indigenous peoples and overseeing the police.[14]

In the years following adoption of the 1988 Constitution, additional laws were passed that legally established new diffuse interests and gave the Ministério Público the powers to defend them, including the Disability Law of 1989,[15] Children's Law of 1990,[16] the Consumer Defense Code of 1990,[17] the Administrative Improbity Act of 1992,[18] and the Antitrust Law of 1994.[19] The Consumer Defense Code is of particular importance because it included amendments to the Public Civil Action Law that allowed the instrument to be used to defend "any diffuse or collective interest," a clause that had been vetoed when the law was originally signed in 1985.[20]

Political Independence

The Brazilian Constitution of 1988 granted the Ministério Público a high degree of independence from other parts of the government.[21] While the 1969 Constitution that preceded it had located the Ministério Público within the chapter setting forth the powers of the executive branch (Kerche 2003: 58), the 1988

Constitution placed it in the section titled "Functions Essential to Justice," separate from those dedicated to the executive, legislative, and judicial branches. Moreover, the constitutional text described the institution's structure and job guarantees with a degree of specificity that helped ensure that the Ministério Público would be substantively independent, not merely nominally independent, from the three major branches of government.[22]

Article 127 grants the Ministério Público "administrative and functional autonomy" similar to that of the judicial branch. It states that the Ministério Público is to prepare its budget proposal within the limits established by the Budget Guidelines Law (Lei de Diretrizes Orçamentárias).[23] The Budget Guidelines Law, in turn, generally establishes a fixed percentage of the state or federal budget that is allocated to the Ministério Público and other branches of government. As long as it stays within its predetermined budgetary limit, the Ministério Público has full autonomy to create new positions and otherwise allocate its resources.[24]

Article 128 determines that the attorney general of each Ministério Público is appointed for a two-year term by the executive—the governor at the state level, the president at the federal level—from among the members of that Ministério Público.[25] At the state level, the article specifies that the governor shall choose the attorney general from a *lista tríplice*, or list of three members selected by the other members of the institution.[26] The attorney general of the Federal Ministério Público, in contrast, is appointed by the president from among all members of the institution over thirty five years of age, and thereafter confirmed by the Senate.[27] A state attorney general may be removed from office upon a vote of the majority in the state legislature.[28] The federal attorney general may be removed by the president upon a vote of the majority in the Senate.[29] Earlier Brazilian constitutions did not include such contingencies for the removal of the attorney general. Rather, the attorney general served at the pleasure of the executive (Kerche 2003: 69).

Article 128 also creates a strong form of tenure for Brazilian prosecutors that gives them a high degree of political independence.[30] After they complete a two-year trial period, they earn life tenure (*vitaliciedade*) and may only be removed from office through a judicial proceeding. They are also guaranteed immovability (*inamovibilidade*), which protects them from being involuntarily transferred to another job post or geographic location, unless such transfer is made in the "public interest" and approved by a majority vote of the institution's leadership body.[31] Finally, the 1988 Constitution specifies that their salaries may not be reduced (*irredutibilidade*). These job guarantees greatly limit the degree to which the attorney general or other institutional leader may interfere or exert influence on the work of an individual prosecutor.[32] Article 128 also establishes several restrictions on prosecutors: it prohibits them from working on the side as private lawyers, receiving honorary fees or private reimbursement for their work, participating in political party activities, and holding any other public office aside from a judgeship.[33] With these provisions, the job securities and job restrictions of Brazilian prosecutors were made essentially equivalent to those of Brazilian judges.

The 1988 Constitution made the Ministério Público independent from the traditional three branches of government. As analyzed by Mazzilli (1999: 105), its independence is established through three different types of constitutional guarantees. First, the Constitution provides for independence in the administration of the institution (*garantias nas atividades-meio*), mainly through its article 127 powers described above. Second, the Constitution provides for independence in carrying out its functions (*garantias nas atividades-fim*). In other words, the Ministério Público is not subordinated to any other governmental organs in the three traditional branches but rather determines which activities it undertakes subject only to the Constitution and other laws. Finally, the Constitution provides individual functional independence to each prosecutor, bolstered by the *garantias dos órgãos e agentes*, or job guarantees, of article 128. Each prosecutor independently chooses how to conduct the investigations and lawsuits in his or her jurisdiction without fear of dismissal, demotion, or involuntary transfer to another jurisdiction. Having emerged from the constitutional process as a powerful and independent institution, the Ministério Público is often referred to as *o quarto poder*, or the fourth branch of government (Mazzilli 1991: 39).

These legal changes signaled a significant institutional transformation in the Brazilian Ministério Público. The combination of institutional independence with the power to investigate and file public civil actions on behalf of a large variety of diffuse and collective interests made the Brazilian Ministério Público a very powerful political actor (Kerche 1997: 32). Comparing it to the Ministério Público in nine other countries, Kerche finds that on the spectrum of independence from political control, the Brazilian Ministério Público is the extreme case of independence (ibid.: 12, 28). Moreover, it has been observed to be almost unique among similar institutions throughout the world in terms of its power to act in defense of public interests (Macedo Júnior 1995: 39).

As stated by one institutional leader, "With the Constitution, [the Ministério Público] gained a lot of new responsibilities and a very modern, advanced new institutional profile—it was given the most advanced profile in the world and I doubt that there is a comparable Ministério Público in any other country of the world" (Bonelli 2001). The next section focuses on explaining how such significant legal changes occurred.

Explaining Legal Reform

Observing the legal changes that granted the Brazilian Ministério Público broad new powers to defend environmental and other public interests raises an important question: Why and how was the Ministério Público, a legal institution traditionally dependent on the executive branch and focused on criminal prosecution, given this new institutional role? An explanation is found in the combination of the political skill of the Ministério Público and a receptive political context. In the post–military dictatorship period of the 1980s, legislators and the Constitutional Assembly were receptive to innovations perceived to enhance and strengthen the democratization of Brazil. The Brazilian Ministério Público, in turn, displayed remarkable political skill in presenting the institution as a force for the protection of rights viewed as central to a democratic society.

Political Skill

The Ministério Público was not a passive observer of the legal changes that transformed the institution. Rather, leaders of the Ministério Público, particularly the São Paulo Ministério Público, played a very active role—engaging in internal institutional debates, helping draft new laws, and lobbying the legislature. With capable leadership and strong organization, the Ministério Público was able to take advantage of the country's democratization process in the 1980s to forge a new role for itself in protecting the newly defined set of "diffuse interests" while simultaneously transforming itself into a more independent and powerful institution. While a favorable political context contributed to the Ministério Público's success, the most important factor was arguably its own political skill and leadership.[34]

In a study of the historical evolution of the Ministério Público in Brazil, Arantes (2002) shows that its institutional reconstruction was the result of a series of changes that were intentionally pursued by the members of the institution.[35] Many of the legislative changes were suggested and lobbied for by the institution itself. As Arantes explains, the Ministério Público began defining a new role for itself in defending societal rather than governmental interests as early as the 1970s. With redemocratization and the emergence of new social movements in the 1980s, it was able to take a lead role in "one of the most radical transformations in Brazilian law—the introduction of collective and diffuse rights into the legal order" (Arantes 2002: 24). The significance of the Ministério Público's political skill is evident through a detailed examination of its contributions to the laws that granted the institution its new powers and authority.

The National Environmental Policy Act

The National Environmental Policy Act of 1981 was the first law to authorize the Ministério Público to act on behalf of a diffuse interest. As early as 1978, several environmentalists and prosecutors concerned about environmental problems had endorsed a new role for the Ministério Público in environmental protection. In the First National Ecological Symposium in 1978, a São Paulo prosecutor made a presentation advocating that the "Ministério Público become active, and that it be given broad powers to prevent, punish, and seek reparations from those that harm the environment" (Guimaraes Júnior 1981: 183).The symposium adopted this as one of its legislative recommendations. In the same year, a professor of ecology gave a speech to a group of prosecutors, including the attorney general, asserting that "the active participation of the Ministério Público is lacking in the process of creating a national conscience to defend the environment" and calling for the creation of a new job title: "Prosecutor for the Protection of Human Health and the Environment" (Tomazi 1981: 141).

The 1981 National Environmental Policy Act responded to these calls, providing that the "Ministério Público of the Union and the States shall have jurisdiction to file civil and criminal liability lawsuits for harm caused to the environment."[36] This provision was suggested and written by a São Paulo prosecutor, Paulo Affonso Leme Machado, who participated in the commission that drafted the law. Machado explains that he suggested it because he "thought that the Ministério Público needed to have some involvement in the [environmental] area" and that it was written quickly after a brief consultation with institutional leaders in the São Paulo Ministério Público (personal interview, 2001).[37]

The 1981 law was passed through the efforts of Paulo Nogueira-Neto, a major figure in the history of Brazilian environmental protection. Nogueira-Neto was the head of the National Environmental Secretariat (SEMA) from its establishment in 1974 until 1986, holding this post under four different heads of state spanning the military dictatorship through democratization (Costa

2003: 76). The 1981 law was passed and signed under the rule of the last military leader, João Baptista Figueiredo. Nogueira-Neto explains that the bill attained the support of both the government and the opposition parties in the legislature and was actually strengthened rather than weakened in legislative committee (ibid.: 77). It was passed almost unanimously by the legislature. According to Nogueira-Neto, when the Confederation of Industries saw the proposed law, it "woke up to the consequences that it could lead to" and urged President Figueiredo to veto thirteen of its twenty-six articles. In Nogueira-Neto's words, "The President consulted me and I recommended that he veto only two of the least significant articles, and he followed my advice. It was quite a victory!" (ibid.).[38] He notes, however, that the Confederation fought hard against regulations implementing the law, the first of which took two years to be enacted.[39]

The Ministério Público of São Paulo took its first action under the 1981 environmental protection law in 1983.[40] Dynamite explosions in a stone quarry caused a rockslide that ruptured an oil pipeline and provoked an oil spill of over 1.5 million liters near Cubatão on the São Paulo coast. The spill was considered to be the worst ecological disaster that had occurred in the country. The São Paulo attorney general appointed one of his prosecutors, Édis Milaré, to work on this case. In November 1983, Milaré filed the first lawsuit pursuant to the National Environmental Policy Act seeking to impose civil liability on the construction company and the state-owned oil company for the environmental harm caused by the spill. The lawsuit was well covered by the press and began building the reputation of the Ministério Público as an actor in environmental protection (personal interview, 2001).

In early 1984, the attorney general created a permanent environmental prosecution office in the city of São Paulo and appointed Milaré as lead prosecutor. The office initially focused on studying the state and environmental laws and providing information and advice to the prosecutors throughout the state who had been designated to protect the environment.[41] Milaré's office also filed several other environmental protection lawsuits that captured public attention.[42]

The Public Civil Action Law of 1985

The São Paulo Ministério Público played a key role in the passage of the Public Civil Action Law of 1985. Building upon the work of a group of Brazilian legal scholars and judges, a group of São Paulo prosecutors drafted the bill that became the Public Civil Action Law. The law gave the Ministério Público the primary role in the protection of the newly emerging set of group rights in Brazil.

In the late 1970s, Brazilian legal scholars began discussing the need for legal protection of group rights, drawing inspiration from the American class action and the "access to justice" writings of the Italian legal scholar Mauro Cappelletti (1978, 1979).[43] In 1982, the São Paulo Association of Judges (Associação Paulista de Magistrados) established a commission of four law professors and judges to draft a law enabling the legal protection of group rights (Arantes 2002: 58). The commission's bill focused on giving civil society organizations the legal power to file lawsuits on behalf of diffuse rights in the area of environment and cultural heritage. It was introduced in the Brazilian legislature in early 1984.[44]

Prompted by the commission's work, Milaré and several colleagues in the São Paulo Ministério Público initiated an institutional discussion about the role of the Ministério Público in the protection of diffuse interests and the ways that the commission's bill might be rewritten to enable the Ministério Público to play a more significant role in this new legal area. With the endorsement of the institution, they authored a new bill based on the one drafted by the commission that strengthened the Ministério Público's role. While both bills gave the Ministério Público as well as civil society organizations the power to file public civil actions, the Ministério Público's version included several innovations that favored the institution. Most important, it created an investigative instrument, the civil investigation, which the Ministério Público could use to collect evidence in preparation for a public civil action (ibid.: 72–73). The Ministério Público's bill also expanded the interests that could be defended in a public civil action to include consumer interests and "any other diffuse interest."[45]

The São Paulo Ministério Público's bill was sent through the São Paulo attorney general to the Federal Ministry of Justice in June 1984, and it was introduced to the national Congress as a proposal of President Figueiredo in February 1985 (see Milaré 1995: 473–93, appendices). Unlike the commission's bill, the Ministério Público's bill received prompt attention and was passed by both houses of Congress by July.[46] The most vocal opposition to the bill came from the professors and judges who had authored the competing bill. They argued that its provisions increased the power of the Ministério Público to the detriment of civil society organizations. As the Ministério Público was at that time still part of the executive branch, they likely feared that the institution would be able to obstruct lawsuits filed against the executive branch (Arantes 2002: 64–65). Along with several lawyers associations and the editorial boards of the two principal newspapers of São Paulo, the commission lobbied the president—now Figueiredo's successor, President José Sarney—for a veto of the offensive provisions. Several business associations also lobbied against the bill (ibid.: 66). The state and federal Ministérios Públicos and governmental agencies linked to environmental and consumer protection urged the president to sign the law in its entirety (ibid.: fn. 84).

On July 24, 1985, President Sarney signed the bill. With respect to the provisions that offended the law professors and judges on the commission, the president adopted the position of the Ministério Público and retained them in full. However, Sarney did exercise his veto power over the phrase "any other diffuse interest."[47] The veto limited the new procedural instrument to the defense of the interests specifically named in the law—the environment, consumers, and cultural patrimony.[48] Sarney justified his veto by citing the "legal insecurity" that arises from the "extremely broad and imprecise reach" of the expression "any other diffuse interest" and stated that the idea "required more reflection and analysis" (Milaré 1995: 496–98).

Given the ultimate importance of the public civil action in environmental enforcement and other areas with political implications, one might expect that the law would have generated greater political resistance. One of the prosecutors who drafted the bill explains that the law's implications were not foreseen:

> It was very difficult [for legislators] to be against an initiative that appeared very "nice" . . . defending the public interest, the environment. . . . It was politically correct, . . . and there wasn't really much motivation to be against, because in the beginning no one believed that it could develop in the way it did, to the point of making the government and companies very uncomfortable. And when those with political and economic power realized its potential, it was already law and they couldn't easily take it back. (Personal interview, 2002)

Six months after the passage of the law, in January 1986, a landmark lawsuit was filed against the twenty-four petrochemical and steel companies that constituted the country's most important industrial district, Cubatão, located in the state of São Paulo. The lawsuit was filed jointly by the São Paulo environmental prosecution office, still led by Milaré, and an environmental nonprofit organization, OIKOS, led by Fabio Feldmann (see Feldmann 1995: 271).[49] The lawsuit requested that the court hold the companies liable for the cost of stabilizing the mountainsides in the nearby coastal mountain range that had become susceptible to landslides; decontaminating the soils, cleaning and recuperating local streams and rivers; and reforesting with native species. The value of the damage was estimated at US$800 million. The case drew national and international attention and was the first of many public civil actions that would make a name for the Ministério Público in the area of environmental enforcement.

The Federal Constitution of 1988

The role of the Ministério Público in the legal defense of the environment and other public interests was consolidated in the Federal Constitution of 1988. Based on its success with the Public Civil Action Law, the Ministério Público lobbied to constitutionalize its new role and the institutional guarantees that it argued to be necessary to fulfill this new role. While the Ministério Público of São Paulo and a couple of other southern states led the lobbying effort, the effort was national in scale as leaders of the Ministério Público throughout Brazil participated in the meetings that defined the Ministério Público's proposal and helped to persuade the Constitutional Assembly to support it. In what has been referred to as the greatest institutional novelty of the 1988 Constitution, the Ministério Público was largely successful in getting the profile it sought (Kerche 1999: 61).

The story of the Ministério Público's success in the 1988 Constitution is a story of strong and organized leadership. A primary objective of institutional leaders was to make the Ministério Público more independent from the executive branch. This quest for political independence had been part of internal institutional discussions for many years, and many prosecutors resented the executive branch's domination of the institution.[50] As Cláudio Ferraz de Alvarenga, a leader of the São Paulo Ministério Público in the 1980s, explains:

> It was an extremely competent group, it was a group of people with great character, people that loved the Ministério Público and thought a lot about a new ideological formulation of the Ministério Público. It was people who drew upon the work of previous members of the institution as well as contemporary work to create a new way of thinking about the Ministério Público that would overcome certain difficulties that the institution had. At that time, for example, the Ministério Público was tied to the executive branch and the executive branch practically controlled the institution. This was something that the prosecutors didn't agree with; they wanted to change this and create a truly independent institution. (Bonelli 2001)

In concrete terms, the Ministério Público argued that the institution should be given its own chapter in the Constitution, outside those of the three traditional branches of government, and that prosecutors should be guaranteed the same job securities and benefits as judges (Kerche 1999: 69–74).

The Ministério Público's interest in increasing its independence from the executive branch dovetailed with its interest in taking a leading role in the protection of the new set of emergent diffuse and collective rights. Its transformation into a defender of societal interests provided a compelling political justification for a higher degree of independence. Alvarenga shows the connection that institutional leaders drew between the institution's political independence and protecting societal rights:

> The great victory was to stipulate in the Constitution that the Ministério Público has administrative autonomy, political autonomy, financial autonomy, and budget-making autonomy. This was the great work of construction. . . . What was always desired was to head in the direction of this autonomy, of this independence—to be able to use this to freely work in defense of society, even when faced with abuses by the executive branch. (Bonelli 2001)

As described further below, the idea of having an autonomous governmental institution take responsibility for defending the general interests of society encountered a receptive audience in the Constitutional Assembly.

The Ministério Público strengthened its position in the constitutional process by presenting a unified proposal agreed upon by state and federal prosecutors from throughout Brazil. In preparation for the 1988 Constitution, a series of national meetings was organized to discuss the future of the institution and determine what the institution would seek in terms of its rights and responsibilities (Mazzilli 1989: 24). In June 1985, the 6th National Conference of the Ministério Público was held in São Paulo, and many papers were presented on the topic of the position and organization of the institution in the future Constitution (ibid.: 22). In October 1985, the National Association of the Ministério Público (Confederação Nacional do Ministério Público; CONAMP) sent a questionnaire to all 5,793 prosecutors throughout the country to gather opinions on future constitutional provisions, and nearly one thousand prosecutors responded (ibid.: 23). And in the First National Meeting of Attorneys General and Presidents of Associations of the Ministério Público, held in 1986, leaders of the Ministério Público from a large number of states endorsed a draft of the constitutional provisions relating to the Ministério Público (Mazzilli 1989: 30).

The Ministério Público submitted this draft as its proposal to the Constitutional Assembly.

During constitutional deliberations, institutional leaders lobbied extensively on behalf of their proposal and continued to maintain a unified position. As Alvarenga describes:

> In the constitutional process . . . we mobilized the Ministério Público from all over Brazil—it was not just us, it was the institution that did this. We had a vision, we knew what we wanted, and we worked like madmen. In terms of coordination, we participated in everything that happened in the Constitutional Assembly, with prosecutors from all over Brazil. When differences arose among the state Ministérios Públicos, we were always able to find an equilibrium point. (Bonelli 2001)

The Ministério Público maintained a continuous and strong presence in the Constitutional Assembly while its proposal was being debated and voted upon (Kerche 1997: 61–67; Arantes 2002: 85–86).

While largely incorporated into the Constitution, the Ministério Público's constitutional proposal did suffer some modifications (Kerche 1997, 1999). The most significant modification concerned the selection and removal of federal and state attorneys general (Kerche 1999: 72). At the federal level, the Ministério Público had proposed that the federal attorney general be appointed by the president, with the approval by the Senate, and removed only for "abuse of power" or "serious omission" as determined by the Federal Ministério Público. After a series of revisions, the relevant provision in the Constitution of 1988 provided that both appointment and removal would be by the president, with the approval of the Senate. For the state attorneys general, the Ministério Público proposed that each Ministério Público would have the power to elect and remove its own attorneys general. The Constitution, in contrast, provides that state attorneys general be appointed by the governors from among a list of three prosecutors selected by the respective state Ministério Público. The legislative branch was given the power of removing the state attorney general.

Another way in which the Constitutional Assembly modified the original proposal of the Ministério Público concerned the ability of prosecutors to participate in electoral politics or hold high-level executive appointments. While the proposal allowed prosecutors to do so, the Constitutional Assembly initially objected because of its concern that prosecutors would use their jobs to promote their own political careers. Drafts of the Constitution thus included a provision prohibiting prosecutors from participating in "political party activities" (ibid.: 73). In the end, however, a compromise was struck that allowed prosecutors who entered the Ministério Público before 1988 to be exempt from this restriction.[51]

Although these modifications imposed several limits on the Ministério Público, they pale in comparison to the powers that the institution was granted in articles 127 through 129.[52] The Ministério Público basically emerged from the process with the constitutional profile it had sought: it would play a primary role in the defense of societal interests and it would have a high level of independence at both the institutional and individual levels (see Mazzilli 1989: 20). Only eleven Constitutional Assembly members out of over five hundred voted against the Ministério Público's new powers (Bonelli 2002).

Prosecutors did not confine their efforts to the constitutional articles that directly referred to the Ministério Público, but also exerted influence in the substantive legal areas that related to their work. In particular, São Paulo environmental prosecutors contributed to the Constitution's environmental law, article 225 (personal interview, 2001). In 1986, Milaré and two other members of São Paulo Ministério Público wrote an article titled "The Ministério Público and the Environmental Question in the Constitution," in which they argued for the need to elevate environmental protection and the Ministério Público's role in this area to the constitutional level (Ferraz, Milaré, and Mazzilli 1986: 15, 20). In coordination with an environmentalist coalition organized by the São Paulo state representative to the Constitutional Assembly, Fabio Feldmann, environmental prosecutors in São Paulo helped to write and lobby on behalf of the environmental article (personal interview, 2002).

Political Context

Given the extent of power granted to the Ministério Público by the 1988 Constitution, some claimed later that the Constitutional Assembly had not understood what it was doing: the Ministério Público's skilled lobby had "tricked" the Constitutional Assembly or the Constitutional Assembly was "napping" when it approved the Ministério Público's proposal (Kerche 1999: 61). While acknowledging the importance of the Ministério Público's effective leadership and organization, Kerche (1999) responds by arguing that the Ministério Público's proposal was consistent with the political culture that dominated the Constitutional Assembly and thus encountered a receptive audience. Viewed in this perspective, the Ministério Público's new profile was not an aberration but rather a component of a larger political project embraced by the majority of the Constitutional Assembly to democratize Brazil in the wake of the military dictatorship.

In the 1980s, large social and political changes were taking place as Brazil began to transition to democracy after almost two decades of military dictatorship. By 1979, when an amnesty law was passed, the political environment had begun to open and there was a surge in the growth of social movements.[53] The period of redemocratization was a time for questioning the authority of the government and exposing the ways that it had violated the rights of citizens during the dictatorship. There was a general lack of confidence in government, particularly in the executive branch. The Ministério Público, however, despite being part of the government, was able to attract praise rather than criticism from social movements during this period. While still formally linked to the executive branch, the Ministério Público aligned itself with societal interests and proclaimed itself a representative of environmental and other social interests.[54]

The key to the Ministério Público's success in the Constitutional Assembly was its ability to present its institutional project as enhancing democracy in Brazil. As explained by Arantes (2002: 77), the Ministério Público went to the Constitutional Assembly "with the discourse that its political independence was essential to the future constitutional democracy and a guarantee for society more than for the institution itself." Given the postdictatorship fervor for democracy, the idea of having the Ministério Público become politically independent of the executive branch and assume the role of defending the democratic legal order and societal rights was well-received.

Research on the political composition of the Constitutional Assembly helps explain why the Ministério Público's proposal received widespread support.[55] In his study of the Constitution's treatment of the Ministério Público, Kerche (1999) argues that the Constitutional Assembly was primarily seeking to democratize the Brazilian state, rather than to minimize it in line with classical liberal ideas of government. The conservative and liberal political parties that participated in the Assembly diverged more on issues relating to executive branch powers and the financial system than on issues relating to democratization. "Even the party or political group with the greatest resistance to democratizing measures was not that distant, in comparison with other issues, from those that most favored them" (ibid.: 68).

While political groups within the Constitutional Assembly differed with respect to how a more democratic order could be attained, the idea of an independent Ministério Público that would protect societal rights appealed across many of these groups. In particular, the idea appealed to the three main currents of political culture that were manifested in the debates of the Constitutional Assembly: the belief that traditional individual rights were insufficient to address social inequalities; the view of the state as a privileged agent for encouraging not just economic progress but also social progress; and the idea that new forms of political participation were needed outside of electoral politics (ibid.; Lamounier and Moura 1990: 83). The Ministério Público's proposal, in which the institution presented itself as a governmental defender of society's collective rights, was highly consonant with this political culture.

Institution Building

After consolidating its new role and status in the 1988 Constitution, the Ministério Público went through a marked period of institution building. The emergence of the new Ministério Público was signaled by institutional growth and selective recruitment, increasing specialization, and a strong institutional esprit de corps. While data are presented below primarily for the state Ministérios Públicos of São Paulo and Pará, this process of institution building occurred throughout the country at both the state and federal levels.

Growth and Recruitment

Even as hiring and salaries tended to stagnate in the public sector in Brazil in the 1990s, the São Paulo Ministério Público was able to hire more prosecutors and offer very attractive salaries. With its growth, the institution became increasingly selective and prestigious. Brazilian law graduates considered the Ministério Público a very desirable place to work. The institution's marked growth attests to its budgetary autonomy and political strength.

The primary indicator of the institution's growth was the increase in the number of prosecutors. Between 1985 and 2002, the number of state and federal prosecutors in Brazil almost doubled, from fewer than 6,000 in 1985 to about 10,000 in 2002 (see Mazzilli 1991: 23; Sadek and Cavalcanti 2003: 209). In São Paulo, the number of prosecutors steadily increased from 849 to 1,620 between 1985 and 2001,[56] and reached 1,689 by 2006.[57] In the state of Pará, the Ministério Público grew from 138 prosecutors in 1988 to 243 in 1995. After about a 10 percent decline in their numbers by 2001 due to a lack of hiring, the number of state prosecutors rose to 254 by 2006.[58] The Federal Ministério Público doubled in size from 271 prosecutors in 1985 to 541 in 2001. Over the next five years, it added again as many prosecutors to reach 826 in 2006.[59]

The physical and administrative infrastructure of the various Ministérios Públicos in Brazil grew to accommodate the new prosecutors. Historically, prosecutors had worked inside the courthouse and had little or no administrative support. By the late 1990s, the São Paulo Ministério Público acquired a new headquarters building, hired 2,500 administrative staff, and became computerized (Bonelli 2002: 157). To pay for these changes, the budget of the Ministério Público of São Paulo grew significantly, particularly in the early and mid-1990s.[60] Similarly in Pará, several buildings were built or remodeled in the capital, and new living and working quarters for prosecutors were constructed in many larger towns throughout the state. Between 1988 and 2000, the number of administrative and technical employees in the Pará Ministério Público grew from 34 to over 500.[61]

Despite its rapid growth, the Ministério Público was able to be increasingly selective in its hiring and maintain high salaries. The Ministério Público recruited by means of a multiphased civil service exam. Candidates were generally recent law graduates, who often spent a year preparing for the exam at an affiliated School of the Ministério Público.[62] The exam included three increasingly selective phases that spanned the course of almost a year—a multiple-choice exam, an essay exam, and an oral exam. Those who were hired were the select few.

In São Paulo, thousands of applicants competed for tens of positions in each civil service exam.[63] While hiring was historically quite selective, it became increasingly selective after 1995. Table 3.1 shows the evolution of hiring in the years between 1989 and 2006 for the São Paulo Ministério Público. In the first half of the 1990s, the percentage of candidates hired averaged 3.3 percent. In the latter 1990s, the average dropped to 1.3 percent, or about 75 candidates for each available position. Finally, in the 2000s, the percentage of candidates hired fell to an average of 1 percent, or one hire for every one hundred candidates.

The sharp rise in the number of applicants in 1996 resulted from a significant salary increase that was announced for São Paulo prosecutors in 1995.[64] Like Brazilian judges, Brazilian prosecutors were well compensated among governmental employees. In 2001, the basic salary of a São Paulo prosecutor who had completed his or her two-year training period was about R$7,000/month

Table 3.1 Hiring in the São Paulo Ministério Público, 1990–2006

Year	No. of Candidates	No. of Hires	Percentage Hired
1990*	3,600	90	2.5
1991*	3,182	134	4.2
1992	1,379	43	3.1
1993	2,287	70	3.1
1994	2,625	70	2.7
1995	2,304	92	4.0
1996	6,832	100	1.5
1997	6,096	70	1.1
1999	5,662	82	1.4
2000	6,659	51	0.8
2002	6,414	91	1.4
2003	8,440	93	1.1
2006	7,356	54	0.7

* Two hiring processes were conducted in the years 1990 and 1991; data for both
are combined.
SOURCE: Diretoria Geral, São Paulo Ministério Público (November 2001); 2003 and
2006 data from CETESB Pollution Control Division (pers. comm., April 2007).

(US$3,030),[65] over twice the average salary of a private lawyer in São Paulo, four
times the average salary of a college graduate employed by the government in
São Paulo, and 35 times the minimum wage.[66] Moreover, salaries increased in
relation to the number of promotions and the length of service. A São Paulo
prosecutor with twenty years' experience who had been promoted to become
an appeals court prosecutor was paid over R$15,000/month (US$6,494).[67] While
similar data were not available from the Pará Ministério Público or the Federal
Ministério Público, prosecutors in those institutions noted the competitiveness
of their civil service exams and were observed to enjoy a similarly privileged
standard of living.

In sum, a prosecutorial career in the Brazilian Ministério Público became
increasingly coveted and remunerative in the aftermath of the 1988 Constitution. Many of the "best and the brightest" of Brazil's law graduates pursued
careers in the Ministério Público. The institution and its prosecutors visibly
gained in prestige.

Specialization

The Ministério Público's growth enabled an increasing level of specialization among prosecutors. When it was smaller, more prosecutors had to be generalists, covering all areas of the institution's work. With the hiring of more prosecutors, more specialization was possible. Moreover, the Ministério Público created specialized administrative units to assist and support prosecutors working in those areas. By the early 2000s, over two thousand state and federal prosecutors counted environmental protection among their responsibilities, and about two hundred prosecutors worked in this area almost exclusively.[68] Specialization was extremely important in developing the Ministério Público's ability to become active in environmental enforcement. However, as shown below, the degree of specialization differed among states. In São Paulo, it occurred to a greater degree than in Pará.

State prosecutors (*promotores de justiça*) start their careers as sole prosecutors in less populated judicial districts of their state.[69] They begin as generalists, prosecuting criminal cases and conducting the institution's traditional civil work as well as the new civil work defending environmental and other public interests. As they receive promotions, prosecutors move to more populated judicial districts where there are more prosecutors, and they have the opportunity to increasingly specialize. At first, a prosecutor may be able to specialize in either criminal or civil matters. Eventually, the prosecutor may be promoted to a larger city—often the state capital—where he or she can specialize in a single criminal or civil area such as the prosecution of homicides or environmental protection. After many years of service, the prosecutor may ultimately be promoted to the small group of appeals court prosecutors (*procuradores de justiça*), the highest echelon of the institution, and may assume positions of institutional leadership. At this level, prosecutors again become generalists, responsible for all the Ministério Público's cases that reach the appellate courts.

With the growth of the São Paulo Ministério Público, all but the most rural judicial districts had at least two prosecutors, allowing one to specialize in criminal matters and the other to specialize in civil matters. In 2001, about 750 prosecutors worked in the state capital (including 200 appeals court prosecutors), and the other 870 prosecutors worked in the other approximately two hundred judicial districts throughout the rest of the state.[70] By 2001, the city of São Paulo had five specialized environmental prosecutor positions, and several other large cities had two or three. In medium-sized towns, prosecutors were often able to specialize in several related areas such as environmental protection, consumer defense, and housing.

State and federal Ministérios Públicos in Brazil supported and furthered specialization by creating area-specific administrative units to assist prosecutors working in areas that required more specialized knowledge. In the environmental area, for example, many state Ministérios Públicos established an Environmental Prosecution Support Center (Centro de Apoio Operacional do Meio Ambiente) at the institution's headquarters in the state capital. The support center is staffed by one or more prosecutors able to give advice about environmental cases to other prosecutors.

In São Paulo, the environmental prosecution office that had been created in 1984 was restructured in 1993 to become an Environmental Prosecution Support Center.[71] Prior to 1993, the prosecutors in the office were authorized to investigate and prosecute cases throughout the state, generally in coordination with the local prosecutor in the applicable judicial district. After 1993, the prosecutors staffing the center lost the authority to prosecute and became exclusively dedicated to providing training and assistance to local prosecutors. The support center grew in the 1990s to include technical staff to conduct analyses and provide support on specific cases to local prosecutors. It also began organizing annual statewide environmental conferences and other activities enabling prosecutors throughout the state to exchange information, opinions, and strategies, and more generally to build a community of prosecutors interested in furthering the institution's work in this area (see Benjamin 1998b; Bonatto 1992).

The Pará State Ministério Público experienced a lower degree of specialization. In 2001, about 90 prosecutors worked in the capital city of Belém (including about 30 appeals court prosecutors) and the other 130 worked in the approximately 100 judicial districts throughout the state.[72] Given the low number of prosecutors per judicial district, specialization was only possible in the state capital and a couple of other large cities. In contrast to São Paulo, the norm was a sole prosecutor in each judicial district.

The Pará Ministério Público began to specialize in environmental protection in 1988 (see Valente 1988). That year, the First Symposium of Pará on the Ministério Público and the Environment was held, in which Édis Milaré and others were invited to speak.[73] As stated by Luis Ismaelino Valente, a Pará state prosecutor who helped organize the symposium, "This was the first time in which environmental issues and especially environmental law were discussed systematically and even academically not only within the Pará Ministério Público but within the state of Pará itself."[74] Soon after, Valente was appointed by the attorney general to be an environmental prosecutor in the state's capital, Belém, and local prosecutors in judicial districts throughout the state were assigned responsibility for environmental protection.[75]

By the early 1990s, Valente had two assistant environmental prosecutors responsible for environmental protection in Belém, and in 1995, an Environmental Nucleus (Núcleo do Meio Ambiente) was established to support and coordinate the environmental work of prosecutors throughout the state.[76] Despite these steps, however, the Pará Ministério Público's environmental work remained limited and lacked the dynamism of the São Paulo Ministério Público's work. The lack of growth in the number of prosecutors after 1995 greatly limited the extent to which prosecutors could specialize in environmental protection, particularly outside Belém. Political factors, discussed in Chapter 4, help explain the lack of institutional growth as well as the weakness of institutional support for environmental prosecution.

Esprit de Corps

In addition to the structural institutional changes, the new Ministério Público was characterized by a high level of esprit de corps in support of its public interest defense work. Scholars have noted that an administrative elite with a strong sense of esprit de corps arises under certain circumstances in public administration (see Kaufman 1960). Describing this phenomenon, Pérez-Perdomo (1995: 317) explains that where esprit de corps is present, "[t]he group is composed of individuals who identify with each other and serve, or say that they serve, the public interest and are usually aware of their own status and privileges." Such esprit de corps is evident in the discourse of prosecutors about the importance of their work.

The Brazilian Ministério Público exhibits the characteristics of strong esprit de corps. A strong group identification prevails among prosecutors deriving from the shared experiences of passing a very selective exam, learning how to be a prosecutor alone in the "trial by fire" conditions of a remote judicial district, and being promoted through the ranks to ultimately arrive back to the capital city, where many of the prosecutors were educated and perhaps even knew each other in law school. Frequent conferences and seminars allow prosecutors to meet, see each other through the years, and follow each other's careers.

The public service ethos is very present in the Brazilian Ministério Público.

As written in 1991 by one São Paulo prosecutor, "There's a lot of strength and idealism, there's a lot of fight in the institution, and there's a lot of work to be done.... [I]n each judicial district of this country, there is a public prosecutor that attends to the public, that pursues criminals rich or poor, that defends the environment, that works on behalf of those injured on the job, the disabled, the workers" (Mazzilli 1991: 19). This type of idealistic discourse about the institution's work is observed in everyday conversation with prosecutors as well.

Brazilian scholars have noted the strong sense of institutional mission among prosecutors. Arantes (2002: 119) calls it an "ideology of political voluntarism" (*ideologia do voluntarismo político*) and finds that it is rooted in two beliefs that are widely held by prosecutors: first, that civil society is too weak and disorganized to defend its own interests; and second, that the government often violates or offends the public interest. These beliefs lead prosecutors to opine that the Ministério Público plays an essential role in defending the public interest against a frequently predatory state. As Arantes states, "From this equation emerges the proposition, instrumental in nature, that 'someone' should intervene in state-society relations in defense of society" (ibid.: 129).

Prosecutors are motivated and energetic in their public interest work, perhaps even to the detriment of the traditional criminal defense work of the institution. A multistate survey of state and federal prosecutors conducted in 1996 showed that while 72 percent of prosecutors prioritized criminal work in the past, only 61 percent planned to do so in the future.[77] In contrast, while 32 percent of prosecutors had prioritized environmental protection in the previous two years, 43 percent planned to prioritize it in the next two years. There were similar increases in plans to give priority to other public interest areas, including fighting political corruption, consumer protection, and advocacy on behalf of the elderly and handicapped. Interpreting these data, Arantes (2002: 118–19) states: "There are strong signs, therefore, that the ideology of political voluntarism is mobilizing an ever larger number of prosecutors to give more attention to diffuse and collective rights, implying stagnation or even decline in terms of priority in the traditional areas of the institution's work like criminal prosecution." Many prosecutors perceive the institution's civil work to be more dynamic and important than its criminal work.[78]

Of course, not all prosecutors are equally enthusiastic about the institution's environmental work. A divide between its older and newer members exists in this regard. As explained by a Brazilian judge, "Those with the longest service in the [Ministério Público] hold a generally [skeptical] position, considering [environmental defense] as a secondary matter or . . . an obstacle to economic development" (Passos de Freitas 2003: 60). But with the institution's rapid growth in the 1980s and 1990s, the average age of Brazilian prosecutors tended to be fairly young. In São Paulo, newly hired prosecutors in the mid-1990s were, on average, 27 years old.[79] The average age of São Paulo prosecutors in 1997 was 37.5 years old, and only a third were over 40.[80] The age profile of prosecutors in other states was similar. A 1996 study of the Ministério Público of seven Brazilian states including São Paulo found the average age of prosecutors to be 33. Similarly, a 1997 study of the Federal Ministério Público found the average age to be 36 (Wiecko V. de Castilho and Sadek 1998: 9). Brazilian prosecutors are often caricatured as being young and idealistic.

In sum, a strong sense of institutional mission and esprit de corps developed in the Ministério Público of Brazil. While not universally shared by all prosecutors throughout the country, many prosecutors in many states held the belief that they were critical actors in defending society's interests against the state. This esprit de corps supported and strengthened the institution's environmental protection work.

Conclusion

In the 1980s, the Public Civil Action Law and the 1988 Constitution conferred upon Brazilian prosecutors legal powers that enabled the country to become a new actor in environmental enforcement. The Ministério Público, which had historically focused on criminal prosecution, gained authority to legally defend the "diffuse and collective" interests of society—environmental and other so-called public interests. Whereas the institution had previously been part of the executive branch, it was reformed into a politically independent "fourth branch" with the power to oversee the legality of the actions of the three traditional branches. These significant changes in the profile of the Brazilian Ministério Público were enabled by a combination of a high degree of political skill by institutional leaders and a favorable political context during the period of redemocratization. Leaders of the Ministério Público from São Paulo were particularly prominent in developing and lobbying on behalf of the institution's new legal and political profile.

After the passage of the 1988 Constitution, the Brazilian Ministério Público experienced a period of institution building that strengthened its capacity to carry out its legal mandate to defend environmental and other public interests. In this period, the number of prosecutors grew and recruitment became more selective. Prosecutors were increasingly able to specialize in the new areas of public interest work, and a strong sense of esprit de corps around this new work developed. While these trends were in evidence throughout Brazil, some prosecutorial institutions experienced them to a greater degree than others. Again, the São Paulo Ministério Público was in the vanguard—it developed the institutional capacity to become a key actor in environmental enforcement. Other state Ministérios Públicos like that of Pará also began building their capacity in environmental enforcement but experienced barriers, as discussed in the next chapter.

4 Confronting Impunity

The Ministério Público became a great threat to all organizations involved with environmental matters—from businesses to the government. It is clear that today in São Paulo everybody worries about the Ministério Público. They always want to know what the Ministério Público thinks of a certain issue.

Coordinator of the Environmental Prosecution Support Center, Ministério Público of São Paulo (personal interview, 2000)

THE INVOLVEMENT OF PROSECUTORS in environmental enforcement had the salutary effect of changing the climate of impunity that had long prevailed in Brazilian environmental law. Prosecutors wield harsh civil and criminal sanctions, they deal with many types of environmental problems, and they challenge a wide variety of actors, including powerful economic and political ones. As one São Paulo prosecutor writes, "through its innumerable investigations and lawsuits, [the Ministério Público] began to question a series of extremely pertinent practices involving large economic interests of private groups as well as the government itself. The Ministério Público's actions began to directly affect public policies and social interests" (Macedo Júnior 1999a: 109). In the view of a scholar and former São Paulo environmental agency official, the Ministério Público became "the most powerful institution in Brazilian environmental politics" (personal interview, 2002).

Prosecutorial enforcement is a particularly communicative way of enforcing environmental laws. As explained by Hawkins (2002: 206), prosecution is a "public act" that makes a statement: it is a "formal and newsworthy means of announcing the enforcement of the law and the defence of public interests." In Brazil, prosecutorial enforcement communicates the importance of environmental law to the general public as well as regulated entities. When reported in the newspaper or on television, the Ministério Público's enforcement cases send a message not just about the particular case, but also about what environmental laws mean and why people should care. With their enforcement cases, prosecutors declare that they take the law seriously and give others a reason to do so as well. As a respected and strong legal institution in Brazil, the Ministério Público confers respectability and strength upon environmental law.[1]

The message that prosecutorial enforcement sends, moreover, is that important actors—those with political and economic power—are also subject to environmental laws. With the prosecutorial enforcement of environmental laws, enforcement cases against the government and large companies became more common. The Ministério Público directly challenged impunity, the commonly held sense that environmental laws could be violated without legal repercussions. As a result of the Ministério Público's actions, "Brazilian society is gaining a sense that crimes committed by the 'powerful' will not be ignored" (Sadek and Cavalcanti 2003: 210). In its environmental enforcement cases against powerful political and economic actors, the Ministério Público reinforces a central element of the rule of law, the idea that the law can be "reliably expected to set the bounds within which all major actors, including the government, will act" (Krygier 1997: 47). This is "equality before the law," in which the law applies to all irrespective of class, status, or power (O'Donnell 1999b: 307–8; Dicey 1959: 203). The environmental enforcement cases against powerful actors communicate to the public that environmental laws apply generally and universally.

The prosecutorial mode of enforcement and its effects are variable across Brazil. State prosecutors are much more active in environmental enforcement in the state of São Paulo than in the state of Pará. In Pará, the environmental enforcement work of a handful of federal prosecutors is more expressive than that of a much larger group of state prosecutors. The São Paulo Ministério Público and the Federal Ministério Público in Pará serve as examples of "energetic enforcement." These institutions have made environmental enforcement an institutional priority. The Pará State Ministério Público, in contrast, has not.

The difference in prosecutorial enforcement activity is partly explained by the extent to which prosecutorial institutions are able to tap resources from environmental agencies and other environmental institutions in their regions. In São Paulo, prosecutors rely extensively on the state's relatively strong environmental agencies to assemble expertise and information for their enforcement activities. Pará's federal prosecutors have similarly established close ties with the office of the federal environmental agency in the state, IBAMA / PA, which has allowed them to bring a large number of successful enforcement actions.

Pará's state prosecutors, in contrast, gain little assistance from the relatively weak state environmental agency. In sum, part of what makes the Ministério Público capable of being a strong actor in environmental protection is the institutional capacity of the environmental agencies in its jurisdiction. Where the corresponding environmental agencies have the technical resources and political resolve to lend support, prosecutors are able to be more productive and successful in their enforcement work.

However, the most critical factor explaining the differences among the activity levels of different prosecutorial institutions in Brazil is the extent of their political independence. The São Paulo Ministério Público and the Federal Ministério Público exhibit a strong degree of political independence from the executive branch, whereas the State Ministério Público of Pará does not. São Paulo prosecutors and federal prosecutors in Pará have felt free to focus on environmental prosecution, which often has placed them in an adversarial position with powerful economic actors and the government itself.

In this chapter, the communicative impact of Brazilian prosecutorial enforcement is described and documented. The first part of this chapter sets forth the civil and criminal enforcement powers held by Brazilian prosecutors, while the second part describes their use in the states of São Paulo and Pará. The final part of the chapter examines differences in political independence among prosecutorial institutions in São Paulo and Pará to help explain the variations in their environmental enforcement activities.

The Powers of Civil and Criminal Enforcement

The Ministério Público has different—and stronger—enforcement powers than the environmental agencies. Under Brazilian law, a single action harmful to the environment may result in administrative, civil, and criminal sanctions; each type of sanction is independent of the application of the others.[2] Environmental agencies are responsible for administrative enforcement while the Ministério Público is generally responsible for civil and criminal enforcement.[3] Before the Ministério Público became involved, polluters were subject only to the threat of administrative sanctions. With an active Ministério Público, the threat of civil and criminal penalties is now much more common. Moreover, prosecutors pursue civil and criminal sanctions in a manner that puts environmental enforcement in the news. As stated by Sadek and Cavalcanti (2003: 209) with reference to the Ministério Público's work on behalf of public interests, "rarely a day passes in which the media does not report an action taken by prosecutors to uphold citizen rights." Its presence as a powerful enforcement actor elevated the importance of environmental law in Brazil.

Polluters fear civil and criminal sanctions more than administrative sanctions. Administrative fines, which are issued only after at least one warning, are generally not very high and are often never paid. While Brazilian environmental agencies are authorized to order the immediate closure of a noncompliant facility, this sanction is rarely used. As shown in Chapter 2, São Paulo's pollution control agency CETESB ordered the closure of fewer than one hundred facilities out of a universe of about 120,000 facilities between 1995 and 2001. Commenting on facility closure as an administrative sanction, Ayres and Braithwaite (1992: 36) explain that "[t]he problem is that the sanction is such a drastic one . . . that it is politically impossible and morally unacceptable to use it with any but the most extraordinary offenses." In São Paulo, agency officials report that the Secretary of the Environment often decides against the agency's recommendation to close a facility, thus limiting the practical use of its strongest administrative sanction.

The involvement of Brazilian prosecutors expands the range of potential sanctions to include civil and criminal penalties. Brazilian law provides for strict civil liability for environmental harm: civil penalties apply regardless of whether the polluter committed the harm intentionally or not. Polluters are liable for remediating the environmental harm or paying damages if the harm is irremediable. As described below, the Ministério Público's civil enforcement powers include strong investigative powers as well as the power to file a civil action or settle the case through the negotiation of an extrajudicial "conduct adjustment agreement."

Simply being under investigation by the Ministério Público often leads to significant changes in polluter behavior. The possibility of a public civil action or criminal prosecution makes polluters willing to submit to a conduct adjustment agreement, wherein the polluter agrees to take certain actions to prevent or remedy an environmental harm. As explained by one agency official in São Paulo, "CETESB also uses threats—the difference is that the maximum that CETESB can do is use its police power to close a factory. The Ministério Público can imprison the owner of the factory. This scares people more" (personal interview, 2002). Another states, "The requirements of the criminal law scared people into changing their ways. I know, for example, that a large number of companies started to implant an internal system of environmental management because they figured that the law was a significant threat, particularly the part about accusing the company directors" (personal interview, 2002). With the threat of civil and criminal sanctions, people have a greater incentive to pay attention to environmental laws.

The Ministério Público's civil and criminal enforcement is particularly useful in seeking environmental compliance among powerful political and economic actors. Large companies, as discussed above, have little to fear in administrative sanctions. Warnings and fines have limited deterrent power, and facility closures are rare. Similarly, organizations that form part of the state or municipal governments are unlikely to be strongly sanctioned by the state environmental agency. The Ministério Público, in contrast to environmental agencies, often has the political independence to pursue such actors. Indeed, the Ministério Público may even have an incentive to pursue powerful actors given that it may enhance the institution's public reputation for independent and aggressive defense of the public interest. Similarly, individual prosecutors may be interested in enhancing their reputations as strong and active prosecutors.[4]

Polluters—particularly large companies—fear the loss of reputation that might result from media coverage of civil or criminal prosecution (see Hutter 1997: 222–23; DiMento 1986: 42–43). Milaré explains that media coverage was very important to the São Paulo Ministério Público's early environmental work: "The press gave fantastic coverage, especially in those first few years . . . We were perceived as one of the few institutions out there doing serious work" (personal interview, 2001). A potential synergy exists between the work of reporters and prosecutors as reporters benefit from getting early leads on big stories, and prosecutors find that media coverage lends impact to their cases. As explained by one environmental prosecutor, reporters and prosecutors make a very strong combination when they work together (personal interview, 2002).

Civil Enforcement Powers

Brazilian prosecutors most often use civil enforcement powers in their environmental enforcement work. The goal of civil enforcement is not to punish the violator, but to force the violator to make the environment "whole"—either by fixing the harm that has been done or by paying damages to an environmental fund. Brazilian prosecutors generally achieve this goal extrajudicially. After investigating, they often seek to settle the case without resorting to formal judicial action. This section discusses the three primary tools of civil environmental enforcement in Brazil: the civil investigation, the conduct adjustment agreement, and the public civil action.

Civil Investigations

The opening of a civil investigation (*inquérito civil*) is the most common starting point of the Ministério Público's involvement in an environmental case.[5] Prosecutors generally open investigations either because they receive a public complaint or an administrative referral or because the prosecutor otherwise determines that an investigation is necessary.[6] The Public Civil Action Law provides that any person has the right to file a complaint and that other governmental officials have the duty to do so. "Any person can and the public servant should provoke the involvement of the Ministério Público, providing it with information about facts that might constitute the objective of a public civil action and indicating the elements of proof."[7] An environmental prosecutor in the Ministério Público of São Paulo estimated that multiple complaints arrive to the Ministério Público each day. Sometimes the complaining individual or organization provides documentation and evidence, but often they send only a letter or a newspaper clipping indicating an environmental harm (personal interview, 1999).

The prosecutor may also open an investigation on his own initiative whenever an environmental harm is suspected because of the prosecutor's personal experience. One environmental prosecutor estimated that he opens at least 80 percent of his investigations on the basis of information he reads in the local newspaper. "Every day, I read the local paper, and I see whether some reported situation falls within our area of responsibility. If so, I cut the article out, sit down at the computer, and open an investigation" (personal interview, 2002). As such, prosecutors do not require notification by a third party in order to begin a process of civil enforcement.

The investigation consists of gathering information about the actual or potential harm. The law states, "the Ministério Público can . . . open a civil investigation, or demand from any public or private entities, certified statements, information, tests, or opinions to be submitted in a determined time period, which cannot be less than 10 business days."[8] Prosecutors may use criminal charges to enforce their demand for information within investigations. The Public Civil Action Law provides that "the refusal, delay, or failure to provide technical information necessary for the filing of a public civil action when demanded by the Ministério Público" constitutes a crime punishable by imprisonment of up to three years and a fine.[9] In the majority of environmental investigations, the prosecutor demands relevant documents or a technical report about a certain problem from the environmental agency.

If the agency fails to comply with the prosecutor's requests, the prosecutor can threaten criminally charges. In situations where the prosecutor doubts the reliability of the agency's information, he may seek an expert opinion from outside the agency.

Prosecutors view the civil investigation as a very important and effective instrument. As discussed further below, between 1984 and 2004, São Paulo prosecutors opened over thirty-six thousand environmentally related civil investigations. An author of the Public Civil Action Law writes: "The extensive practical use and the success of the civil investigation—when legal doctrine was not even well established on the meaning of the concept of a 'diffuse interest'—undoubtedly surpassed even [our] most optimistic projections" (Ferraz 1995: 63).

Conduct Adjustment Agreements

Once the prosecutor has sufficient information about the problem under investigation, the prosecutor generally tries to settle the case extrajudicially rather than taking the matter to court. The majority of the Ministério Público's environmental investigations result in settlement agreements, called "conduct adjustment agreements."[10] Negotiated with the responsible party, these agreements determine the actions that the party must take to remedy the harm and the monetary penalties to be applied if the agreement is not complied with. In the case of noncompliance, the prosecutor may enforce the agreement in court. Such lawsuits are won almost automatically, given that the conduct adjustment agreement represents the accused party's admission to causing the harm and his or her acceptance of the stated penalty (Akaoui 2004: 87–88). Moreover, prosecutors often find parties quite willing to sign conduct adjustment agreements, as parties recognize that their failure to do so may result in a public civil action or criminal prosecution.

Environmental prosecutors cite many reasons for preferring to resolve cases using a conduct adjustment agreement. Perhaps most important, it avoids the time and expenses associated with the judicial process. As one prosecutor states, "There are drawbacks to the formal legal process that affect the parties directly, tiring them out emotionally and causing them financial losses" (Fink 2001: 114). Another São Paulo prosecutor calls the conduct adjustment agreement "the quickest and most efficient option for both remediation and prevention of harm" (Ferraz and Guimaraes Júnior 1999: 27, fn. 15; see also Cappelli 2000: 59). Given the utility of the conduct adjustment agreement, many environmental prosecutors view filing a public civil action as a last resort (ibid.; Fink 2001: 114).

Prosecutors emphasize that conduct adjustment agreements allow cases to be resolved in more environmentally beneficial ways. Fink (2001: 113) calls extrajudicial resolution of environmental conflicts "more meaningful than the cold command of a judicial decision." The quality of the agreement is higher than that of a judicial decision because the remedy can be custom designed. A negotiated agreement may be more likely to be fulfilled than a judicial order, as a wrongdoer voluntarily assumes responsibility and there is a shared understanding that the negotiated solution is possible to carry out (ibid.: 131–35). Through the negotiation process, the wrongdoer is also educated about the importance of environmental laws and the impact of his behavior.

Significantly, the use of a conduct adjustment agreement leads to an enforcement process that is more cooperative and less adversarial. In the words of one Brazilian legal scholar, "Filing a lawsuit . . . causes the parties' interests to move further apart, it is very uncertain and risky for all parties. . . . In contrast, the conduct adjustment agreement brings interests together, finds the points of convergence, and tries to resolve the environmental problem."[11] As discussed in Chapter 1, the academic literature on environmental regulation has found many benefits to a cooperative enforcement approach, including less legal uncertainty, lower compliance costs, and less defensiveness among regulated entities. Prosecutors find similar benefits in using conduct adjustment agreements.

Public Civil Actions

Where prosecutorial investigation and attempts to negotiate a conduct adjustment agreement fail to achieve results, prosecutors may file an *ação civil pública* (public civil action). The decision to do so is considered by many prosecutors to be nondiscretionary: where there is proof of environmental harm and the case has not been resolved extrajudicially, the prosecutor has a duty to file a public civil action.[12]

Public prosecutors can use the public civil action both to impose liability where environmental harm has occurred and to prevent environment harm. In cases where the harm has already occurred, a court may order the responsible party to pay money damages to a governmental environmental fund or require the party to take a certain action (*obrigação de fazer*) or to abstain from taking a certain action (*obrigação de não fazer*) to further environmental protection.[13]

Except where the environmental harm is considered irreparable, prosecutors generally seek a court order requiring the party to take some protective action rather than payment of money damages.

Where environmental harm is threatened by a party's activities, a court may issue a *mandado liminar* (preliminary injunction) ordering a party to take or abstain from taking a certain action as an emergency measure before the court makes a final decision on the merits of the case. To be granted a preliminary injunction, the Ministério Público must show that its case has a good legal foundation (*fumus boni iuris*) and that absent such an emergency order the objective of the lawsuit will be lost because the interest being defended will be irreparably damaged (*periculum in mora*).

Unlike the power to open an investigation, the power to bring a public civil action is not exclusive to the Ministério Público. Environmental public civil actions can also be filed by a variety of other governmental actors, including environmental agencies and environmental groups that have been established for at least one year.[14] However, the Ministério Público has brought over 90 percent of such lawsuits (Cappelli 2000: 55). Environmental agencies generally choose to enforce the law using administrative sanctions—warnings, fines, and facility closures. Environmental groups often choose to make a complaint to the Ministério Público rather than filing lawsuits themselves. In some cases, the environmental group becomes a co-plaintiff with the Ministério Público.

Criminal Enforcement Powers

Prosecutors may also use criminal sanctions to enforce environmental laws. While criminal sanctions for some environmentally harmful activities have existed in Brazil for many years, the passage of the Environmental Crimes Law (Lei de Crimes Ambientais) of 1998 enhanced the possibility of criminal penalties for environmental law violations. Under this law, legal entities such as corporations as well as individuals may be held criminally liable (article 3) (Benjamin 1998a).

The law specifies criminal penalties for violations in five areas: fauna, flora, pollution, cultural and historical preservation, and administration of environmental laws. Crimes against fauna and flora include the unauthorized hunting of wildlife, punishable by six months to a year in jail and a fine (article 29), and intentional damage to protected forests, punishable by one to three years in jail, and/or a fine (article 38). The crime of intentionally causing pollution at levels that result or may result in harm to human health, death of animals, or significant destruction of flora carries a penalty of one to four years in jail and a fine (article 54). The crime of intentionally causing damage to historical or cultural monuments incurs a penalty of one to three years of jail and a fine (article 62). When the harm is caused by a negligent action rather than an intentional action, the penalty is generally about half as severe.

With respect to the administration of environmental laws, the law criminalizes certain acts by environmental agency officials. The act of issuing a permit out of accordance with environmental regulations and the act of making false or misleading statements in the course of processing an environmental permit are punishable by a fine and one to three years in jail (articles 66 and 67). If an agency official negligently issues an illegal permit, the penalty is three months to one year in jail.

In contrast to civil enforcement, the Constitution does not clearly give Brazilian prosecutors the power to conduct criminal investigations.[15] Rather, criminal investigations are widely viewed as being the responsibility of the judicial police, who may then refer cases for criminal prosecution to the Ministério Público. Alternatively, as discussed below, an environmental agency may collect evidence that supports a criminal indictment and refer the case to the Ministério Público. When criminal charges are filed for violations carrying a penalty of fewer than two years of jail, the alleged violator has the right to negotiate a plea bargain with the Ministério Público (Brito, Barreto, and Rothman 2005). Plea bargains are not permitted when the alleged violator has negotiated a plea bargain in the previous five years or has previously been incarcerated.

The Absence of Prosecutorial Discretion

Discretion is a concept that remains foreign to Brazilian prosecutors. As explained by the American legal scholar Kenneth Culp Davis, a public official has discretion "whenever the effective limits on his power leave him free to make a choice among possible courses of action and inaction" (Davis 1969: 4). Davis and more recent commentators often criticize the expansive nature of prosecutorial discretion in the American legal system. In contrast, Brazilian prosecutors officially adhere to the *princípio da obrigatoriedade* (principle of obligation), also called *princípio da legalidade* (principle of legality).[16] This principle holds that a prosecutor has the obligation to file criminal charges in every case where sufficient evidence of the defendant's guilt exists.[17]

The principle of obligation developed in the context of criminal actions, but Brazilian prosecutors generally consider it applicable to the civil context as well. It is consonant with the civil law tradition's foundational premise that the legislature makes the law: the legislature decided that a certain action was a crime and all persons who committed the crime should be prosecuted. It is also consonant with the rule of law ideal that all cases should be adjudicated in a courtroom with independent, objective judges. As explained by a Mexican scholar: "To allow for discretion substitutes the judgment of the legislator with the judgment of the prosecutor, whose judgment is completely personal and thus susceptible to error" (Castro 1998: 95).

Some civil law countries that traditionally abided by the principle of obligation have introduced more prosecutorial discretion into their criminal law systems. The Peruvian criminal law code, for example, was reformed in 1991 to allow the Ministério Público to exercise the *princípio de oportunidad* (principle of opportunity or principle of expediency). This principle holds that prosecutors may decline to file criminal charges in cases where they determine that criminal penalties are not necessary and the offender does not deserve criminal penalties.[18] The penal codes of Bolivia, Chile, Costa Rica, El Salvador, Guatemala, Honduras, Paraguay, and Venezuela also allow for some exercise of the principle of opportunity (Duce and Riego 2006: 28, Table 2). The principle of obligation has been relaxed as prosecutors have assumed new functions in line with the transition from an inquisitorial criminal law system to an accusatorial one (ibid.: 27).

In terms of the Brazilian Ministério Público's environmental work, the principle of obligation means that once a prosecutor becomes aware of potential or actual harm, whether by public complaint or otherwise, the prosecutor is obligated to take action to investigate the harm. And when the investigation reveals that harm occurred that could be remedied through further extrajudicial or judicial action, he or she must pursue the case as necessary to remedy the harm. If the investigation does not reveal an adequate basis for further action, the investigation may be terminated and archived.[19] As stated by Mazzilli (2001: 78) in his discussion of the Ministério Público's work in the defense of environmental and other diffuse interests: "It is not acceptable that the Ministério Público, having identified a hypothesis under which it should act, chooses not to . . . if the Ministério Público is alerted that the law has been violated, it is not acceptable that it abstains from acting or intervening for reasons of convenience." Most environmental prosecutors in Brazil formally adhere to the principle of obligation.[20]

Civil and Criminal Enforcement in Action

Prosecutors in the states of São Paulo and Pará have used their civil and criminal enforcement powers to different extents and in different ways. In the state of São Paulo, prosecutors are very involved in environmental enforcement, and they almost exclusively utilize civil enforcement instruments—investigations, conduct adjustment agreements, and public civil actions. Federal prosecutors in Pará are also energetic in their environmental enforcement work, and, notably, they have begun to heavily utilize criminal environmental enforcement. State prosecutors in Pará, in contrast, display a lack of energetic enforcement. They have largely been confined to using only investigations and conduct adjustment agreements and to pursuing cases that do not involve powerful political and economic actors.

While the strength of the Ministério Público's environmental enforcement varies throughout the country, a 1996 survey showed that 32 percent of Brazilian prosecutors emphasized environmental protection in the preceding two years, and that 43 percent planned to during the following two years (Sadek 1997: 59). Moreover, in a 1997 survey of federal prosecutors, environmental protection received the best evaluation of all areas in which the Ministério Público works: 55 percent of prosecutors opined that the institution did an excellent or good job defending the environment (Wiecko V. de Castilho and Sadek 1998: 22).

The State of São Paulo

The São Paulo Ministério Público is active in the defense of a variety of public interests, but its work in environmental protection is particularly strong. Each year, the Ministério Público sponsors a conference dedicated to environmental enforcement, and several of the most well-regarded scholars of environmental law in Brazil have been São Paulo prosecutors.[21] The Federal Ministério Público also plays an important role in environmental protection in São Paulo.

Enforcement by State Prosecutors

In November 2001, the 5th Annual Environmental Conference of the Ministério Público of São Paulo was held in the touristy town of Campos do Jordão, several hours from the capital. The majority of the two hundred attendees were state prosecutors, although several representatives of the Federal Ministério Público, environmental agencies, environmental police, and other governmental institutions were also invited to participate. Prominent prosecutors, scholars, and judges gave speeches discussing current themes in environmental law and the significance of the Ministério Público's environmental work. Through formal and informal activities, state prosecutors discussed and developed ideas about how to improve environmental prosecution. The mood was one of celebrating past achievements and inspiring new ones.

Environmental protection is an area in which the Ministério Público of São Paulo has a strong history of action. In the 1980s, Édis Milaré developed environmental protection as a role of the São Paulo Ministério Público and traveled to other states to help their Ministérios Públicos begin working in this new area. In the 1990s, another dynamic institutional leader, Antonio Herman Benjamin, headed the Environmental Prosecution Support Center of the Ministério Público of São Paulo and began organizing statewide conferences and other activities to develop the institution's environmental practice. In 1997, Benjamin also organized the first annual international conference on environmental law in Brazil, which attracted prosecutors as well as other environmental legal professionals from throughout Brazil and other countries.

There is an expanding group of prosecutors in São Paulo that views environmental protection as one of the institution's most important functions. Some of them are advanced in their careers, having started out in less populated areas of the state where they were responsible for all of the institution's work, criminal and civil. They have been promoted to larger cities, where they are able to specialize in environmental prosecution. Others are at the beginning of their careers and, while they are responsible for many different types of cases, they find time to dedicate to environmental work. One young prosecutor explains that environmental prosecution feels more rewarding than other areas of her work, and she is motivated by the camaraderie with other environmental prosecutors (personal interview, 2002).

Prosecutors, of course, vary in their commitment to environmental protection. Some prosecutors might do only the minimum, opening investigations when they receive public complaints and governmental referrals. Other prosecutors go beyond their basic professional obligation. They are zealous environmental advocates, confident about their importance in environmental protection.[22] They take the initiative in finding out about environmental problems in their jurisdiction through establishing contacts with community groups and participating in local events and campaigns. They see their role as solving environmental problems—often extrajudicially—rather than merely fulfilling their obligation to investigate and file a public civil action.

In her study of São Paulo state prosecutors involved in the defense of children's rights, Silva (2001) sketched two classic types. On the one hand are *promotores da gabinete*, prosecutors who are relatively passive in their work, waiting for the problem to come to them. These prosecutors fulfill their responsibilities of responding to public complaints with investigations and public civil actions, but do not go beyond their basic duties. The passive prosecutor "does not see himself as an authority that should continually oversee the government's implementation of policies and social programs" (ibid.: 99). On the other hand are *promotores de fatos*, active prosecutors who expend their time and energy to discover problems and use prosecutorial instruments more creatively and strategically to solve them. As Silva explains, active prosecutors "tend to expand prosecutorial functions beyond the judicial sphere, turning themselves into true political actors in their communities" (ibid.: 100). These opposing types also apply to differences in the styles of environmental prosecutors.

Data on the usage of investigations, public civil actions, and conduct adjustment agreements by the São Paulo Ministério Público show how prosecutorial enforcement grew.[23] Between 1985 and 2004, São Paulo state prosecutors opened almost 37,000 environmental investigations,[24] 5,890 in the year 2004 alone.[25] Table 4.1 and Figure 4.1 show that the annual number generally grew after 1984, with particularly precipitous growth after 1996.[26]

The prosecutors of the São Paulo State Ministério Público also filed 4,250 environmental public civil actions between 1984 and 2004 (see Table 4.1 and Figure 4.1). While the number of investigations grew consistently throughout this period, the number of public civil actions increased between 1984 and 1992 but stayed fairly constant in the 1990s, averaging about 240 per year from 1991 to 2002. In 2003 and 2004, the number of public civil actions filed by São Paulo prosecutors increased to about 410 per year.

With the power to settle cases extrajudicially, granted by amendments to the Public Civil Action Law in 1990, prosecutors increasingly chose to resolve cases extrajudicially rather than through litigation (see Fink 2001).[27] Prosecutors of the São Paulo Ministério Público negotiated about one thousand environmental conduct adjustment agreements in the year 2000—four times the number of public civil actions filed in the same year.[28] The use of conduct adjustment agreements by environmental prosecutors is common throughout Brazil. In the state of Rio Grande do Sul, for example, only 70 environmental public civil actions were filed as compared to about 550 conduct adjustment agreements in 2001

Table 4.1 Environmental Investigations and Public Civil Actions by the State Ministério Público of São Paulo, 1984–2004

Year	Investigations	Public Civil Actions	Year	Investigations	Public Civil Actions
1984	3	5	1995	643	250
1985	10	18	1996	830	204
1986	41	41	1997	1,515	203
1987	53	55	1998	2,747	234
1988	129	131	1999	3,559	272
1989	209	145	2000	3,974	229
1990	288	169	2001	4,756	249
1991	553	257	2002	4,979	256
1992	529	284	2003	4,816	412
1993	644	217	2004	5,890	407
1994	691	218	TOTAL	36,859	4,256

SOURCE: 1984–97 data compiled from the author's analysis of a database for this period from the Environmental Prosecution Support Center of the São Paulo Ministério Público; 1998–2004 data acquired directly from the support center.

Figure 4.1 Environmental Investigations and Public Civil Actions by the State Ministério Público of São Paulo, 1984–2004

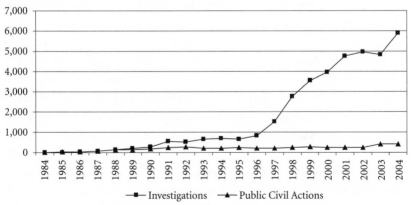

SOURCE: 1984–97 data compiled from the author's analysis of a database for this period from the Environmental Prosecution Support Center of the São Paulo Ministério Público; 1998–2004 data acquired directly from the support center.

(personal interview, 2002). It is estimated that the Brazilian Ministério Público resolves about 90 percent of its cases without litigation (Sadek 2000: 28).

In cases where public civil actions are filed, prosecutors commonly request injunctive relief from the court.[29] As described above, preliminary injunctions require a showing that the case has a solid legal foundation and that a possibility of irreparable harm exists. Environmental prosecutors are often able to meet this standard, given that polluters are strictly liable under Brazilian environmental law and many types of environmental harm are arguably irreparable. By obtaining preliminary injunctions, prosecutors have had a significant degree of success in stopping or delaying proposed projects and activities with alleged irregularities in the environmental permitting process. While precise data are not available for São Paulo, prosecutors state that the majority of environmental public civil actions include requests for a preliminary injunction. In the state of Rio Grande do Sul, the lead environmental prosecutor estimates that 99 percent of environmental public civil actions seek preliminary injunctions (personal interview, 2002).

Another significant aspect of the São Paulo Ministério Público's environmental enforcement work is the range of environmental problems that are addressed. The most common type of environmental harm alleged in the 2,197 public civil actions filed by the Ministério Público of São Paulo between 1984 and 1997 involved deforestation and other violations of Brazilian forestry laws (35 percent).[30] Deforestation and devegetation in areas of the Atlantic Rainforest (Mata Atlântica) and in erosion-prone areas are extremely restricted under Brazilian forestry code and other laws, requiring a special permit that can only be obtained for works of public utility or social interest.[31] The prevalence of these lawsuits is also explained by the fact that prosecutors are routinely informed of such violations by the São Paulo Environmental Police (Comando de Policiamento Ambiental), and thus these are the problems about which prosecutors hear most and have the information available to file a public civil action.[32]

Other issues dealt with by the Ministério Público in the lawsuits filed between 1984 and 1997 include water quality (13 percent), land use and construction (12 percent), air quality (9 percent), solid wastes (9 percent), and mineral extraction (8 percent). Water quality cases brought by the Ministério Público most often involved lack of domestic sewage treatment, but many cases dealt with industrial water pollution, oil spills, fish kills, water treatment, and other water quality issues. Land use and construction cases are those involving the construction of subdivisions, buildings, or roads in a way that causes environmental damage and, in many cases, without the necessary environmental permits. With regard to air quality cases, it is worth noting that the majority involved rural air pollution from the practice of burning sugarcane fields to facilitate harvest. Solid waste cases involved both industrial and residential solid wastes and most often dealt with illegal dumping and the impact of unprotected landfills. Mineral extraction cases most often involved extraction of sand and other construction materials, but also granite, calcium, gold, and other minerals.

The remainder of the cases involved noise levels (6 percent), wildlife and animal protection (4 percent), historical preservation (3 percent), and other assorted issues (1 percent). Noise pollution cases involved factories, music clubs, evangelical churches, and other establishments that produced illegally high noise levels. Wildlife and animal protection cases involved illegal hunting and animal mistreatment. Historical preservation cases generally sought to protect historical buildings such as churches, railroad stations, and plazas in urban areas.[33]

A comparison of the number of enforcement actions initiated by São Paulo prosecutors with the number of sanctions issued by São Paulo's pollution control agency CETESB demonstrates the significance of prosecutorial enforcement in the state. As described in Chapter 2, CETESB issued on average about 4,600 warnings and 2,700 fines each year between 1990 and 2001. By 2001, the annual number of investigations conducted by the Ministério Público had grown to almost equal the number of warnings issued by CETESB. The number of public civil actions filed each year was almost one-tenth the number of administrative fines issued each year throughout the 1990s. And in 2000, the number of conduct adjustment agreements negotiated by São Paulo prosecutors was about half the number of administrative fines issued by CETESB that year. The volume of prosecutorial investigations, civil actions, and conduct adjustment agreements clearly contributed substantially to environmental enforcement in the state of São Paulo.

The São Paulo Ministério Público's enforcement work greatly benefited from the assistance of São Paulo's relatively strong environmental agencies. As noted above, the office of the São Paulo Environmental Police routinely sends information about forestry violations to São Paulo prosecutors. According to one study, one-third of the environmental complaints received by São Paulo city environmental prosecutors between 1990 and 2001 came from governmental offices (Maciel 2002: 83–84). The author of the study interprets the data to indicate "the existence of strong cooperation between these two spheres of state power in public policy implementation."

Prosecutors also receive a great deal of technical information and assistance from São Paulo environmental agencies in the course of their civil investigations.[34] In each investigation that São Paulo prosecutors open, they generally contact the appropriate state agencies asking for information about the company or landowner under investigation and the environmental problem at issue. When they negotiate conduct adjustment agreements, they often request the assistance of environmental agency officials in fashioning an appropriate course of action. Moreover, agency staff are often made responsible for verifying the violator's progress in complying with the conduct adjustment agreement. The São Paulo Ministério Público is able to build upon and benefit from the substantial capacity that exists within the São Paulo state environmental agencies.

No data were available on the number of criminal prosecutions for environmental violations, and environmental prosecutors were not aware of any criminal environmental prosecutions. There are several reasons that São Paulo state prosecutors rely exclusively on civil enforcement. First, they perceive civil enforcement to be more effective and appropriate. As stated by a São Paulo environmental prosecutor, "In the civil sphere, we have a much more powerful tool: strict liability. We do not have to argue about guilt—it doesn't matter if the offender acted intentionally or not. In the criminal sphere, you have to prove a guilty mental state."[35] Civil enforcement is also geared toward preventing and remedying environmental harm, which prosecutors often express to be their priority, rather than punishment.

Another important reason that prosecutors rely heavily on civil enforcement involves organizational aspects of the Ministério Público. São Paulo state prosecutors who specialize in environmental protection in midsize and larger cities are considered civil rather than criminal prosecutors. As such, they do not have the authority to act in the criminal sphere.[36] The specialized environmental prosecutor must refer the potential criminal case to a criminal prosecutor, who also handles all other types of criminal cases. Given that criminal prosecutors are not specialized, other criminal cases may take priority. In rural judicial districts, prosecutors are authorized to do both civil and criminal work, but these prosecutors have followed the lead of specialized prosecutors in relying on civil enforcement in their environmental cases.

Enforcement by Federal Prosecutors

The Federal Ministério Público in São Paulo is also very active in environmental prosecution, particularly in cases involving large projects in which the federal government is involved. However, given that there are many fewer federal prosecutors than state prosecutors, the number of investigations is much lower. In 2002, two federal prosecutors worked exclusively on environmental problems (including historical preservation and protection of indigenous peoples) in the São Paulo metropolitan region, consisting of the city of São Paulo and fourteen surrounding municipalities. In 1999, these prosecutors opened 38 environmental investigations; by 2001, this number had doubled to 70.[37] On average, they filed 3 environmental public civil actions per year.[38] No criminal prosecutions were reported.

The State of Pará

In the state of Pará, the prosecutorial mode of environmental enforcement is also operative. Yet it is the enforcement work of the Federal Ministério Público rather than the Pará State Ministério Público that is most prevalent and visible. Moreover, federal prosecutors in Pará have extensively used instruments of criminal enforcement as well as civil enforcement. The state Ministério Público has been considerably less active in environmental prosecution.

Enforcement by State Prosecutors

The Pará State Ministério Público's environmental prosecution work has focused on environmental problems in Belém, the capital of Pará. There, the Ministério Público has a specialized environmental prosecution office staffed by two prosecutors responsible for the city of Belém.[39] State prosecutors working outside the capital have not become significantly active in environmental prosecution.

Data on the activities of the environmental prosecution office in Belém suggest that the Pará State Ministério Público has been very limited in both the number and types of cases it pursues.[40] Environmental prosecutors in Belém opened a total of 273 investigations between the years 1998 and 2001. Over these four years, the number of investigations per year remained relatively constant, with an average of 68. In addition, 33 environmental public civil actions were filed in the fourteen years from 1988 to 2001. The number of lawsuits per year peaked in 1991 with 11, and tended to decline over the following years. In the years 2000 and 2001, no environmental public civil actions were filed by the environmental prosecutors of Belém. This apparent decline in the environmental enforcement activity of the Pará State Ministério Público is discussed further below.

Of the environmental public civil actions that were filed by the environmental prosecutors of Belém from 1988 to 1999, over one-third (36 percent) dealt with the issue of noise pollution.[41] Mineral extraction accounted for eight cases (24 percent), historical preservation for five cases, illegal construction for four cases, water pollution for two cases, and harm to vegetation and wildlife for two cases. The same areas of emphasis are evident in the environmental investigations conducted by the Belém prosecutors. A full 50 percent of the 273 investigations conducted in the four years from 1998 through 2001 concerned noise pollution. Another 15 percent concerned air pollution, many of these in combination with noise pollution. Eight percent concerned harm to vegetation and wildlife, 7 percent concerned cultural and historical preservation, and 5 percent concerned solid waste disposal. The remaining 15 percent dealt with a wide variety of other problems including water pollution, basic sanitation, illegal construction, mining, and the illegal sale of forest products.

As in São Paulo, conduct adjustment agreements were used frequently, as indicated by data on the outcomes of one environmental prosecutor's investigations: of 45 investigations opened in 1998, over two-thirds (31 investigations) were concluded with a conduct adjustment agreement; about one-quarter (12 investigations) were terminated and archived because the issue had been resolved in the course of the investigation; and the remaining two investigations became public civil actions. The outcomes of this prosecutor's 1999 investigations were similar.

While the Pará State Ministério Público does not collect statewide data on environmental prosecution activities outside the capital, evidence suggests that few, if any, environmental public civil actions were filed in the 1990s. In her study, Dourado (1993) documents the existence of eight public civil actions by prosecutors outside Belém filed between 1988 and 1991. However, persistent questioning of several of the most environmentally active prosecutors in the state revealed no information about any environmental lawsuits filed outside Belém after the mid-1990s. The number of environmental investigations was also unavailable but estimated to be quite low.

As told through the data on investigations and lawsuits, the story of the State Ministério Público of Pará differs from the stories of other prosecutorial institutions included in the present research. Environmental enforcement did not become an area of emphasis and dynamism in the State Ministério

Público of Pará. The number of investigations did not rise precipitously as in São Paulo, but rather stayed constant at a relatively low number. The number of lawsuits filed declined over the decade to zero. Moreover, the domination of the caseload by noise pollution cases signals the prosecutors' tendency to deal with cases of limited environmental consequence rather than those involving complex problems or powerful economic and political interests.

However, when compared with administrative enforcement conducted by Pará's state environmental agency SECTAM, the Pará State Ministério Público's record does not look quite as weak. Its 273 investigations opened between 1998 and 2001 compare with 840 warnings and fines issued by SECTAM over the same period. In the context of the state of Pará, even the relatively low level of activity of the state Ministério Público arguably represents a significant contribution to environmental enforcement.

Moreover, the weak environmental enforcement work of Pará state prosecutors finds partial explanation in the weakness of the state environmental agency. Pará prosecutors who have tried to use the agency as a technical resource for their work have often been disappointed. As stated by one, "there are many issues that SECTAM does not have the ability to respond to, and others that they don't want to respond to because it is against their interest" (personal interview, 2002). SECTAM has had some success in using political channels to avoid responding to information requests that state prosecutors have sent. Other reasons underlying the absence of energetic enforcement in the Pará State Ministério Público are explored below.

Enforcement by Federal Prosecutors

In 2002, the Federal Ministério Público's delegation in Pará had six prosecutors, with three spending part of their time on environmental matters. Despite their small number, these prosecutors' environmental activities often made news headlines. In an April 2002 news article, the chief federal prosecutor in Pará declared that environmental protection had been, and remained, a priority in the work of Pará federal prosecutors: "Environmental issues were always a priority of the Federal Ministério Público, and this has been demonstrated and emphasized with our work over many years, including our efforts to promote the integration and joint action of administrative agencies that deal with environmental problems."[42] He further explains that the Federal Ministério Público's work has concerned not only preserving forests but also the environmental impact of large economic projects such as hydroelectric plants and the impact of illegal logging on indigenous tribes.[43]

The extent to which federal prosecutors in Pará have prioritized environmental protection is evident in prosecutorial data. Of the 494 investigations opened by the Federal Ministério Público in Pará between 1996 and 2001, 70 (28 percent) concerned environmental problems. As measured by the number of public civil actions, the emphasis on environment is even greater. Federal prosecutors in Pará filed 106 public civil actions between 1987 and 2001. The subjects of these lawsuits are illustrated in Figure 4.2. Of these lawsuits, 62 (58 percent) concerned environmental issues—28 dealt with preservation of historical buildings, 21 dealt with illegal logging, and the remainder concerned river channelization projects, protected areas, and preservation of archeological sites. A judicial injunction was sought in about 80 percent of these lawsuits. The nonenvironmental areas in which federal prosecutors primarily filed civil actions in these years included political corruption, employment law, consumer protection, education, and taxation. While no data were available on extrajudicial resolution of environmental cases in the Federal Ministério Público, a federal environmental prosecutor asserted that conduct adjustment agreements are often more effective and explained that he "only takes a case to court as a last resort, because when you bring it to court you lose the control needed to resolve it in a better way" (personal interview, 2002).

Figure 4.2 Environmental Public Civil Actions by the Federal Ministério Público in Pará by Subject Area, 1987–2001

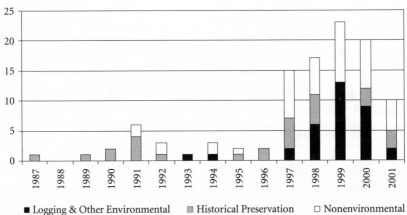

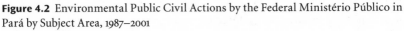

SOURCE: Database constructed from analysis of all public civil actions kept at the Federal Ministério Público's state headquarters in Belém, Pará, May 2002.

What is most notable, however, about the environmental enforcement work of the Federal Ministério Público in Pará is the increasing reliance on criminal prosecution. Accounting for the decrease in the number of environmental civil actions in 2000 and 2001, federal prosecutors explained that they began to use criminal prosecution to pursue environmental violations much more frequently in these years. They found criminal prosecution to be more efficient and also found a way to request civil penalties as part of the criminal case. Data on criminal prosecution in 2001 show the predominance of environmental prosecution in its criminal caseload. In 2001, 92 out of 306 criminal prosecution cases (30 percent) concerned environmental violations. Other criminal cases were primarily in the areas of social security; improper usage of public funds; telecommunications; false identity; and drug trafficking.

Almost all criminal environmental cases filed in 2001 by the Pará federal prosecutors were based on information about criminal violations forwarded by the federal environmental agency in Pará (IBAMA/PA).[44] As discussed in Chapter 5, in the few years prior to 2001, Pará's federal prosecutors had criminally prosecuted several high-level IBAMA/PA officials for administrative improbity. By 2001, IBAMA/PA had a new state director who sought to cooperate with federal prosecutors, referring to them as "essential partners." Like São Paulo state prosecutors, Pará federal prosecutors were thus able to rely on and benefit from the technical competence of an environmental agency. This clearly contributed to the number and success of their enforcement actions.

A 2005 study of forestry-related cases filed by federal prosecutors in the federal court of Belém between 2000 and 2003 sheds further light on criminal environmental enforcement in Pará (Brito and Barreto 2005). The study analyzed a sample of 55 criminal prosecutions that resulted from over 1,200 notices of criminal violations sent by IBAMA to the Federal Ministério Público in Pará. Of the 55 cases, 53 percent were against legal entities and 47 percent were against individuals. The study showed that the Ministério Público relies on extrajudicial resolution in its criminal enforcement work as well as in its civil enforcement work. Federal prosecutors sought to negotiate a *transação penal* (plea bargain) in 91 percent of the cases. In many of these cases, however, procedural problems such as difficulties in locating the alleged violators prevented the successful conclusion of negotiations and collection of monetary penalties. In about 20 percent of the cases, plea bargains were negotiated and the alleged violators were complying with their agreements. The large majority of these plea bargains (95 percent) involved requirements that the violator perform some type of social assistance, usually involving a donation of food or medicine. Only a very few (3 percent) required any type of environmental remediation.

The study found substantial time delays in both the extrajudicial and judicial processes of punishing offenders. In cases where plea bargains were struck, it took an average of six months for the agreements to be negotiated, and sometimes longer for them to be complied with. In the almost 10 percent of cases that became criminal actions, it took an average of eight months between the issuance of the administrative fine by IBAMA and the beginning of the criminal action. This delay allowed time for offenders to change addresses, which then often led to additional delay. While the study clearly provides evidence that the environmental crimes law is being used by the Federal Ministério Público, it concluded that the law "has not yet succeeded in eliminating the incentives to log illegally" (Brito, Barreto, and Rothman 2005: 19).

The Ministério Público's focus in Pará on criminal prosecution is very different from that of São Paulo. This difference finds some explanation in what Hochstetler and Keck (2007: 151) call the "politics of state absence" that characterizes much of the Brazilian Amazon. They explain that the problem of law enforcement in the Amazon is not just a matter of weak institutional capacity on the part of environmental agencies, but a symptom of the weakness of the state's overall presence in the region. With the absence of the state, power relations in the natural resource sector resemble those of organized crime. As stated by Federal Police Marshal Jorge Barbosa Pontes in a newspaper interview in 2002, "We are not dealing with small bandits, but with a mafia."[45] Given the prevalence of a criminal mentality and modus operandi in the exploitation of Pará's forests, prosecutors may view criminal prosecution as the most suitable vehicle for their enforcement work.[46]

The Significance of Prosecutorial Independence

Much of the variation observed in the extent and degree of civil and criminal environmental enforcement by prosecutorial institutions in Brazil can be related to prosecutorial independence. The independence of Brazilian prosecutors, as discussed in Chapter 3, has two main components.[47] The first component is the political independence of the Ministério Público as an institution. The Brazilian Constitution of 1988 provides for such independence by largely removing the institution from the control of the three branches of government. The second component of prosecutorial independence is the functional independence of its prosecutors. This allows individual prosecutors to pursue cases in the manner they deem appropriate, largely free of influence by prosecutors that form the leadership of the institution. Functional independence is rooted in constitutional provisions guaranteeing strong job protections to individual prosecutors. Both prongs of prosecutorial independence are formally established in law, but vary in the extent to which they are a reality throughout Brazil.

Too Little Independence: Barriers to Energetic Enforcement

The prosecutorial mode of environmental enforcement did not develop to the same degree in all parts of Brazil. The State Ministério Público of Pará serves as an example. As described in Chapter 3, it began doing environmental work in 1988 with the passage of the new federal constitution. Yet, as evident from the small number of investigations, lawsuits, and other enforcement activity, the Pará State Ministério Público has not emerged as an important actor in the same way as its counterpart in São Paulo has. While the number of investigations and lawsuits grew in the first five years of its work from 1988 through the early 1990s, the data indicate stagnation and even decline in the institution's environmental prosecution since the mid-1990s. Unlike São Paulo, it has not expanded and become more active. Rather, the prosecutorial mode of enforcement has been constrained by political and institutional factors.

Writing in the mid-1990s, Ismaelino Valente, the first environmental prosecutor in the Pará Ministério Público, acknowledged the ineffectiveness of the institution's work in addressing the state's significant environmental problems and sought to explain it. As he states, "the action of the Ministério Público in defense of the environment in the Amazon is reduced to isolated cases, generally of a small scale, such as the pollution of air or small streams resulting from the industrial activity of small companies . . . completely overlooking the large environmental problems of the Amazon such as deforestation, pollution of rivers by mercury, and the ecological chaos in unregulated mining areas" (Valente 1995: 224–25).

According to Valente (1994: 24–27), both external and internal barriers constrained the Pará State Ministério Público's effectiveness. Barriers external to the institution included the disorganization and complexity of environmental laws; the lack of technical assistance and information available to prosecutors; and the lack of communication with both environmental agencies and federal prosecutors in the state. Internal barriers included the lack of a defined institutional policy on environmental issues; the lack of an action strategy that might lead to articulated action by prosecutors; and the lack of financial resources for planning, education, and the confrontation of powerful interests that cause environmental degradation (ibid.: 27–28).

In a 1993 study of the effectiveness of the Pará State Ministério Público's environmental work, Dourado (1993) emphasized the magnitude of the state. She explained that the Ministério Público is plagued by the same problems that inhibit the effectiveness of other state governmental entities, namely the large distances between towns that make transportation and communication difficult. In a similar vein, a federal prosecutor in Pará explained that the Pará state government is essentially not present in many areas of the state: "This is a serious problem. . . . Sometimes you even have a judicial decision, but it doesn't arrive to the place because the government does not have a strong enough presence. A few policemen might be stationed nearby, but how are a half-dozen people going to enforce the law against the guy who owns all the land in the area?" (personal interview, 2002). The reach of the legal system does not effectively extend to these areas (see O'Donnell 1999b: 313).

While not directly stated and discussed by Valente or other early commentators, the most fundamental factor constraining the State Ministério Público of Pará is its lack of independence from the executive branch. The state governor from 1994 through 2002 was openly critical of federal prosecutors' involvement in environmental protection in the state. Reacting to the Federal Ministério Público's challenge to a new state highway, for example, he declared in a press interview that "no one is going to give us lessons about protecting the environment."[48] He further criticized prosecutors for defending monkeys rather than people, and he implied that federal prosecutors had political motives in opposing the state's development of canals, dams, and highways.[49] Given the state governor's view of the environmental work of the Federal Ministério Público, it is not surprising that the Pará State Ministério Público's environmental work encountered political barriers.

Despite the constitutional provisions that favor the political independence of the Ministério Público, Pará governors managed to retain influence over the work of state prosecutors through their control of the state budget process and their power to appoint the attorney general.[50] When state prosecutors are asked why the Pará Ministério Público has not grown in the environmental area, the lack of budgetary resources is most commonly cited. The state does not have enough prosecutors, and prosecutors in rural areas end up being responsible for all prosecutorial functions not only in one judicial district but often in several districts. In such situations, criminal prosecution and other more traditional prosecutorial functions take precedence over newer areas such as environmental defense. Lack of institutional support for environmental enforcement work is also evident in the absence of an Environmental Prosecution Support Center dedicated to assisting prosecutors in environmental cases. Acknowledging political interference, a state prosecutor explains that the governor does not allocate money to environmental enforcement because "environmental law in certain ways hurts the interests of those that have the economic power and these people have a lot of political influence" (personal interview, 2002).

The Pará state governor's appointment of the attorney general also allows him some control over the activities of prosecutors. The attorney general is able to keep individual prosecutors in line through the promotion process. In Pará, almost all state prosecutors are from Belém, the state capital. As new prosecutors, they must begin their careers working in rural parts of the state, but they seek to be promoted as quickly as possible to areas close to the capital. As explained by a federal prosecutor, "the prosecutor can't go against the attorney general or others who are powerful in the institution, because they make the decisions about your promotions" (personal interview, 2002). Discussions with prosecutors revealed several examples of cases in which prosecutors who became active in environmental defense felt pressure from others in the institution to change their position or be less aggressive. As reported by a federal prosecutor: "One [state prosecutor] that worked a lot with me was called to the office of the attorney general and told he could be suspended, that he could be punished because he had filed an action against the state government. This is unthinkable in a place like São Paulo and it is unthinkable in the Federal Ministério Público, but it is a local reality in Pará" (personal interview, 2002).

Pará's state prosecutors may also lack independence from city governmental officials in the localities where they work. As explained by a federal prosecutor, many state prosecutors in rural areas are in need of resources such as an administrative assistant and computer access, and municipal governments often provide them with such resources. This, however, may compromise the prosecutor's independence from local officials. Stories circulated about mayors and other municipal officials in Pará with ties to illegal logging operations, but no investigations of such allegations had been opened by state prosecutors (personal interview, 2002).

While the Pará State Ministério Público's relatively low level of political independence has prevented the development of an energetic environmental enforcement practice, some state prosecutors have become involved in environmental protection in another way that is worthy of mention. In the mid-1990s, State Prosecutor Raimundo Moraes became involved in the internationally funded "Pilot Program to Conserve the Brazilian Rain Forest." With funds from the program, Moraes helped to establish an Environmental Nucleus within the Pará State Ministério Público in 1996.[51] With additional program funds, Moraes designed and coordinated a graduate-level course in environmental law offered to state prosecutors and other environmental professionals in the state. First offered in 1999 and again in 2002, approximately 25 prosecutors and 35 others participated in the courses (personal interview, 2002). Through this work, Moraes and the state Ministério Público have become important actors in state environmental policy, though not specifically in environmental enforcement.

Other states, particularly those in the northern Amazonian region of Brazil, have state prosecutorial institutions that are similarly constrained. Indeed, in the regional context, the State Ministério Público of Pará is considered a leader in terms of its involvement with environmental protection. As the only state Ministério Público receiving funding directly from the pilot program, the Pará State Ministério Público has been more consistently and deeply involved in state environmental policy than those of other Amazonian states. In 2000, the Ministério Público of Pará coordinated the First Regional Conference on the Ministério Público and the Pilot Program to encourage prosecutors from other states to become more involved and to establish a regional network of environmental prosecutors to allow greater coordination of their activities.[52]

As illustrated through the case of the State Ministério Público of Pará, not all prosecutorial institutions in Brazil are equally involved in enforcing environmental laws. In Pará, political and institutional barriers have prevented the state Ministério Público from becoming a significant actor in environmental enforcement. The barriers that are apparent in Pará are operative in other states to varying degrees. Even in São Paulo, where the Ministério Público is very energetic, some prosecutors perceive a lack of full independence from the executive branch. According to one environmental prosecutor, the executive branch retains a level of influence over the institution's budget that "ends up inhibiting more rigorous action in matters relating to potential infractions by actors tied to the state government" (Proença 2001: 144). In other words, the extent to which prosecutorial institutions are subject to political influence is a matter of degree. Even where such influence does not preclude energetic enforcement, it may still weaken it.[53]

Independence: Enforcement Against Powerful Actors

The willingness of Brazilian prosecutors to confront powerful economic and political actors in their environmental cases, clearly present among São Paulo prosecutors and federal prosecutors in Pará, is a key aspect of the prosecutorial mode of enforcement. As described in Chapter 3, the 1988 Constitution provided for a large degree of independence for the Ministério Público as an institution and for individual prosecutors. According to prosecutors and others, this independence is essential to their ability to challenge powerful interests in their advocacy on behalf of public interests. Indeed, many of the Ministério Público's environmental cases, particularly those that make news headlines, are against the government or large companies.

A significant percentage of the Ministério Público's environmental lawsuits are against the Brazilian government, whether municipal, state, or federal. The Ministério Público's power to challenge the legality of government actions was established in the 1988 Constitution, which states as one of its functions "to ensure that the government and publicly relevant services effectively respect constitutional rights."[54] This constitutional mandate was avidly adopted by institutional leaders in the early 1990s. In 1990, the São Paulo state attorney general declared the Ministério Público "a weapon of society against the state inserted into the state apparatus itself" (Pozzo 1990). And articulating a view commonly held by prosecutors, a São Paulo prosecutor explains, "we generally have a government that is abnormally large, inefficient, bureaucratic, sometimes even corrupt, that ends up being the cause of some of the most serious national problems. . . . As such, the Ministério Público should defend the interests of society above all against the actions of the government itself" (Ferraz 1993: 10).

According to one environmental prosecutor, the reasons why the government is often a defendant include the lack of honesty in public administration; the direct involvement of the state in activities provoking environmental degradation; and omissions in the exercise of the state's police power (Proença 2001: 144). In the majority of the Ministério Público's cases against the government, prosecutors accuse the government of causing environmental harm directly. Municipal governments have often been sued for failing to treat sewage or handle solid wastes in accordance with environmental laws. State and federal governments have been sued for environmental harm caused by infrastructure projects such as roads, dams, and energy facilities. The Ministério Público has also filed cases that challenge the legality of the environmental permitting process. In such cases, the environmental agency and the government itself are often included along with the private developer as defendants. In a handful of cases, environmental agency officials have also been named individually as defendants, charged with acts of administrative dishonesty or omission.[55]

A governmental entity was named as a defendant in almost one quarter of the environmental public civil actions filed by the Ministério Público of São Paulo between 1985 and 1997.[56] In studies of similar actions filed in the state of Rio de Janeiro, Fuks (1999: 61) and Araujo (2001: 98) also find that about one quarter of the lawsuits include the government as a defendant. In Pará, over one-half of the cases of Federal Ministério Público (56 of 106 cases, or 52 percent) were filed against the government—most commonly the federal government. In the cases prosecuted by the State Ministério Público of Pará, the government was a defendant less frequently. The government or an agency of the government was the party under investigation or the defendant in 9 percent of investigations and 12 percent of the environmental public civil actions filed by Belém prosecutors between 1988 and 2001.

The Ministério Público has also displayed a willingness to confront powerful economic interests. An early example is the São Paulo Ministério Público's 1986 case against the 24 petrochemical and steel companies operating in Cubatão.[57] While a final judicial decision was never reached, the lead prosecutor, Milaré, credited it in 1995 with having brought about important changes in the Cubatão region and beyond. "Even with the delay and even without any decision, this case has partially accomplished its mission. It made the 24 companies install pollution control mechanisms. Cubatão today is much better than it was in 1985."[58] In a statement about the case several years later, he opined that it had served its pedagogical and historical purpose: "It was because of this case that many companies began to worry about the environment."[59]

An employee of the Ministério Público who had previously been a manager at CETESB had an insider's view of why the Ministério Público was more effective in confronting powerful economic interests than the environmental agency. As a manager at CETESB, he tried to close down a unit of Petrobras, the Brazilian petroleum company, but the closure order was never granted by the state secretary of the Environment. Upon retiring from CETESB, he became a technical expert at the Ministério Público of São Paulo and had the opportunity to work on the same case "from the other side." As he explains, "There is a lack of courage in the agency—but it is not really a matter of courage—it is a matter of [having its judgment compromised] and being subservient to broader governmental policy" (personal interview, 2001). A similar view was expressed by an official at the Pará state environmental agency, SECTAM: "There are situations in which the government does not have the courage to confront the big interests alone, and that leaves only the Ministério Público, which is the best one to do this. So I think the Ministério Público, acting in this role, is important" (personal interview, 2002).

The passage of the Environmental Crimes Act of 1998 further solidified the Ministério Público's ability to confront and change the behavior of powerful economic actors. As explained by the coordinator of the São Paulo Environmental Prosecution Support Center, "After the passage of the environmental crimes law, there was a change in the posture of the large companies. Almost none of them work anymore without the help of environmental consultants, lawyers, and engineers. Many with development projects that normally would have tried to obtain permits without passing through the environmental impact process do not dare to do this now" (personal interview, 2000). The strengthening of environmental laws combined with the presence of a strong and independent enforcement actor made companies begin to incorporate environmental compliance into their business operations.

Too Much Independence? The Problem of Consistency

Where the Ministério Público is a large institution, as it is in São Paulo, and there are many environmental prosecutors acting independently of each other, the problem arises of consistency in their enforcement responses. Consistency in the application of the law is itself a component of the rule of law. As explained by O'Donnell (1999b: 307), the "minimal (and historically original) meaning" of the rule of law is that "whatever law there is, this law is fairly applied by the relevant state institutions." He continues to explain that "fairly" means, among other things, that the application of legal rules is consistent across equivalent cases. If the law is applied differently in similar cases, it is hard for people to learn to rely on the law.

Consistency in prosecutorial activities has been a subject of study in other national contexts as well. American scholars have identified and discussed a tension between the goals of individualizing criminal justice decisions and promoting their consistency (see Ohlin 1993).[60] In his seminal study of California prosecutors, Carter (1974: 7) argued that "attempts to impose organizational control over individual prosecutors either failed, or to the extent they succeeded, tended to impair the quality of case dispositions." Johnson (2002: 154–55) finds that a combination of cultural and structural factors allows

Japanese prosecutors to more regularly attain both the goals of individualized justice and consistency.

In Brazil, an important barrier to consistency in prosecutorial environmental enforcement is the strong emphasis on the functional independence of each prosecutor. Each prosecutor acts independently in the cases he handles in his judicial district. The independence of prosecutors was shown above to contribute to energetic enforcement. Their independence allows them the freedom to determine how to proceed in each case without interference from institutional leaders or other prosecutors. This, in turn, contributes to their ability to challenge the actions of powerful political and economic actors.

However, where numerous prosecutors are responsible for and energetic in environmental enforcement, as in the São Paulo Ministério Público, inconsistency in enforcement responses is likely. Responsible only for their own judicial district, prosecutors do not systematically consider how the problems in their jurisdictions relate to or compare with problems in the other judicial districts of the state. Moreover, the extent and zealousness of a prosecutor's activity with regard to environmental problems varies according to his interests and knowledge. As a result, similar cases are often not treated in a like manner by prosecutors. As explained by Proença (2001: 149, 150), an environmental prosecutor in São Paulo, the Ministério Público's defense of environmental and other public interests "has occurred in a fragmented way, without an effective institutional effort to formulate long-term strategic goals that guide the overall work of its prosecutors." He argues that rather than responding to all problems within its jurisdiction that come to its attention, as it does presently, the institution should define criteria by which to select the most relevant and urgent problems and focus its institutional resources on confronting them.

The need for institutional planning was recognized soon after the passage of the 1988 Constitution. In a speech to São Paulo prosecutors in 1990, Attorney General Pozzo explained that the institution needed to define institutional objectives and priorities in order to fulfill its constitutional mission. Observing that the Ministério Público had historically acted in response to either judicial needs or to the complaints of the public, he called its work more "reactive" than "active" and recommended that the institution base its work in objectives, priorities, and concrete action plans, ceasing to act only when provoked externally (Pozzo 1990: 372–73, 376). He also recommended the creation of mechanisms that encouraged cooperation among prosecutors in the same judicial district and in other districts (ibid.: 377).

Formalizing this institutional reform effort, the 1993 Organic Law of the Ministério Público of São Paulo instituted several mechanisms with the potential to enhance consistency.[61] The law established the Environmental Prosecution Support Center and other support centers devoted to specific substantive areas to provide assistance to prosecutors throughout the state, thus reducing discrepancies in prosecutorial action due to lack of knowledge and interest. It also legislated the preparation of annual action plans for each area of prosecutorial activity, including environmental protection. The following types of plans are required under the law: (1) a general action plan to be written annually by the attorney general with input from the prosecution support centers and other prosecutors, defining the goals of the institution; (2) a prosecutorial action plan to be written annually by each prosecutor or group of prosecutors working together in the same location, defining its local goals consistent with the general action plan; (3) integrated action plans to be written by prosecutors in a group of districts regarding a joint goal; and (4) special projects to be devised by the attorney general to address a special need.[62]

More recently, the Environmental Prosecution Support Center in São Paulo also made attempts to strengthen coordination among prosecutors. Between 1996 and 1998, the support center created and sponsored the meetings of *grupos especiais* (thematic work groups) in which prosecutors tried to establish lines of action for recurring problems (Maciel 2002: 117, fn. 32; Proença 2001: 149, fn. 10). The support center also advocated on behalf of the establishment of regional prosecutorial positions in certain watersheds and other well-defined environmental regions to develop regional strategies and enhance coordination among local prosecutors.[63]

Attempts to direct or coordinate the environmental work of local prosecutors, however, were criticized as a threat to the functional independence of each prosecutor. Prosecutors argued that establishing regional prosecutorial positions violates the *princípio de promotor natural* (natural prosecutor principle), which holds that the type and location of a legal offense determines which prosecutor is responsible for the case (Kerche 2003: 96).[64] Traditionally, each local prosecutor is assigned to a single geographic district where the prosecutor is assigned responsibility for all or a subset of the types of cases handled by the Ministério Público. If a regional prosecutor's office were established, the regional prosecutor would impliedly have authority to act over a larger geographic area, thus coming into conflict with the natural prosecutor principle. This principle is viewed as a key aspect of prosecutorial independence because it prevents the attorney general and other institutional leaders from moving prosecutors on or off cases for political reasons.[65]

Similarly, the extent to which the action plans called for by law can bind and obligate an individual prosecutor was widely debated within the institution. Mazzilli, a member of the São Paulo Ministério Público and a prolific author on the structure and role of the institution, denied the legitimacy of such action plans, arguing that "the functional priorities of the Ministério Público are already established by the law and by the individual decisions of the prosecutors, by virtue of their freedom and functional independence" (Mazzilli 1995). This position is reflected in the statement of an environmental prosecutor, "The action plan does not bind me, it does not obligate me to act in the priority areas of the plan. It can't, in part because priorities change from region to region, so what is a priority in a different part of the state is not a priority here" (personal interview, 2002).

Others argue that the action plans should bind each prosecutor and that prosecutors should be accountable for fulfilling the goals of the plan. In the view of Macedo Júnior (1999a: 136), the proposition that plans established by the institution are not at least as binding as the complaint of an individual was "patently contrary to common sense." Another prosecutor similarly placed the importance of institutional plans over arguments defending individual prosecutorial independence: "He who does not execute these goals can't invoke the principal of functional independence in his defense because this principle cannot serve to protect those that fail to follow democratically defined institutional goals" (Goulart 1998: 118, fn. 176). In part as a result of this debate, the development and implementation of institutional plans did not become important aspects of the Ministério Público's work.[66] While they have been prepared each year since 1993, they are criticized for being too general and lacking usefulness, and they are not considered an important reference point for environmental prosecutors (Proença 2001: 155–56).

To fill the gaps in institutional planning, groups of environmental prosecutors have at times taken the initiative to establish mechanisms to coordinate their work. An innovation that emerged in the environmental prosecution office in São Paulo city is indicative. Recognizing that many of the cases they were working on individually overlapped in terms of subject area, the five environmental prosecutors in the office instituted *protocolados gerais* (general investigations), which are more far-reaching and open-ended than a typical investigation (see Maciel 2002: 117). While an individual investigation might focus on the air pollution caused by a single bus company in a certain part of the city, for example, the general investigation would have as its objective the characterization of harms caused by all municipal buses in the entire city. In 2002, there were seventeen general investigations being carried out by the São Paulo city environmental prosecution office. Subjects of investigation included air pollution, noise pollution, leaking underground storage tanks at gas stations, and illegal squatting in the watershed of the city reservoir.

In the case of the Federal Ministério Público in Pará, the lack of consistency in enforcement responses was not a significant problem. A small number of federal prosecutors have been responsible for filing all the environmental cases, and there has thus been greater consistency in the way that similar cases are dealt with. Given that most of the federal prosecutors work in the capital Belém, there are greater opportunities for coordination and discussions about priorities. Almost all the historical preservation cases, for example, have been litigated by one federal prosecutor who has worked in the state for over fifteen years, and almost all the illegal logging cases have been filed by two federal prosecutors who have worked together closely in Pará since the mid-1990s. It is likely, however, that if the activities of the Federal Ministério Público were viewed from the perspective of the country as a whole rather than from a single state, similar issues regarding consistency would become evident.

Conclusion

Brazilian prosecutors challenge impunity through civil and criminal enforcement of environmental laws. Prosecutorial enforcement makes headlines and sends a message that environmental laws will be enforced. Cases against powerful economic and political actors communicate that the law applies generally and universally, a key element of the rule of law.

Both the State Ministério Público of São Paulo and the Federal Ministério Público in Pará serve as examples of energetic environmental enforcement. Environmental prosecutors in these institutions have actively used their civil and criminal enforcement powers, even in cases against governmental officials and large companies.[67] Both institutions have been able to harness the help of environmental agencies in their jurisdictions to furnish information about violations and other technical assistance. The State Ministério Público of Pará, in contrast, was less energetic in environmental enforcement, with civil and criminal enforcement activities remaining at a low level.

Prosecutorial independence is the most significant factor enabling energetic enforcement. In the case of the Pará State Ministério Público, evidence points to a lack of actual prosecutorial independence in spite of the constitutional guarantees that have enabled it in the São Paulo Ministério Público and the Federal Ministério Público. In São Paulo, the extent of prosecutorial independence was so high that it arguably jeopardized the consistency of enforcement responses. Prosecutors defended their independence by resisting or rejecting any attempts to coordinate or create plans for the environmental enforcement work of the institution. The resulting inconsistency in the levels of enforcement across prosecutorial jurisdictions could arguably compromise the rule of law ideal of "equality before the law," as some polluters could be treated much more harshly than others.

5 Making Agencies Accountable

> *In Brazil we have a Ministério Público that is extremely active
> in the defense of public interests, including environmental
> interests. The Ministério Público is creating new positions
> throughout the country, and there is nothing that IBAMA
> does that the Ministério Público is not checking up on.*
>
> **Eduardo Martins, president of IBAMA, as reported in**
> ***Jornal do Comércio* (Recife, February 8, 1998)**

IN THE PROSECUTORIAL APPROACH to enforcement that emerged in Brazil, prosecutors have the power to oversee the work of the environmental agencies. Constitutional and other legislative changes granted the Brazilian Ministério Público a variety of powers that enable it to become a "watchdog" of the agencies.[1] Using its legal powers, the Ministério Público makes environmental agency officials accountable for their decisions and actions.

More specifically, the Brazilian Ministério Público constitutes an agent of "horizontal accountability" for Brazilian environmental agencies.[2] O'Donnell defines horizontal accountability as "the existence of state agencies that are legally enabled and empowered, and factually willing and able, to take action that spans from routine oversight to criminal sanctions or impeachment in relation to actions or omissions by other agents or agencies of the state that may be qualified as unlawful" (O'Donnell 1999a: 38).[3] O'Donnell (2003, 1993) argues the absence of horizontal accountability to be a primary source of the weakness of Latin American democracies.[4] In its absence, governmental corruption, improper use of public resources, and impunity for state actors may become the norm (Mainwaring 2003: 4).

The Ministério Público's oversight of environmental agencies has the effect, in a variety of ways, of making environmental agency officials more accountable. Using their investigative instruments, prosecutors may monitor, find facts and generate evidence regarding the legality of agency decisions and actions in particular environmental cases. Prosecutors may request both information about and explanations for agency decisions. In other words, agency officials are "answerable" to prosecutors (Schedler 1999: 14). But beyond this power of inquiry, prosecutors also make agency officials "sanctionable" for unlawful actions or omissions. Using their civil and criminal enforcement processes, they may impose "material consequences" that punish improper behavior (ibid.: 15–16). With these mechanisms of accountability, the law becomes an instrument for preventing and redressing the abuse of political power. Prosecutorial enforcement contributes to the construction of a culture of lawfulness within environmental agencies.[5]

This accountability takes different forms depending on the Ministério Público's relationship with the environmental agencies, and indeed upon a particular prosecutor's relationships with a particular agency official. The São Paulo Ministério Público routinely oversees the São Paulo environmental agency through a large volume of "information requests" sent as part of prosecutorial investigations, with the occasional use of civil sanctions. The Federal Ministério Público in Pará has more extensively used civil and criminal sanctions against agency officials, but ultimately developed a close working relationship with an agency director they considered trustworthy. The Pará State Ministério Público, lacking energetic enforcement as described in Chapter 4, has not developed an effective practice of oversight of Pará's state environmental agency.

Placing prosecutorial institutions in a position to oversee environmental agencies raises questions about governmental effectiveness. Accountability is often in tension with governmental effectiveness, defined as the ability of governments to obtain good policy outcomes (Mainwaring 2003: 4). As discussed by Nonet and Selznick (2001: 64), fidelity to the rule of law implies a susceptibility to legalism, "a disposition to rely on legal authority to the detriment of practical problem solving." In terms of regulatory enforcement, Kagan (1994: 385–86) explains that from a rule of law perspective, "administrative officials should be closely constrained by objective legal rules, formal procedures, and review mechanism," but that effective regulation "requires cooperative problem solving, elicited by negotiation about the sensible application of legal rules." The form of agency accountability that arose in São Paulo, with its high volume of information requests, illustrates this tension.

Prosecutorial oversight also raises the question of "who guards the guardians?" (Shapiro 1988). This is the problem of "second order" accountability: how to hold institutions of accountability accountable (Schedler 1999: 25–26).

This question is particularly relevant when the guardian is a nonelective, autonomous state institution like the Brazilian Ministério Público that can make other (sometimes elective) state institutions answerable and sanctionable. The Ministério Público, like any locus of political power, is itself vulnerable to inefficiencies and abuses of power. While mentioned in this chapter, this issue is addressed at greater length in Chapter 7.

The first section of this chapter discusses the various instruments that prosecutors may use to oversee environmental agencies in Brazil. The second and third sections describe how prosecutorial oversight functions in the states of São Paulo and Pará, respectively. The final section discusses the various consequences of prosecutorial oversight, highlighting its legalistic tendencies as well as its accountability effects.

Prosecutorial Oversight

As a role that has developed through practice, the accountability of agencies to the Ministério Público is not a clearly established or delineated institutional relationship. Prosecutors may use a wide range of instruments to oversee agencies, spanning from routine information requests to criminal prosecution. This section describes the primary instruments of oversight, with a description of their legal basis and general use.

Most commonly, prosecutorial oversight occurs informally through prosecutorial investigations as prosecutors request information from an agency about a particular environmental problem or case. Under the Public Civil Action Law of 1985, prosecutors have the power to require government agencies to submit information to them as part of their investigations.[6] Failing to submit requested information constitutes a crime, punishable with one to three years of jail and a fine (article 10). Using this power, prosecutors make demands on the environmental agency, requiring information from the agencies in almost all investigations that they open. Through the agency's responses, prosecutors find out what, if any, actions the regulatory agency has taken related to a particular environmental problem or case. They find out, for example, how frequently inspections occurred, what the inspections found, and how the agency reacted. In the course of their investigations, prosecutors may call meetings or *audiências* (hearings) with agency officials to get further information.

Where a prosecutor identifies a potentially illegal act or omission in the agency's work, there are several steps the prosecutor may take. Perhaps most often, the prosecutor continues to investigate the case, with a greater focus on the agency's actions. The prosecutor may solicit more detailed information from the agency, thus signaling a growing interest and attention to the case or problem. This alone may result in changes. The prosecutor may also solicit a technical opinion from an expert outside the agency to evaluate the agency's work. On the basis of the information gathered in this investigation, the prosecutor may try to negotiate a conduct adjustment agreement in which the agency agrees to change its behavior.

Alternatively, the prosecutor may make a written "recommendation" to inform the agency of an illegality or other problem in its work and make suggestions regarding how the agency should change in order to comply with the law.[7] As explained by Machado (1999: 344), the Ministério Público might send a recommendation to the agency "for the preparation of or changes to an environmental impact study; regarding the time and place of a public hearing; for inspections where environmental harm is threatened or has occurred; for administrative sanctions to be levied; or so that the agency does not issue a permit or authorization before the conclusion of a prosecutorial investigation." Rather than making a written recommendation, many prosecutors choose to raise such issues less formally in the course of an investigation.[8]

The prosecutor may also take judicial action in response to an illegal agency action or omission through a public civil action based on environmental harm, a public civil action based on administrative improbity, or criminal prosecution of agency officials. Where the agency has acted or failed to act and thus caused or threatened to cause environmental harm, the prosecutor may file an environmental public civil action against the agency (see Ackel Filho 1990; Topan 1994). As highlighted below, an important subset of these cases have regarded the agency's implementation of environmental permitting laws, particularly those requiring the preparation of environmental impact studies for projects and activities that may cause significant environmental harm. In both São Paulo and Pará, the Ministério Público has used environmental public civil actions to suspend projects based on alleged illegalities in the permitting process (see also Fearnside 2000: 260). As discussed in Chapter 4, these actions generally seek a court order forcing the defendant to take or abstain from taking a certain action to remedy the harm, but may also seek money damages.

The prosecutor may also file a public civil action based on the federal Administrative Improbity Act (Lei de Improbidade Administrativa) of 1992.[9] Addressing corruption and other illegal behavior of governmental officials, this federal law prohibits three categories of acts or omissions: those that result in illegal enrichment (article 9); those that result in loss to the public coffers (article 10); and those that offend the principles of public administration, namely honesty, impartiality, legality, and loyalty to the institution (article 11). While not a criminal law, the civil sanctions provided for by the law are considered very severe and are levied against agency officials as individuals rather than against the agency or government as an entity.[10] In addition to having to return any illicit gains and compensate any loss to the public coffers, sanctions may include loss of one's public job, loss of political rights such as the right to vote and hold public office for up to ten years, payment of a significant monetary fine, and ineligibility for government contracts, fiscal incentives, or benefits for up to ten years. Moreover, the public official charged with improbity must retain a private lawyer for his or her legal defense, implying an additional financial burden. The Administrative Improbity Act significantly enhanced the powers of the Ministério Público to investigate and prosecute public officials (see Arantes 2004: 15; 2002: 102; Salles 1999: 36).[11]

Members of the Ministério Público of São Paulo played an important role in proposing amendments to and lobbying on behalf of the federal Administrative Improbity Act. A state prosecutor who participated in this process explains that he became aware through the newspaper in 1992 that President Collor had sent an anticorruption law to Congress, but that the proposed law was actually a slightly modified version of a 1945 law and thus a "mere political gesture, not meant to be worth anything" (personal interview, 2002). Upon learning this, the state prosecutor assembled a group of prosecutors who proposed more than fifty amendments to the bill and called upon the National Federation of the Ministério Público to lobby at the federal level on behalf of the amendments. He explains that as the bill was progressively amended by each house of Congress, it "got better than the politicians really wanted it to be." Despite last-minute attempts to weaken it by some members of Congress and the president, a very strong bill was passed into law.

In recent years, prosecutors have written extensively on the possibility of using the Administrative Improbity Act against environmental agency officials who, in their view, do not comply with the Constitution and other environmental laws (see Vieira de Andrade 1999). These writings often analyze the possibility of charging agency officials under article 11, which lists "an action aiming to reach a goal prohibited by law or regulation" as an offense to the administrative principle of impartiality or legality.[12] As discernible in these writings, a wide

range of official acts might be considered by prosecutors to violate these principles, including issuing a permit before all legal requirements have been met
(Akaoui 1998: 97; Sobrane 1999: 55); failing to adopt measures to impede the oc-
cupation of or other illegal activities in protected areas (Pazzaglini Filho 2000:
120); permitting a landfill in an inappropriate place or the disposal of untreated
sewage (Rodrigues de Souza 1999: 90); an omission in the use of agency police
power (Dawalibi 1999: 101); and the failure to place the public interest over private interests (Bello Filho 2000: 78).

In addition to the Administrative Improbity Act, administrative acts may
also be punished criminally under the federal Environmental Crimes Law of
1998.[13] This law contains a section dedicated to crimes committed by agency officials, including making a false or misleading statement in the environmental
permitting process (article 66); issuing a permit in violation of environmental laws (article 67); and allowing someone to fail to fulfill a legal or contrac-
tual obligation relating to environmental protection (article 68). The penalties
for these crimes include imprisonment of one to three years and a fine. More
broadly, the law criminalizes a large range of behaviors that may cause environmental harm, such as the operation of an industrial facility without the appropriate environmental permits, and makes environmental officials jointly liable
for the crime if they become aware of such a situation and fail to take action. As
stated in the law, "the environmental official who knows of an environmental
infraction is obligated to take action immediately through the administrative
process, under penalty of joint liability" (article 70).

The São Paulo Ministério Público also played an important role in the passage of the federal Environmental Crimes Law through the participation of
Antônio Herman Benjamin, coordinator of the São Paulo Ministério Público's
Environmental Prosecution Support Center from 1996 to 2000. Benjamin suggested in 1996 to Brazil's Minister of Justice, Nelson Jobim, that a "commission
of specialists" be named to consider and draft an environmental crimes law
(personal interview, 2001). The Minister of Justice agreed, and Benjamin became the *relator geral* (general secretary) of the commission. After becoming
aware that a bill was already being debated in Congress regarding administrative penalties for environmental offenses, the commission was able to add
significant new sections on environmental crimes, and the bill passed into law
as the Environmental Crimes Law in 1998.

While these instruments are available to all Brazilian prosecutors under
federal law, their relative use varies by prosecutorial institution and, to some

extent, by individual prosecutor. The next two sections illustrate this variability by describing prosecutorial enforcement by state and federal prosecutors in the states of São Paulo and Pará.

São Paulo: State Oversight Through Civil Investigations and Actions

In São Paulo, state prosecutors are present in the day-to-day life of the state environmental agency with a substantial effect on how the environmental agency approaches and carries out its work. Agency officials receive "information requests" from prosecutors conducting environmental investigations on a daily basis, and they are regularly called to take part in official meetings in prosecutors' offices. In a few headline cases involving alleged illegalities in environmental permitting, São Paulo state prosecutors have also filed public civil actions against the agency and several of its officials. Everyone in the agency has an opinion about the Ministério Público, and often about particular prosecutors. While most CETESB officials think the Ministério Público plays "a very important role," they sometimes resent individual prosecutors for having threatened or accused other agency officials. Indeed, as discussed below, prosecutors take divergent approaches in overseeing agencies. Some adopt a "hardliner" approach, viewing agencies as fundamentally corrupt and inept; others view agency officials as potential allies in environmental protection and seek to cooperate with them.

Information Requests

The Ministério Público's work often overlaps with the work of agencies as prosecutors investigate environmental problems brought to their attention. In this parallel enforcement activity, they have strong powers to enlist the help of the environmental agencies—requesting documents, answers to particular questions, or the preparation of a technical report.[14] They generally do so by sending formal requests for information to the relevant environmental agency. Agency officials often resent how the Ministério Público's information requests add to their daily workload. Many think that the requests constitute an obstacle to conducting more important environmental protection activities.

São Paulo prosecutors make heavy demands on the state agency responsible for pollution control, CETESB, and other environmental agencies. In the years from 2000 through 2004, prosecutors sent an annual average of over 3,910 requests for information to CETESB (see Figure 5.1). This number is more than

Figure 5.1 Information Requests Sent by the State Ministério Público of São Paulo to CETESB, 1996–2004

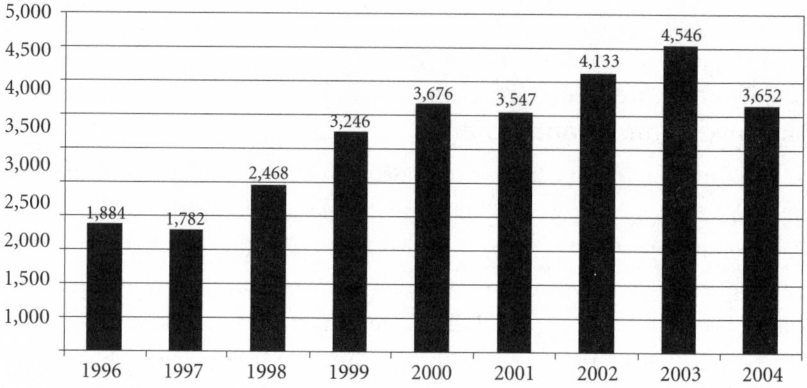

SOURCE: 1995–2001 data from "SIPOL Total Activities, 1995–2001," pers. comm., CETESB Pollution Control Division (January 2002); 2002–2003 data from "SIPOL Total Activities, 2002–2006," pers. comm., CETESB Pollution Control Division (April 2007).

double the number of requests sent annually in 1996 and 1997. Reports for the year 2001 prepared by eleven regional offices of CETESB showed that they spent almost one fifth (19 percent) of their enforcement-related time fulfilling the information requests of prosecutors.[15] Other divisions of the São Paulo Secretariat of the Environment also registered significant increases in information requests. Between 1995 and 2001, the number of requests sent from the Ministério Público and the courts to the São Paulo State Department of Natural Resource Protection (DEPRN) increased sixfold from 1,276 to 7,689.[16]

The information requests are highly variable in form and substance, but they generally include a series of questions about a particular environmental case or problem and the agency's handling of it. Often the request requires a visit by an agency inspector to a facility or site to update or gather new information. In some cases the prosecutor requests that a formal technical report be prepared. A prosecutor's request for information about a hazardous waste site and the ensuing set of interactions between the Ministério Público and the agency provides an example. In his initial request for information, sent to one of CETESB's regional offices, the prosecutor asked the following:

Does the landfill activity require a permit from CETESB? For what activities?

Does the activity require a permit from other government organs? Which?

What are the wastes that are being disposed of at the site?

Does a permit exist (either from CETESB or other government organs) for the activity being realized at the site?

Is there environmental harm? If so, what is it?

Who is responsible for the landfill?

What are the laws that deal with this topic?

What is the volume of waste disposed of daily at the site?

What is the volume of waste that has been disposed at the site?

Are there water bodies being harmed by the disposal?

Six months later, after requesting an extension from the initial sixty-day time period, CETESB sent a response to the prosecutor with answers to each question. The prosecutor called a meeting with CETESB officials and the party responsible for the landfill three months after he received CETESB's answers. At this meeting, a conduct adjustment agreement was written and signed in which the parties agreed to take a series of preventative actions and prepare a study of the landfill's environmental impacts under the guidance of CETESB. Another meeting was held several months later to monitor the party's compliance with the conduct adjustment agreement, and the prosecutor followed up with a request for information to CETESB to find out whether the responsible party had completed the report and whether CETESB had completed its technical analysis of it. In the agency's last interaction with the prosecutor in this case—a year and a half after the initial information request—CETESB sent the report and its analysis to the prosecutor.

A second example further illustrates how oversight occurs in the course of prosecutorial investigations. In a case concerning contaminated soils and groundwater at a gas station, the São Paulo prosecutor initially requested technical information about storage tank leakages; the existence of contamination and measures being taken to clean it up; and the economic value of the irremediable harm. CETESB responded a couple of months after it received the request by informing that CETESB had asked the company to submit a remediation plan. The prosecutor wrote at regular intervals to find out whether it had been submitted and what actions were being taken. After three years and the exchange of a total of twelve requests for additional information and progress updates, prosecutors in the case were considering filing a public civil action against the company.[17]

While these demands are a valuable mechanism for enabling prosecutorial oversight of a wide variety of agency decisions and actions, they also impose a burden on the agency. A CETESB regional manager explains how responding to prosecutorial information affects agency inspectors:

> As much as you deny it, responding to a demand from the Ministério Público or from the court is more stressful than other tasks. With other tasks, you have time to do them and you are not worried. With the Ministério Público, every inspector is afraid from the get-go. They fear that if the prosecutor does not like the response he gets—if he doesn't understand it or if it wasn't what he wanted to hear—he will be subject to questioning by the prosecutor. People don't talk much about this, but it is more work not just quantitatively but qualitatively. (Personal interview, 2001)

Moreover, information requests utilize agency time and resources in a way that reduces the ability of the agency to focus on more important environmental problems.[18] As stated by one CETESB official: "When a prosecutor wants to know about some type of air emission, he doesn't care to know if it is important in the overall scheme of air pollution problems. He wants to know about that type, so that's what we focus on. So we have to suspend our routine activity to attend to an issue that, within the general context, is absolutely insignificant" (personal interview, 2002). In the annual reports prepared by CETESB regional offices throughout the state, regional managers made note of the impact of the Ministério Público's information requests on their workloads. As reported by one regional manager: "In order to be able to respond to this demand within the stated deadlines, we have had to allocate resources that should have been used in other programs such as enforcement activities for priority pollution sources, landfills, and sanitary waste systems."[19] In sum, the time that agencies spend fulfilling the information requests of prosecutors may compromise their ability to carry out more environmentally significant activities.

Environmental Permitting Cases

The São Paulo Ministério Público also exercised oversight through filing civil actions that challenged agency compliance with laws requiring an environmental impact study (EIA). Prosecutors interpreted the Constitution and federal laws to require the preparation of an EIA in various situations in which the São Paulo state environmental agency did not require one.[20] Two cases in which prosecutors filed actions against environmental agencies and their officials became particularly important reference points. In the Volkswagen case, state prosecutors filed a public civil action based on an alleged violation of environmental impact laws against the agency and other defendants. In the Xuxa Water Park case, prosecutors took the more extreme step of filing a public civil action based on an alleged violation of the Administrative Improbity Act against individual agency employees.

The Volkswagen Case

In April 1996, the Ministério Público filed an environmental public civil action against Volkswagen of Brazil, the city of São Carlos, the São Paulo Secretariat of the Environment, and CETESB concerning the construction of an auto assembly plant and test drive area near the city of São Carlos. The new Volkswagen plant was a high-priority project for the state and for the city, and some construction had begun before the necessary environmental permits were obtained. Ultimately, the agency issued a permit determining that the project did not present the potential for "significant environmental degradation" and thus did not require an EIA.[21]

State prosecutors accused defendants of violating a 1986 CONAMA resolution that required the preparation of an EIA for a proposed "industrial district," a name by which the proposed auto assembly plant and test drive area had been called in promotional materials for the project.[22] Referring to the strong political support for the project, the prosecutor suggested that construction had begun before the necessary permits were obtained to make it "impossible for a judge to say no to the project."[23] The public civil action sought a court decision that federal law required an environmental impact study. The lawsuit also requested a preliminary injunction to stop all construction, invalidate the environmental permit that had been issued, and prohibit the agencies from issuing any other permits until after the approval of the EIA.

The agency argued in response that, while the project had been referred to as an industrial district, it really was not one because only one industrial facility was proposed. The agency moreover argued that, under state law, the list contained in the federal law was suggestive rather than conclusive regarding the need for an environmental impact study. In other words, the state environmental agency argued that it had the discretionary power to determine whether a particular project of a type listed in the federal law actually presented the potential of significant environmental degradation. If so, then an EIA is required. In this case, the agency had determined that the proposed project did not present such a potential.

The preliminary injunction was not granted based on the judge's reasoning that the company would have the resources to make reparations for any eventual environmental harm. Given the denial of the injunction, the construction continued and the plant became operational in October 1996.[24] However, the Ministério Público ultimately won the lawsuit in January 2000 when the judge ruled that an EIA was indeed required by federal law and that no new activities, including the installation of the test drive area, could be developed in the area without the preparation of an EIA.[25]

The Xuxa Water Park Case

In July 1998, a prosecutor of the São Paulo Ministério Público accused three officials of the State Secretariat of the Environment as well as a private company of administrative improbity.[26] This was the first case in which state prosecutors filed charges against state environmental agency officials under the 1992 Administrative Improbity Act.[27] Agency defendants included the acting state secretary, the director of the permitting division, and the director of the environmental impact evaluation division.

The private company, Embraparque, had applied for a permit to build a theme park near the São Paulo coast, to be named Xuxa Water Park after a famous television personality. The proposed theme park would require the deforestation of an area of Atlantic Rainforest with special protected status under the Brazilian Constitution. The agency issued a preliminary permit to Embraparque, exempting the company from the preparation of a full environmental impact study.

The prosecutor charged the officials with violating the provision of the 1992 Administrative Improbity Act that prohibits actions "aiming to reach a goal prohibited by law or regulation."[28] The prosecutor argued that the permit that was issued was an act contrary to legality because the officials issued the permit without requiring the preparation of an environmental impact study and before receiving an opinion from the federal environmental agency, allegedly required because of the special federal protection status of the area affected by the project. In addition to an injunction invalidating the permit, the prosecutor requested the court to order the dismissal of the agency officials from public office and a monetary penalty.

The court's decision in July 1999 determined that there had been illegality in the permitting process, but that it did not rise to the level of improbity required for violation of the law.[29] As such, the judge declared the administrative act, namely the issuance of the permit, void, but he did not impose other penalties on the defendants. Both parties appealed and the decision of the appellate court, issued in December 2001, reversed the trial court in favor of the defendants.[30] The appellate court determined that the agency officials had properly acted within their legal authority under state environmental laws in issuing the permit.

While the public civil action was ultimately decided in favor of the agency officials, it put them and others on notice that prosecutors could use the Administrative Improbity Act in this way. Such a lawsuit implies a substantial personal and professional burden for the defendants, as explained by one of the defendants in this case:

> It is worse than you can imagine to have someone call you dishonest in this way. It changes your life. It comes out in the paper and you feel that people are looking at you. . . . This kind of harm is irreparable. And when the court eventually says that in fact you did nothing wrong, it is not publicized. Rather, people keep thinking of you as the defendant in the lawsuit. (Personal interview, 2002)

This official clearly harbored resentment toward the prosecutors that filed this case, but she still expressed support for the idea that the Ministério Público should oversee the agencies. She opined that there was a small group of environmental prosecutors that lack *bom senso* (common sense) and overreach their authority. The majority of environmental prosecutors, however, were reasonable in her view. She asserted that the Ministério Público is an important institution in environmental protection, though perhaps in need of some oversight itself.

Variations in Oversight: Hardliners and Cooperators

The manner in which a prosecutor uses his or her oversight power, and the resulting relationship between the Ministério Público and the environmental agency, often depends on the perspective and personality of the prosecutor. With the high degree of individual autonomy, prosecutors vary significantly in their approaches. Some prosecutors cultivate a cooperative relationship and limit their use of the more coercive oversight instruments. Others approach the agency in a threatening manner, making clear their willingness to seek civil and even criminal sanctions against agency officials.

In the São Paulo Ministério Público, environmental prosecutors may be categorized generally into two groups. Some are referred to by colleagues as "hardliners." These environmental prosecutors tend to view the environmental agency as corrupt and inept, as a force against—rather than for—environmental protection. In the words of one prosecutor, the environmental agency is "our biggest enemy" because it issues environmental permits freely for anything the governor and private parties want to do (personal interview, 2001). Agency officials view these prosecutors as extremists, sometimes using colorful language such as "radicals" or "fascists."

Such prosecutors are more likely to threaten and treat agency officials as incapable and dishonest and, ultimately, to file charges under the administrative probity and environmental crimes acts. As stated by one:

> I observe that the agency takes a long time to respond to us. So I decided on the following approach—I demand a response in 30 days, and I know the date it leaves here and the date it arrives there. I use the verb "to order"—which is what it is. I am not asking, I am ordering, and I say so. . . . If they don't respond in this time, I give one more time period of 10 days. If they still don't respond, I refer the case to the police to open a criminal investigation against the official that didn't respond to me. That's the way I do it. (Personal interview, 2001)

Other prosecutors attribute deficiencies and delays in the agency to forces beyond the control of agency officials, whom they view as lacking resources and staff as well as individual autonomy. These prosecutors may be dubbed "cooperators" as they are more likely to utilize informal mechanisms, particularly meetings and other personal communication, in reaction to perceived deficiencies in the environmental agency. Agency officials comment that such prosecutors are "reasonable" and that they treat agency officials with respect. Describing one such prosecutor, an agency official states:

> He is great. He sits down with you and he says, "You are the technical expert—what has to be done and what is the time period in which it can be done?" When it is this way, and we sit down together and agree on how the case should proceed, it is perfect—we are participating, we are given the chance to say what we have to say. (Personal interview, 2001)

In a similar way, agency officials differ in their level of transparency and responsiveness toward prosecutors. Some officials resent the interference of prosecutors in their work; others take the view that the Ministério Público is faithfully fulfilling its constitutional role. Some are slow to respond to prosecutorial requests; others treat them with priority and special attention. Some choose to have minimal communication with prosecutors; others cultivate communication. A CETESB regional manager who developed cooperative relationships with local prosecutors explained, "In this region, I always have contact with prosecutors so that we don't have conflicts. You discuss things and they tell you what they need, and you tell them what you need as well" (personal interview, 2002).[31]

In one legendary case, a regional manager was demoted because he was not adequately responsive to prosecutors. The regional manager refused to provide certain information requested by prosecutors on the basis that such requests involved issues such as noise pollution that he considered outside CETESB's jurisdiction. After several polite refusals, an angry prosecutor complained to the environmental secretary and, ultimately, the regional manager was demoted. As explained by another regional manager: "The Ministério Público has this power. The issue was that he stood up for himself, he did what he thought was right . . . and the prosecutor did not like that" (personal interview, 2002). Such cases are not very common, but they are well known among agency officials.

In the São Paulo Ministério Público's oversight of agencies through civil lawsuits, the distinction between hardliners and cooperators is also evident. Hardliners in the São Paulo Ministério Público have advanced the position that environmental impact study must be prepared for any project of a type listed in a 1986 resolution passed by the National Environmental Council, CONAMA.[32] The São Paulo state environmental council, however, passed a state resolution that qualifies this list and allows for more administrative discretion about whether a full EIA is required.[33] Hardliner prosecutors have taken the view that state environmental laws that give agencies more discretion about when to require an EIA are out of conformity with federal law and even unconstitutional. Agency officials, on the other hand, view these state resolutions as their primary legal references.

This conflict in legal interpretation led to cases like the Volkswagen and Xuxa Water Park cases in which the Ministério Público attacked the state laws through lawsuits against the agency or its officials. As explained by an agency lawyer: "One thing I see as very problematic about the Ministério Público is that there have been cases against individual agency officials for not requiring an EIA in cases where a state norm exempts the applicant from preparing an EIA. They should attack the government for establishing the norm and get it declared illegal, not the agency officials that apply it" (personal interview, 2002).

A CETESB regional manager explained that in areas where the agency and the Ministério Público differ in their interpretations of the law, he felt that he had to follow the Ministério Público's interpretation. As he stated, "the last thing I want is to have an administrative improbity action filed against me" (personal interview, 2002).

While much depends on the personalities of the prosecutor and agency officials involved, the general tone of the relationship may also be set at the institutional level. Where the head of the environmental agency, or the governor himself, and the attorney general or a close assistant have political or personal differences, the relationship between the institutions may be more conflictive overall. In the mid- to late 1990s, such a situation existed in the relationship between the São Paulo Ministério Público and the State Secretariat of the Environment. After the leadership of each institution changed, the institutional relationship generally improved (personal interview, 2000).

Pará: Federal Oversight Through Criminal and Civil Actions

In the state of Pará, prosecutorial oversight has taken different forms than in the state of São Paulo. As described in Chapter 4, the Federal Ministério Público in Pará is energetic in environmental enforcement in a manner similar to the state Ministério Público in São Paulo. And as in São Paulo, the work of federal prosecutors in Pará has had a very large impact on its counterpart environmental agency, IBAMA / PA. Federal prosecutors were instrumental in exposing corruption on the part of two IBAMA state directors and thereafter formed a close working relationship with their successor. Federal prosecutors have also been very active in overseeing the environmental permitting processes for large infrastructure projects in the state such as shipping canal and power plant construction projects. Their oversight work in these areas is described in the first and second parts of this section. The Pará State Ministério Público, in contrast, had not developed a significant degree of oversight of the state environmental agency, SECTAM. As explained in Chapter 4, it has lacked sufficient political independence to energetically enforce environmental laws. This weakness in oversight is described in the final part of this section.

The IBAMA Corruption Cases

The Federal Ministério Público offers an example of strong prosecutorial oversight of an environmental agency. Over several years, federal prosecutors investigated and prosecuted IBAMA agency officials for corruption in the implementation and enforcement of federal forestry laws.[34] After two state directors of IBAMA/PA were accused of corruption and removed from their posts, a state director came in who cultivated a very transparent relationship with federal prosecutors in the state. This relationship involved extensive communication and cooperation between federal prosecutors and agency officials.

Federal law required that logging companies that want to commercially extract logs from private land in the Amazon region submit a Sustainable Forest Management Plan (Plano de Manejo Florestal Sustentavel; PMFS) to IBAMA.[35] The plan had to contain information about the characteristics of the forest stand, harvesting techniques, and regeneration of the commercial species as well as protection measures for noncommercial species and water bodies, a projected annual harvest, and an analysis of the costs and benefits of the project.[36] After approving the sustainability plan, IBAMA issued a document called the Authorization for the Transport of Forest Products (Autorização para Transporte de Produto Florestal; ATPF) that must accompany the logs and sawn wood in transport.

In many cases, however, companies submitted a PMFS for an area where logging was legally possible, and then used the resulting ATPF to transport logs extracted from areas where logging was legally impossible, such as protected areas and Indian reservations. Companies could also misrepresent the amount or types of species to be extracted. PMFSs were often approved and carried out without adequate field inspections by the agency. In 1997, the Brazilian intelligence service estimated that about 80 percent of all logging in the Amazon was illegal.[37]

Beginning in 1998, federal prosecutors filed a set of civil and criminal cases targeting the illegal practices in the logging industry and related corruption in IBAMA/PA.[38] In February 1998, federal prosecutors in Pará filed criminal charges against the state director of IBAMA/PA Paulo Koury as well as his ex-chief of the technical directorate, three forestry company owners, and a forestry engineer contracted by the company.[39] The charges alleged criminal theft and fraud for illegally extracting mahogany from federal lands and Indian reservations. The company owners and their contractor were charged with acquiring an ATPF from IBAMA based on false information submitted in the PMFS. The IBAMA employees were charged with giving authorization while knowing that it was factually false and illegal.

In December 1999, Pará's federal prosecutors filed the first public civil action based on administrative improbity against IBAMA officials in the state. The federal prosecutors named as defendants four IBAMA officials of Pará, including the former state director Paulo Koury, as well as the representative of a private company.[40] Charges were based on evidence that the IBAMA officials had approved authorization for the company on several properties lacking proof of land title and sufficient geographic specification to accurately locate the property. The improbity suit requested that the accused public officials disgorge illegally gained benefits, lose their public job, pay a civil fine, and be made ineligible for public service or public contracts for a period of five years.

In February 2000, the new state director of IBAMA/PA, Paulo Castelo Branco announced his discovery of another fraudulent authorization that four IBAMA officials had signed in his absence and opened an internal investigation.[41] Then in late April 2000, Castelo Branco made a public statement that corruption, bribery, and falsification of documents were rampant in IBAMA/PA and requested that the Federal Ministry of the Environment take control of the state office to conduct a full investigation. Federal prosecutors also filed another criminal case in May 2000 charging three IBAMA/PA enforcement officials for receiving bribes in exchange for lax inspections.[42]

In late May, the evolving corruption scandal in IBAMA/PA took a surprising turn.[43] Castelo Branco, who had become known for exposing the corruption of other IBAMA/PA officials, was caught in the act of requesting and receiving a bribe of R$1.5 million (US$820,000)[44] from the largest logging company in the state to make their outstanding fines "disappear." Federal prosecutors were involved in orchestrating the arrest, and they filed criminal charges against Castelo Branco that carried a maximum sentence of fifteen years in prison.

In June 2000, a new state director of IBAMA/PA was appointed. Selma Bara Melgaço had been an IBAMA employee for many years and had a reputation for technical expertise and trustworthiness. Over the two years in which she held the position as state director, Melgaço cultivated a close relationship with federal prosecutors. She significantly increased transparency and communication with federal prosecutors by having frequent meetings and opening a variety of agency records to them. As she explained, "I go to [the Ministério Público] to consult with them on how we can get something done, and they help out. It is essential. It is an essential partner to us (personal interview, 2002). While she admitted that the Ministério Público sometimes seemed to be "interfering" in agency business, she opined that this was its correct role. As she stated, "I don't mind being investigated. Those that have something to hide are those that will complain" (personal interview, 2000).

IBAMA began coordinating extensively with the Federal Ministério Público as well as the Federal Police to confront corruption in the early 2000s, as described in Chapter 2. This multiagency law enforcement effort resulted in the arrest of over 500 people for environmental crimes throughout the country over several years, including 116 IBAMA employees. In the wake of the 2005 "Operation Curupira," in which 49 IBAMA employees were arrested for participating in a fourteen-year-old illegal logging scheme in the Amazonian state of Mato Grosso, the minister of justice praised the extent to which governmental agencies had worked together: "The action involved the Federal Ministério Público, the Ministry of Justice, the Federal Police, the Ministry of the Environment, and IBAMA. . . . The crime is organized, so we have to be organized."[45] This coordinated attack on corruption at the national level had its roots in those first cases in which federal prosecutors in Pará and other states exposed corruption in IBAMA at the state level.

Environmental Permitting Cases

Another important locus of prosecutorial oversight in Pará involved the permitting process conducted by environmental agencies. Federal prosecutors in Pará filed a series of high-profile public civil actions against the government and private parties regarding the legality of the environmental permitting process for large government-sponsored infrastructure projects. Notably, the Pará State Ministério Público joined federal prosecutors in filing one such action, and the action succeeded in stalling the construction of a new commercial shipping canal that was favored by the state governor. These cases were very controversial: environmental groups complained that agencies failed to require environmental impact studies or that prepared studies were inadequate; project proponents argued that environmental impact studies were costly and useless bureaucratic hurdles; agencies claimed they lacked resources to monitor and evaluate environmental impact studies; and powerful economic and political actors generally decried the involvement of the judicial branch in environmental permitting decisions (Moraes 2005: 37–38). Importantly, these headline cases served to demonstrate that even large infrastructure projects viewed by politicians as integral to economic development were subject to environmental laws.

In 1998, federal and state prosecutors in Pará jointly sued the federal government, the state government, the Pará Dock Company (Companhia Docas do Pará), and a private construction company to halt construction of the Marajó Canal (Hidrovia Marajó) (Moraes 2005: 209). The government planned to build the Marajó Canal across the Island of Marajó, off the coast of Pará, to expedite passage from Belém to the capital of the neighboring state of Amapá.[46] In April 1998, the state government issued a request for construction bids. After the state government signed a contract for construction of the canal in July 1998, state and federal prosecutors filed a civil action in federal court alleging that the construction contract was illegal because it was signed before the necessary environmental permits had been issued.[47] The following month, the state environmental agency SECTAM issued the necessary environmental permits. However, in September 1998, the federal court granted the plaintiffs an injunction that suspended the construction contract because an environmental impact study had not been prepared.

In 2000, the Pará State Ministério Público removed itself as a plaintiff in the case. Federal prosecutors continued in the litigation, and the injunction remained in force for several years until the prosecutors determined that the environmental impact study was complete. Due to the extensive legal controversy, the Hidrovia Marajó was never built. Para's governor Almir Gabriel openly expressed his irritation with the federal prosecutors. As reported in the news, he asserted that the state of Pará was suffering because of the actions of the Federal Ministério Público: "My patience is running out. We already sent our people to talk to the [federal attorney general], to tell him about this unbearable situation that we have here in which young prosecutors say they are defending societal interests and keep projects of extreme importance from happening that would generate employment and economic activity in our economy and in places like Marajó, which has to develop economically or it will never improve."[48] In the face of such political pressure, neither the state environmental agency nor the state prosecutors would likely have been able to demand the completion of the environmental impact study.[49]

Another headline case filed by Pará federal prosecutors involved the government's plans to build the Belo Monte dam and hydroelectric plant on the Xingu River, a tributary of the Amazon River (Moraes 2005). Federal prosecutors filed a civil action against Electronorte, Brazil's state-owned power company in charge of the project, as well as against the organization that had been contracted to perform the environmental impact study. Prosecutors based the case on a narrow legal argument, namely that the Constitution required that the federal government conduct the environmental permitting process of projects that affect indigenous lands. Since the dam would affect indigenous lands and the state environmental agency was conducting the permitting process, the case was easily won (see Fearnside 2006). As the prosecutor explained: "If you have to argue whether the water quality is going to be affected or other technical issues, it would be more difficult to win because the judge is not necessarily going to accept your technical argument" (personal interview, 2002). Like the Hidrovia Marajó case, federal prosecutors succeeded in the Belo Monte case in halting a large governmental infrastructure project on environmental grounds. As further explained in the next section, Pará state prosecutors would have been unable to sustain a similar challenge because of the state government's support of the project.

The Weakness of State Oversight

Whereas the São Paulo Ministério Público and the Federal Ministério Público in Pará realized their potential to oversee their counterpart environmental agencies, the Pará State Ministério Público did not. Pará state prosecutors are clearly aware of the large deficiencies in the enforcement work of the environmental agency. As stated by one, "Most environmental harm in the state occurs without the knowledge or consent of the ... environmental agencies" (personal interview, 2002). Prosecutors say that SECTAM lacks both the political resolve and the institutional resources to conduct inspections and other enforcement activities.

The Pará State Ministério Público, however, does not have sufficient political independence or power to make much of a difference.[50] Like the agency itself, prosecutors are subject to the state government's general lack of interest in enforcing environmental laws. To the extent that Pará prosecutors tried to use their oversight instruments, SECTAM officials accused them of interfering in matters entrusted to the agency. SECTAM also successfully fended off state prosecutors' demands for technical assistance from the agency. A high-level official explains that when SECTAM received information requests, agency officials "talked with the Attorney General" to explain to him that the Ministério Público needed to "educate" prosecutors about the limits of the agency's technical capacities (personal interview, 2000). The agency also suggested that the Ministério Público should make some payment for the agency's technical assistance, as do companies when the agency provides its technical services for a permitting process. The state Ministério Público has not filed any civil or criminal lawsuits against SECTAM or its officials.

In sum, instruments of prosecutorial oversight that are well-established in the work of the São Paulo State Ministério Público and the Federal Ministério Público in Pará are inoperative in the work of the Pará State Ministério Público. Accordingly, SECTAM officials give little importance to the work of Pará state prosecutors. As explained by one state prosecutor, "agency officials are not afraid of prosecutors but they like to keep a certain distance . . . The agency thinks the Ministério Público is bothersome" (personal interview, 2002). Often, agency officials are simply able to ignore the state Ministério Público. At most, they view state prosecutors as an annoyance.

The Legalistic Turn

Where the prosecutorial mode of enforcement is strong, as in the cases of the São Paulo Ministério Público and the Federal Ministério Público in Pará, the Ministério Público pushes the agency toward a more legalistic approach to regulatory enforcement. Prosecutors seek to limit administrative discretion and force agencies to abide to a greater degree by formal legal rules and procedures. At its extreme, a legalistic approach may result in the "literal application of a legal rule," without regard to "common-sense notions of fairness and social utility" (Kagan 1978: 6). In other words, prosecutorial oversight may push agencies toward a counterproductive degree of legalism in which legal fidelity is gained at the cost of administrative effectiveness. While a higher degree of legalism may be warranted where agencies are not adequately attentive to the law or use their discretionary powers improperly, it may also obstruct environmental problem solving and decision making.

Many of the conflicts that arise between the São Paulo Ministério Público and CETESB may be traced to a difference in their basic approaches to environmental enforcement. The prosecutorial approach—particularly that of the "hardliners" discussed above—tends toward the strict application of the letter of the law. Agency officials, in contrast, generally view the enforcement process as a long-term process of communication and negotiation. Following the literature on environmental enforcement in advanced industrialized countries, the "legalistic turn" that prosecutors bring to the enforcement process could thwart opportunities for cooperation (Kagan and Axelrad 2000). On the other hand, if the approach of an environmental agency has been more of a "negotiated non-compliance," the Ministério Público's intervention may have more positive implications (Gunningham 1987).

In the view of the law-trained prosecutors, the letter of the law dictates what should happen in enforcement. They generally consider the Constitution's environmental provisions and other environmental laws to be comprehensive and clear, particularly with regard to the government's obligation to protect the environment. In the prosecutorial approach, every time a violation occurs, the agency should be there to sanction it. When it isn't, the Ministério Público considers this a failure or omission of the agency.

Many prosecutors consider agency information and decision making to be inappropriately influenced by political and economic interests. As stated by one prosecutor, "I have a very pessimistic view of environmental agencies. Why? Because I believe that the agencies and their officials don't like the law when it creates barriers to implementing measures and policies that the government wants. They don't like the law when it creates barriers to development that favors business profits" (personal interview, 2001). Another states, "Why doesn't CETESB function as it should? Because it suffers from a lot of political influence. Because of politics, these agencies do not have the independence that they should have. So it is very difficult for them to form good environmental policies. . . . If a manager is very aggressive, industry gets him removed" (personal interview, 2001).

While also claiming to adhere to the law, CETESB has an approach more typical of a governmental agency. The agency does not expect to detect and punish all violations, but rather views itself as having to make difficult decisions about how to allocate its enforcement resources. As explained by one CETESB official, the Ministério Público "has a way of reading the law, an understanding of the laws and of CETESB that is very legalistic and focused on the letter of the law. For example, if the law prohibits burning, then it is always prohibited. The law has to be enforced, and CETESB has to be enforcing it. There is no interest in the extent or severity of the burning. Every time an event of this type occurs, the state should be there to enforce the law, and if the state isn't there, it has failed" (personal interview, 2002).

Moreover, agency officials often view prosecutors as naïve and idealistic in their expectation that political and economic factors should be irrelevant to enforcement decisions.[51] As one agency official commented:

For someone to become a prosecutor—with the incredible power that a prosecutor has, he should have attained a certain level of maturity. . . . What occurs is exactly the opposite—many of the promoters are young, recent graduates, with lots of idealism. This is great, but they don't have their feet on the ground. They lack knowledge of life, of reality, of the difficulties of operating a business—especially in this country, which is not easy. (Personal interview, 2000)

Indeed, an ongoing struggle ensues over which institution, and which approach, will be primary in the enforcement of environmental law. These differences lead each institution to criticize the enforcement approach of the other and assert its ineffectiveness. Observing that the environmental agency does not share their legalistic approach, prosecutors feel that the agency is not doing its job of enforcing the law and that they, the prosecutors, end up having to do it instead. Agency officials criticize prosecutors for trying to substitute their technical and legal judgments for those of the agency.

The confrontation between the differing approaches of the Ministério Público and the environmental agencies has played out in the courts as a challenge to the agencies' administrative discretion.[52] Prosecutors tend to view administrative discretion as an excuse used by the agency for failing to implement or enforce environmental laws. As one environmental prosecutor writes, "the word 'discretion' has been truly vulgarized, becoming for some representatives of the government a justification for illegalities, arbitrary acts, inactivity, omission, etc." (Fink, Alonso Jr., and Dawalibi 2000: 86). Prosecutors argue that the Constitution and environmental laws obligate the government to protect the environment, leaving little, if any, room for discretionary power. Prosecutors thus seek to narrow the range of agency activities and decisions that are immune from judicial review. At stake in the legal struggle over administrative discretion is the extent to which the Ministério Público is able to challenge and possibly change governmental environmental policies (see Arantes 2002: 102).

Recent legal scholarship, much of it written by São Paulo prosecutors themselves, emphasizes that the passage of environmental laws progressively restricted, or even removed, administrative discretion in the environmental area (Akaoui 1998; Benjamin 1992; Ferreira da Costa Passos 2001; Topan 1994; Vieira de Andrade 1999). Benjamin (1992: 27), for example, argues that preventative regulatory instruments such as environmental zoning, environmental planning, and environmental impact studies placed limits on administrators' discretionary power: "The role [of the EIA] is to limit, in the sphere of environmental decision making, the administrator's freedom to act." Others point to the many duties imposed on the government and its environmental agencies by laws such as the National Environmental Policy Act and the environmental provisions of the Constitution (Vieira de Andrade 1999: 210–13). Most Brazilian prosecutors are skeptical of administrative discretion. A 1996 survey of state and federal prosecutors revealed that 87 percent agreed fully or in part with the statement, "The Ministério Público has the obligation to require the government to protect the rights established by the Constitution, other laws, and electoral promises. When there is a law guaranteeing a right, there is no administrative discretion" (Arantes 2002: 134).[53] Only 11 percent disagreed, and 2 percent expressed no opinion.

Some environmental prosecutors thus take the position that administrative discretion has no place in the implementation and enforcement of environmental law. As explained by one São Paulo prosecutor:

> The principle of administrative discretion permits the administrator . . . to do his work in the way he understands he should—or not do it at all. In the environmental area, there is very little room for discretion. The Constitution didn't give this margin of liberty to the administrator. It tells the administrator what he must do—defend and preserve the environment. To the extent that the administrator does not defend or preserve it, that is an illegality. So the administrator really doesn't have discretion to decide if he will or won't do something in a given case. If the law says he can't, he can't. That's it. There is no discretion. I don't think discretion exists in environmental law. (Personal interview, 2002)

Agency officials, in turn, defend their discretionary powers in practical terms, explaining that without discretionary powers, they would be unable to take any action:

> For example, the polluter has two technologies that he can use. If the two technologies produce the same results, the administrator can decide which one should be used. And the Ministério Público has no place to say that instead of one technology another should have been used if I can show that they produce the same results. There is a parcel of administrative discretion for the environmental agency—and there has to be because I have to be able to make a decision. I can't ask for the Ministério Público's blessing on every decision I make. If I had to ask their blessing, I would lose the position of being the permitting agency, and the Ministério Público would become the permitting agency. An area of discretionary activity exists, wherein the Ministério Público cannot insert itself. To do so, would to be to take away my legal authority. (Personal interview, 2001)

These mutually incompatible perspectives on administrative discretion have led to considerable conflict, and the legal doctrines regarding the exercise of discretion by agency officials continue to evolve.

Prosecutors have even argued that the budget authority of the executive branch, an area in which courts traditionally deferred almost absolutely to the executive branch, is amenable to judicial review. João Carlos Figueireido, a judge and scholar of administrative law explains, "The administrator is not completely free to make his own budget. There are values prioritized by the federal and state constitutions. In this area, sometimes, the administration has no discretion because the contrary would be to give him the power to reject the priorities that were constitutionally established" (quoted in Mancuso 1999: 40). Despite these arguments, courts have generally sided with the administrator when the dispute involves public spending (Valery Mirra 1989: 44; 1999). A series of environmental public civil actions filed against São Paulo cities in the 1990s to force them to build sewage treatment plants were generally lost in court on this basis. The courts tended to agree that the executive branch has, at the very least, the discretionary power to determine how to allocate scarce budget resources (Fink, Alonso Jr., and Dawalibi 2000: 86).

Enhanced Accountability

The Ministério Público's oversight provides many of the benefits of horizontal accountability. As conceptualized by O'Donnell (2003: 34–35; 1999a: 41), horizontal accountability serves to counteract two powerful forces: corruption, defined as unlawful advantages that public officials obtain for themselves or their associates; and encroachment, defined as unlawful ways in which one state agency intrudes upon the proper authority of another. As expressed in the statements of agency officials, opportunities for both corruption and encroachment are reduced by prosecutorial oversight. In the words of one prosecutor, the Ministério Público helps "make the agency the environmental agency that it should be" (personal interview, 2002).

The Ministério Público's oversight of agencies also improves agency performance in other important ways. Most notably, the direct or implied involvement of prosecutors in administrative enforcement cases strengthens the agency's ability to gain compliance. In addition, it gives agency officials leverage and backing in difficult enforcement cases. Agency officials who want to increase the strength of administrative enforcement instruments are able to threaten violators with the possibility of civil and criminal enforcement. In these ways, the accountability engendered by prosecutorial oversight not only prevents enforcement lapses but also reinforces the agency when it is already committed to enforcing the law.

While sometimes resentful of prosecutors, most agency officials expressed strong support for an energetic Ministério Público. One CETESB official told the story of one manager who was fired after a prosecutor presented the agency's director with a document that suggested corruption. In his view and the view of others, fear of the Ministério Público serves as a powerful deterrent to illegal or improper administrative behavior. As stated by a former São Paulo agency official:

> The impact is positive. It is going to improve [the agency]. Why? Because the Ministério Público has the power to get even the agency manager fired. It can charge those that don't do what should be done with improper official behavior. There is practically a sword at the back of the agency official that reminds him that if he doesn't do what he is supposed to correctly, the Ministério Público is going to file charges against him. (Personal interview, 2001)

Prosecutors also believe that their work has this impact. "I have no doubt in saying that the agency thinks several times before committing an illegal act. It knows that it could have serious problems with the Ministério Público. Because if word of an illegality arrives to us, we are going to make that official liable—criminally liable—and make him lose his job" (personal interview, 2002).

A federal prosecutor in Pará notes the Federal Ministério Público's effect on environmental agencies as one of its biggest successes: "You perceive when you call SECTAM or IBAMA that they have become more careful, that they are more worried about corruption in their ranks—not that corruption no longer exists—but there is a fear. It is in this area where we have the most visible action and that the largest return is generated. Comparing with the past, it is a significant advance" (personal interview, 2002). The first environmental prosecutor in São Paulo, Édis Milaré, similarly opines that the Ministério Público had the effect of making São Paulo environmental agencies work "with more commitment and seriousness" (personal interview, 2002).

Prosecutors note that their presence is particularly important in environmental permitting cases when a government project is under review. In such cases, environmental agencies may suffer from encroachment by other state agencies that want the project to move forward as quickly as possible. As explained by a federal prosecutor in Pará, "The government treats environmental agencies as secondary agencies, as agencies that have no independence. When the government is the developer as well as the permitter, there is [no independence]. In this situation, our work ends up being useful because it creates fear and the environmental official takes into account that the Ministério Público could come after him later" (personal interview, 2002). The horizontal account-ability provided by the Ministério Público makes the environmental agency bet-ter able to assert its jurisdiction over the environmental aspects of the project.

Beyond making agencies more resistant to corruption and encroachment, the Ministério Público's involvement in environmental enforcement lends force to agency officials interested in enforcing the law rigorously. Whether prosecutors are active in the case or not, the agency may invoke the name of the Ministério Público to secure compliance. Moreover, the agency may invite the Ministério Público to participate in its more difficult enforcement cases in order to strengthen the environmental position legally and even politically. In some cases, particularly where the environmental agency administrators are politically or ideologically aligned with environmental interests, the Ministério Público and agency cooperate extensively, strengthening each other through sharing information and coordinating their strategies.

Environmental agency officials in São Paulo can use the Ministério Público as leverage in their compliance negotiations with regulated entities even when the Ministério Público is not involved. One CETESB official explains that while he does not directly threaten a polluter with a criminal sanction, he may "re-mind" the polluter that such sanctions exist (personal interview, 2002). Accord-ing to another, the "big argument" he uses to convince project developers to conduct environmental studies is that "you are not going to be stopped halfway down the road with a lawsuit. . . . This is what we try to show the developers—you have to try to avoid the conflict" (personal interview, 2000). Yet another CETESB official explains how just mentioning the Ministério Público power's to investigate helps her gain compliance. Referring to the Ministério Público as a "partner," she states:

> When you don't get the result you want using the administrative tools you have, your partner can obtain it with the mere reminder that this partner exists. When you are discussing the situation with the violator and he tries to negotiate out of the requirement you are making, you can say, "I can't do that because if I don't require this of you, the Ministério Público will ask me why not, and what will we do then? Are you going to want to be questioned by the prosecutor? 'No.' So are you going to do it? 'Yes, we'll do it.'" (Personal interview, 2001)

According to this official, results that sometimes took the environmental agency months to obtain are now achieved much more quickly.

In other cases, the Ministério Público strengthens agency enforcement efforts through its direct involvement in a case. When administrative enforcement has not resulted in compliance, the agency may refer the case to the Ministério Público for civil or criminal enforcement. As one of the first environmental prosecutors in São Paulo recalled, "When the Ministério Público began to act, we observed that the environmental agencies welcomed its participation because the agencies were clearly deficient in terms of making people respect the law. The fines were almost laughable given the wealth of the polluters, and the agencies did not have other instruments" (personal interview, 2002). He explained that the agencies would refer difficult cases to the Ministério Público, thus bringing into play potential civil and criminal penalties that the polluter feared.

Present-day agency officials in São Paulo also acknowledge this impact. "When the Ministério Público is involved, it's not just an administrative action—the legal part comes in. So if the polluter doesn't resolve the problem, he is not subject to just the administrative penalties of CETESB but also a criminal action. So it is a greater force that we have to require the polluter to fix the problem" (personal interview, 2002). The official further noted that the involvement of the Ministério Público changed the behavior of the polluter: "They don't want the name of their company involved in a criminal action. It is one thing to have an administrative fine against you or even have your operations temporarily closed down by the agency. But a criminal case is different—that would be in the news."

The relationship that developed between federal prosecutors and the IBAMA / PA state director, Selma Bara Melgaço, provides another example of how the Ministério Público may strengthen administrative enforcement. Working in close cooperation with federal prosecutors, Melgaço subjected proposed and active forest management plans to stricter verification and inspection. As plans were suspended or cancelled for legal irregularities, their number fell from 1,300 to 150 over the course of about one year.[54] The agency also referred more cases to federal prosecutors for criminal enforcement, allowing a significant increase in the number of criminal prosecutions for forestry law violations, as documented in Chapter 4.

Prosecutorial and administrative enforcement efforts may also reinforce each other in the negotiation of a conduct adjustment agreement.[55] Often prosecutors request that the environmental agency participate in structuring and enforcing the agreement. The agency takes part in the negotiating discussions and often takes responsibility for monitoring the polluter's compliance with the agreement. One official explained that such a joining of forces produces results.

"I have had very good experiences with the Ministério Público when we have prepared conduct adjustment agreements together. In such cases, the Ministério Público brings a weight to the process that is very important, and CETESB also has a lot of weight in technical matters. So I think that when this relationship exists, the work becomes extremely positive" (personal interview, 2002).

Finally, agency officials believed that the Ministério Público's involvement could facilitate cooperation and coordination with other governmental entities that the agency was unable to achieve alone. After the Federal Ministério Público's crackdown on illegal logging in Pará, IBAMA was able to obtain a formal institutional agreement among the various state and federal agencies responsible for land titling and indigenous peoples to support the agency in its enforcement work. The IBAMA / PA state director states, "without the force that the Ministério Público has, we would not be able to have this articulation" (personal interview, 2002). A prosecutor in São Paulo similarly cites the Ministério Público's ability to coordinate other actors as one of its strengths. "Because of the stature and the independence of the Ministério Público, it can call together the city manager, the director of the environmental agency, and other leaders to get information, and people are a little bit afraid. This is what I think needs to be exploited—this ability to coordinate entities" (personal interview, 2000).

Conclusion

The Brazilian Ministério Público fits the definition of an institution of horizontal accountability. It is legally enabled and empowered to oversee and punish the unlawful acts of other state agencies. Its involvement in environmental enforcement holds the potential to significantly enhance the accountability of environmental agencies.

The manner in which prosecutorial institutions in Brazil use their oversight powers varies. In São Paulo, CETESB officials primarily experience prosecutorial oversight as a series of questions by prosecutors about their handling of particular environmental cases and problems. Cases in which prosecutors have filed civil lawsuits against the agency and its officials form a powerful backdrop to these more routine interactions between agencies and the Ministério Público. Within the São Paulo Ministério Público, some environmental prosecutors are "hardliners" in their dealings with the agency while other prosecutors seek to develop cooperative relationships with agency officials.

The Federal Ministério Público in Pará served as another example of strong prosecutorial oversight. While few in number, Para's federal prosecutors successfully responded to rampant corruption in IBAMA with civil and criminal lawsuits against the agency's state directors and other enforcement officials. When the opportunity was presented, the federal prosecutors formed a close working relationship with an IBAMA state director they considered trustworthy. The Pará State Ministério Público, in contrast to other prosecutorial institutions included in the study, lacked the means to oversee its counterpart state environmental agency.

Where prosecutorial oversight is strong, it may introduce a greater degree of legalism into Brazilian environmental enforcement. In the case of São Paulo, prosecutors sometimes erred on the side of legalism in their interactions with CETESB. In holding CETESB officials to the letter of the law and narrowing their discretionary powers, prosecutors may prevent the agency from finding the best solutions to environmental problems and otherwise getting "the work of society done."[56]

Yet, in both CETESB and IBAMA / PA, there were clear accountability effects from prosecutorial enforcement. Despite being inconvenienced and discomfited by the work of prosecutors, agency officials generally think the Ministério Público is doing "important" work. In addition to making the agency more resistant to corruption and encroachment, prosecutorial enforcement reinforces the authority of agency officials as they deal with regulated entities. With prosecutorial enforcement, environmental laws are more present and more powerful in the daily work of agency officials.

6 Making Justice Accessible

*If the Ministério Público didn't exist, we wouldn't achieve a
third of what we do. . . . We pressure the Ministério Público,
and the Ministério Público pressures the environmental agency
or goes after the problem itself—that is how stuff gets done.*

**Environmental activist, Núcleo Amigos de Terra / Brasil
(personal interview, 2002)**

THE BRAZILIAN MINISTÉRIO PÚBLICO'S environmental enforcement work had a significant impact on how environmental problems and conflicts are resolved in Brazil. Environmental problems, previously dealt with almost exclusively by politicians and executive branch administrative agencies, increasingly became legal issues in which prosecutors and courts were involved. The Ministério Público's environmental work contributed to solving a historical problem of the Brazilian legal system—the problem of "access to justice." Through its extrajudicial and judicial work, the Brazilian Ministério Público provided a new forum for the resolution of environmental conflicts and other conflicts involving public interests.[1] Environmental interest groups came to view the Ministério Público as a partner in their work, and they increasingly took their concerns and problems to prosecutors and ultimately to the courts.

Access to justice is an element of classical definition of the rule of law. Raz, for example, includes in his conception of the rule of law that "the courts should be easily accessible" (Raz 1979: 217).[2] Embodying the ideal that people should be able to get disputes resolved without excessive delay or expense, access to justice may also be furthered by the availability of nonjudicial forums for the legal resolution of conflicts (see Ungar 2002; Cappelletti and Garth 1981: 14–15). Access to justice assumes, moreover, that people view the law as a practical means of furthering their interests. As Hendley (1996: 3) documents in the case of the Soviet Union, courts were very accessible but little used. People did not embrace the law "as a mechanism for remedying wrongs and advancing interests." The law was not "mobilized" by people when they felt their rights had been violated because it did not offer adequate remedies (ibid.: 16, 33). A society's belief that laws "do and should count" is revealed in, among other things, "the degree of willingness to use laws 'on the books' to protect and advance one's interests" (Krygier 2002: 13405). In sum, for access to justice to be meaningful, people must believe the law is theirs to use.

The Brazilian Ministério Público became a key player in expanding access to justice for environmental interests through its involvement in the passage of the Public Civil Action Law and its extensive work on behalf of environmental interests under this law. As described in previous chapters, the Ministério Público established specialized prosecutorial positions for environmental defense and dedicated substantial institutional resources toward developing environmental enforcement as one of its areas of activity. As the Ministério Público began to play this new role in environmental protection, individuals and civil society organizations increasingly called upon prosecutors to take action. However, as shown throughout this book, the extent and way in which prosecutors are involved in environmental enforcement differ among prosecutorial institutions. The degree to which their work enhances access to justice accordingly varies.

Where the Ministério Público is active in environmental enforcement, its new role has implied the establishment of a "new judicial arena for solving conflicts that before then did not have access to the justice system" (Arantes 1999: 84). Environmental groups often lack legal resources and prefer to bring complaints to the Ministério Público rather than filing a public civil action themselves. By using extrajudicial instruments, particularly investigations and conduct adjustment agreements, the Ministério Público came to serve as a forum of dispute resolution itself. Moreover, as discussed in Chapter 4, the Brazilian Ministério Público has filed thousands of environmental public civil actions, many on the basis of a complaint by a concerned citizen or an environmental group. While environmental public civil actions may be filed by a variety of other nongovernmental and governmental actors, about 97 percent of environmental public civil actions have been filed by the Ministério Público (Macedo Júnior 1999a: 107). The Ministério Público has thus served as the primary vehicle through which environmental interests have received access to the courts, lending significant judicial force to environmental protection laws.

In sum, the Brazilian Ministério Público's work in enforcing environmental laws has meant "access to justice" for environmental problems. The Ministério

Público became a partner to individuals and groups concerned about the environment and transformed itself as well as the courts into a public resource for the consideration and resolution of environmental problems and disputes. In doing so, the formal environmental rights of the 1988 Constitution and other laws became significantly more effective. As evaluated by a well-known Brazilian legal scholar:

> Several years after the introduction in Brazil of the legal defense of collective and diffuse rights . . . the balance is frankly positive. After some resistance and ups and downs, predictable given the natural difficulty of fully understanding the complexity of the new norms, it can be said that collective processes are now part of judicial praxis. The large number of lawsuits and the adequate judicial response to them clarified the new technical procedures and demonstrated the commitment of those with jurisdiction [to file lawsuits]—especially the Ministério Público. . . . It can certainly be said that public civil actions transformed civil procedure as a whole, which is now in tune with the accompanying social and political reality. . . . It is through these lawsuits that Brazilian society has exercised, in the most articulated and efficient manner, the rights of citizens. (Grinover 2000: 148)

The two sections below illustrate the changes in the Ministério Público and the Brazilian judiciary that have enhanced access to justice for environmental interests. The first section discusses the Ministério Público's partnerships with civil society organizations and how it became the environmental lawyer and negotiator of society. It also analyzes the "prioritization problem," a byproduct of the Ministério Público's responsiveness to public complaints. The second section describes changes undergone by the Brazilian judiciary, partly as a function of the Ministério Público's work, that made it increasingly able and willing to resolve environmental and other public interest cases. The problem of judicial delay and the debate regarding the "judicialization of politics" are also explained. Where relevant, differences between São Paulo and Pará are highlighted and discussed.

Access to Prosecutors

The Brazilian Ministério Público pursued and solidified a new role for itself in defending environmental and other public interests in the 1980s and 1990s by helping to pass the Public Civil Action Law, by lobbying in the Constitutional Assembly, and by building institutional capacity in these new areas. The

Ministério Público established itself as a sort of superombudsman, an official representative of society with the legal powers to file civil and criminal charges.[3] Indeed, the Ministério Público actively lobbied in the Constitutional Assembly against the creation of a more traditional ombudsman institution on the basis that it would be able to fulfill this role better than a new institution (see Arantes 2002: 86–91; Mazzilli 1991: 35; Ferraz 1991).

A traditional part of the role of the Brazilian prosecutor is attending to the public (Silva 2001: 84; Mazzilli 2001: 146). Fulfilling this role differs depending on where the prosecutor works, whether in a large city or a small town (Silva 2001: 84–85; Maciel 2002: 99). Prosecutors who work outside of the large cities generally set up hours on a daily or weekly basis during which they are available to give legal advice to the local community. In these communities, prosecutors are well-known figures—they are one of a handful of governmental officials who live in the town—and community members often expect the local prosecutor to do something about various sorts of problems they are having, particularly problems involving the provision of governmental services. Prosecutors try to resolve problems "with a quick phone call" or by directing people to the appropriate person at another governmental agency (Silva 2001: 84). Sometimes the information they receive results in the opening of an investigation regarding an actual or potential harm to the public interest. In larger cities, prosecutors also consider attending to the public one of their functions, but it takes a different form. Information about relevant community problems usually arrives to prosecutors from the press, other governmental officials, and organized civil society groups (ibid.: 84–85).

Once a prosecutor becomes aware of a potential or actual harm to a public interest, whether by public complaint or otherwise, the widely adhered-to principle of obligation holds that the Brazilian Ministério Público has the legal duty rather than merely the legal right to act.[4] The majority of environmental investigations by the Ministério Público are opened on the basis of some sort of public complaint or governmental notification of actual or potential harm to the environment. A study of the São Paulo Ministério Público's environmental prosecution office in the capital city concluded that about three-quarters (77.5 percent) of investigations between 1990 and 2001 were initiated on the basis of information provided by a third party (Maciel 2002: 83, 87). About half of these provocations came from individuals or groups in society, including neighborhoods, environmental organizations, unions, and professional organizations. The other half came from other governmental entities, such as the police, municipal governments, and environmental agencies. The other quarter (22.5 percent) of the investigations were initiated by prosecutors without external provocation, presumably based on a prosecutor's personal observation or awareness of an environmental problem. A study of the Rio de Janeiro State Ministério Público provided a similar profile of the origins of cases, with about half of all cases (51.0 percent) initiated in response to a public complaint, a quarter (22.8 percent) initiated in response to a governmental referral, and the other quarter (26.2 percent) initiated by the Ministério Público without direct provocation by a third party (Fuks 1999: 65).[5]

Prosecutors strongly endorse the view that the Ministério Público should enhance access to justice. A multistate survey of Brazilian prosecutors conducted in 1996 found that 78 percent of prosecutors agreed in full or part that "the majority of the population does not have access to justice," and 86 percent agreed in full or in part that "the Ministério Público should be a channel for social demands in the quest for greater access to the courts, transforming the courts into a suitable arena for the solution of collective conflicts." Of prosecutors interviewed, 93 percent agreed that the judge cannot merely apply the law but must be sensitive to the social context, and 72 percent agreed that a commitment to social justice should outweigh the strict application of the law (Arantes 1999: 95). As viewed by a São Paulo prosecutor, "The Ministério Público is the institutional instrument through which the most important social questions can be submitted to the judicial branch for consideration" (Ferraz 1993: 10).

Prosecutors also strongly expressed their view that the Ministério Público had already contributed significantly to access to justice. Almost all respondents opined that the new responsibilities given to the Ministério Público by the 1988 Constitution had improved the delivery of justice in Brazil (94 percent) and that the Ministério Público was the institution (governmental or nongovernmental) that had most contributed to the expansion and consolidation of public interest rights (89 percent) (Sadek 1997: 53, Table 9). Over three-quarters (77 percent) positively evaluated the institution's work in defending public interests through the use of investigations and public civil actions since 1988 (Sadek 1997: 54, Table 11). Also, federal prosecutors evaluated the institution's work on behalf of environmental interests above all other areas, with 55 percent saying that it had done excellent or good work in the environmental area in the past ten years (Wiecko V. de Castilho and Sadek 1998: 22).[6]

The "Lawyer of Society"

The Ministério Público established a new role for itself in the 1980s as the "lawyer of society," the legal representative of society's interests. It opened its doors to public complaints dealing with harm to the public interest, including environmental interests, and developed instruments to respond to them. In doing so, it increasingly became seen by civil society organizations as a strong and important partner, one that would listen to their problems and take action, whether extrajudicial or judicial, to resolve them.[7] As noted above, the Brazilian Ministério Público has filed the vast majority of all environmental public civil actions (Macedo Júnior 1999a: 107).

It is estimated that about one thousand environmental groups exist in Brazil (Ames and Keck 1997: 7). The Brazilian environmental movement grew quickly in the 1980s, from forty environmental groups in 1980, to four hundred in 1985, and to nine hundred in 1991 (Viola and Nickel 1994: 174). The majority of environmental organizations are in the more urbanized and industrialized southern and southeastern regions of the country (Peritore 1999: 125; Biderman Furriela 2002: 159). Most are small, with an annual budget of less than US$5,000, and focused on a single issue such as the protection of a certain local park or the water quality of a certain stream (Biderman Furriela 2002: 159; Ames and Keck 1997).[8] About a third of environmental organizations have paid staff, and only a handful have lawyers on staff capable of bringing environmental public civil actions.

Environmental groups that wanted legal assistance were more likely to look to the Ministério Público than to a private lawyer. As explained by an environmental prosecutor in the São Paulo Ministério Público, there are three bases for strong partnerships between the Ministério Público and nongovernmental organizations. First, the Ministério Público lowers the costs and risks borne by organizations because it does the investigation and legal work; second, the complaints brought by organizations to prosecutors serve as an efficient information flow about potential violations of rights; and third, organizations can help amplify the effects of the Ministério Público's work through their connections with the press (Macedo Júnior 1999b: 257).

Indeed, many environmental organizations came to rely on the Ministério Público for assistance in addressing the environmental problems they were concerned about. As stated by one environmental activist, "If the Ministério Público didn't exist, we wouldn't achieve a third of what we do.... We pressure the Ministério Público, and the Ministério Público pressures the environmental agency or goes after the problem itself—this is how stuff gets done" (personal interview, 2002). Environmentalists considered the Ministério Público more responsive than governmental environmental agencies. As explained by a São Paulo environmentalist:

> For us, as an organization, [and] for the universe of nongovernmental organizations, the Ministério Público has been that organ of support—first you send a letter to the responsible agency, looking for action to be taken, and you don't get any answer, then you look for help at the Ministério Público. We arrived to the point where at the same time we would write a letter to CETESB or another responsible governmental agency, we would also write a letter to the Ministério Público because we knew that we would not get any response from the agency. (Personal interview, 2002)

He further spoke of the special relationships that often developed between environmentalists and prosecutors: "every prosecutor that you were able to conquer was treated like a beloved spouse. It was a love affair."

Even the few environmental organizations with lawyers on staff tended to rely on the Ministério Público to file public civil actions. According to a lawyer at one such organization, "For nongovernmental organizations it is more difficult to use lawsuits. It's more expensive—you have to have a scientific study, you have to prepare extensively. This requires time, human resources, money— so they say 'Let's work in other areas. The Ministério Público can work with lawsuits. We can do the parts that the Ministério Público cannot do'" (personal interview, 1999). Another environmental lawyer observes, "The market for lawyers that work in environmental protection is filled by the prosecutors of the Ministério Público. The citizen goes to the Ministério Público rather than hiring a lawyer" (personal interview, 1999).

Brazilian prosecutorial enforcement stands as an example of "state-society synergy" (Evans 1997, 2002a), involving a reciprocal relationship between civic engagement and effective state institutions, in which each strengthens the other. Where synergy is present, "[m]obilized communities can have an impact in particular arenas of deliberation and decision making within particular agencies, even if the state as a whole is focused on other agendas" (Evans 2002b: 21). With prosecutorial enforcement, citizens and communities gained greater access to the environmental enforcement process, and they played a direct role in activating the enforcement process. Environmental groups found an ally in the Brazilian Ministério Público and became able to participate to a greater degree in environmental decision-making processes through their partnerships with prosecutors.

A visible example is provided by the Ministério Público's lawsuits to enforce environmental permitting laws that require environmental impact studies. Throughout the country, Brazilian prosecutors filed public civil actions against governmental and private actors alleging irregularities in the environmental permitting process.[9] In one well-publicized case, federal prosecutors in Pará were granted an injunction that suspended plans for the construction of the Belo Monte hydroelectric plant. The proposed plant would dam an Amazon River tributary, the Xingu River, to construct the third-largest hydroelectric plant in the world.[10] Belo Monte was one of the first of more than seventy dams proposed by the Brazilian government that together would flood about 3 percent of the Amazon forest (Fearnside 2001: 377).

In this case, the state-owned power company, Electronorte, sought an environmental permit for the construction of the plant from the Pará state environmental agency, SECTAM.[11] Federal prosecutors filed suit with the argument that the project required a federal environmental permit from IBAMA because the Xingu River was a *bem da União*, or federal property. Prosecutors also alleged that the terms of reference for the environmental impact study had been formulated without sufficient participation from the scientific community, public agencies, and societal groups affected by the project. Finally, prosecutors argued that the project required explicit congressional authorization before the EIA was conducted due to the Xingu River's use by indigenous peoples. The injunction granted by the lower court in May 2001 was ultimately affirmed in October 2002 by the Federal Supreme Court (Moraes 2005: 37–39).

Underlying this legal action was an alliance between federal prosecutors and a network of civil society organizations that included environmental groups and more than a hundred local grassroots organizations in the region (Scholz et al. 2004: v). As explained by Scholz et al. (2004: 49), this alliance succeeded in suspending the Belo Monte permitting process "through the focused use of legal instruments as well as by working with the press, exchanging information, and organizing public campaigns and gatherings." In a close study of the Belo Monte case, Moraes (2005) argues that this case supports the hypothesis that societal actors look to the Ministério Público and the Judicial branch to vindicate their rights and guarantee public participation in situations where the executive branch tries to limit the expression of public opinion. In his opinion, the parties' legal arguments and the legal process served to raise awareness of and solidify constitutional rights relating to public participation in the political process.

The Ministério Público's strength as an environmental advocate clearly varied among Brazilian states and regions. Maciel (2002: 33) studied the interactions between the São Paulo Ministério Público and society and found that its environmental work had been guided by a dynamic of "openness" and "permeability" toward the interests and values of societal actors. She analyzed how the São Paulo Ministério Público's receptivity to and cooperation with environmental leaders in the 1980s gave the institution a high degree of public visibility, which in turn helped it gain more powers to defend societal interests in the Federal Constitution of 1988 (ibid.: 36–37). She also found that the Ministério Público's attentiveness to the complaints of societal actors inhibited the institution from developing a strategy of environmental enforcement that was capable of preventing, rather than merely responding to, environmental problems (ibid.: 77–79).

In Bahia, a relatively poor state in northeastern Brazil, Sanches Filho (1999: 55) observed that the defense of public interests by the Ministério Público had not achieved the same degree of importance as in southern states such as São Paulo. Rather, criminal work remained the institutional priority: "The new 'social' profile [of the Bahia Ministério Público] is still in a phase of consolidation as the Ministério Público is not sufficiently prepared for its new functions, which brought a series of difficulties for prosecutors, especially the oldest prosecutors, who constructed their whole career on criminal work and have to adapt and learn enough to work in these newer areas (environment, consumer, children and youth, ethnic issues, etc.)."

A similar emphasis on criminal prosecution over environmental and other public interest work was observed in the Pará State Ministério Público. Few linkages between Pará's environmental organizations and state prosecutors were apparent. Indeed, relative to São Paulo and many other Brazilian states, Pará had a small number of organized environmental groups. In an early-1990s study, Dourado (1993: 140) counted 17 environmental groups, of which 12 had fewer than 56 members. A 2002 survey by the Brazilian Institute of Geography and Statistics (Instituto Brasileiro de Geografia e Estatística; IBGE) documented a total of 41 nongovernmental groups focused on environmental protection in the state of Pará. Of these, three-quarters of the groups had no employees, and only three groups had ten or more employees.[12]

Dourado's study found that most of Pará's environmental groups focused on environmental education and had practically no contact with the Ministério Público or the courts (ibid.: 141–44). Similarly, in 2000, a representative of one of the largest environmental organizations in Pará, Environmental Research Institute of the Amazon (Instituto de Pesquisa Ambiental da Amazônia; IPAM), stated that the organization had little contact with the state Ministério Público. To her knowledge, the organization had never sent information to the Ministério Público that might lead to an investigation or legal action (personal interview, 2000). Debert (2000: 237–38) similarly found that civil society organizations in other areas of social interest in Pará, such as women's rights and Afro-Brazilian rights, also had very little contact with, or even awareness of, the state Ministério Público's role in defending collective and public interests. These findings accord with the fact that the Pará State Ministério Público had not made the representation of environmental and other public interests an institutional priority.

Extrajudicial Lawyering

In addition to providing access to justice as a "lawyer of society," the Ministério Público resolves many environmental cases without resorting to the judiciary. As discussed in Chapter 4, prosecutors in both São Paulo and Pará were more likely to negotiate extrajudicial conduct adjustment agreements than to file public civil actions. As stated by one environmental prosecutor in São Paulo, "We always try to resolve cases through conduct adjustment agreements without going to court. . . . The majority of my cases are resolved this way—70 percent, maybe 80 percent of my cases" (personal interview, 2002). In sum, the emergence of the Ministério Público as a negotiator on behalf of environmental interests is a significant aspect of how the prosecutorial mode of enforcement has provided "access to justice" for environmental claims.

Prosecutorial reliance on conduct adjustment agreements reflects the lack of effectiveness of judicial resolution. Prosecutors often cite delays and other difficulties of the judicial process as obstacles in their environmental protection work.[13] In a study of the São Paulo Ministério Público's anticorruption work, Arantes (2002: 147) similarly found that the Ministério Público used extrajudicial agreements to "compensate for the low procedural effectiveness" of its lawsuits. He further asserts that such agreements "undoubtedly have more of a real impact." Environmental prosecutors almost universally view conduct adjustment agreements as a faster and more effective way of resolving a case.

While Brazilian prosecutors relied heavily on extrajudicial resolution in both São Paulo and Pará and at both the state and federal levels, an important difference existed in the use of extrajudicial resolution by Pará state prosecutors. In contrast to the prosecutors of the São Paulo State Ministério Público and the Federal Ministério Público in Pará, prosecutors of the Pará State Ministério Público relied exclusively on extrajudicial resolution because filing actions in the state courts was not a viable alternative. Without the ability to make a credible threat of filing and winning a judicial action, Pará state prosecutors had less bargaining power. They were more limited in the types of cases they could seek to confront and resolve extrajudicially, and they shied away from cases against powerful economic and political actors. Instead, they spent their time on cases with little political and economic significance, often against an individual or a small business.

The Prioritization Problem

According to the principle of obligation, prosecutors must respond to all environmental problems that they become aware of. Fidelity to this principle of responsiveness comes at the cost of prioritization.[14] The citizens or groups that complain most get the prosecutors' attention, while other more significant environmental problems are ignored. The problem is illustrated well by an environmental prosecutor in São Paulo:

> Ninety percent, the great majority, of investigations and cases that the Ministério Público handles begin with complaints—generally from nongovernmental organizations or citizens.[15] The Ministério Público does not choose its agenda. We have little control over our work, little ability to set our own priorities. For example, one of the problems that is most reported and must be followed up on is noise pollution—a bar, restaurant, or disco that is disturbing a neighbor. I don't mean to say this isn't a big problem—it is for the person who lives next door. But in a city like São Paulo, it is far from being the most important environmental problem. Another problem that is often reported is the cutting of a handful of trees. From the point of view of forming priorities for the city of São Paulo, this is practically insignificant. The institution does not have a mechanism that allows the few existing prosecutors to pay attention to the most significant issues. (Personal interview, 2000)

Unable to set his own agenda because of the need to respond to all problems that come to his attention, one São Paulo city environmental prosecutor explained that he is faced with two types of problems in his daily work: the "unsolvable and the insignificant." On the one hand, there are "very difficult problems like river pollution, watershed protection, and urban zoning violations;" on the other, "we have the local disco and the cutting of a handful of trees" (personal interview, 2000). Unable to resolve the unsolvable problems and constantly dealing with insignificant problems, he questioned the effectiveness of his work.

The emphasis on small, isolated problems was evident from the types of environmental harm alleged in public civil actions adjudicated by the São Paulo Ministério Público.[16] The largest category of cases, over one-third of all lawsuits filed between 1984 and 1997, involved deforestation and devegetation of erosion-prone areas. Of these, 75 percent concerned less than 5 hectares or 500 trees; 50 percent concerned less than 1 hectare or 100 trees; and 35 percent concerned areas of less than 0.5 hectare or 50 trees.[17] Many cases concerning land use conversion related to the construction of a single building and the associated environmental impact. In the category of mineral extraction, over two-thirds of the cases involved the extraction of sand for civil construction, a type of mining with smaller environmental impact than many other types. Noise pollution cases, constituting 6 percent of the total, generally involved small establishments—restaurants, bars, and churches—that disturbed a limited number of neighbors.[18] In sum, prosecutors often filed public civil actions regarding relatively little harm.

Some prosecutors have argued for reforms that would change the current practice of responding to all complaints and problems. Proença (2001: 163) asserts that the Ministério Público should increase its effectiveness by "restricting itself to cases with the most social impact and visibility." Another São Paulo prosecutor points out that the Ministério Público has so many legal functions that fulfilling them satisfactorily requires that the institution define priorities and plans of action (Goulart 1998: 116). Reformers advocate the development and use of institutional criteria for selecting the most significant and urgent problems and focusing resources on confronting them.

Other prosecutors strongly defend the principle of obligation. As stated by one environmental prosecutor:

> Does the Constitution at any point say that the Ministério Público can choose which environmental questions to act on or not? No. The only thing that the Ministério Público has to find out—and this is what it finds out through the

investigation—is whether there was or wasn't environmental harm or risk. If there is risk or actual harm, then the Ministério Público is obligated to take action. (Personal interview, 2002)

And as another environmental prosecutor explains:

The prosecutor can't decide that, say, the illegal cutting of a tree is something that, by his criteria and for reasons of convenience and suitability, he is not going to do anything about. He may say he prefers to work against the big polluters, and I understand. But if I start to think this way, then everyone who cuts trees is going to think that they will suffer no consequences—and if you sum the number of trees cut that this would imply, we may have a problem much larger than a big pollution case. Or with regard to the Ministério Público's role in a case of noise pollution, I can't just say this isn't an important issue and close the file. At the minimum, I have to call the responsible party in, tell him he must stop producing noise above the legal limits and write up a conduct adjustment agreement. This is the obligation that we have as prosecutors and this has to be maintained. (Personal interview, 2001)

Prosecutors who defend the principle of obligation often express that they feel unable to determine which environmental problems are important and which are not. Given the lack of criteria by which prosecutors can judge the significance of environmental problems brought to their attention, they argue that prosecutors should respond to all of them equally.

Access to the Courts

In the 1980s and 1990s, the Brazilian judiciary also changed in ways that provided greater access to justice for environmental and other public interests. It became more independent of the other two branches of government and more willing to contest the constitutionality and general legality of their actions. By bringing environmental and other public interest-related conflicts to the courts, the Ministério Público contributed to these changes in the Brazilian judiciary. One of the legal scholars who introduced the idea of public interest rights in Brazil in the early 1980s explains that the filing of public civil actions "meant making the judge a principal actor in resolving cases that . . . are extremely socially and politically important. Because of public civil actions, the judiciary abandoned its frequently distant and remote stance, and became a protagonist in large national controversies" (Grinover 1999: 46).

Yet, these changes in the Brazilian judiciary certainly did not remove all barriers to the use of public civil actions to address environmental problems. Rather, the inefficiencies of judicial resolution created persistent problems for the Ministério Público and the prosecutorial approach to environmental enforcement. Moreover, the new level of involvement of the judicial branch in public interest issues previously confined to the political sphere led to questions about the "judicialization of politics." These aspects of the expansion of access to the courts for environmental claims in Brazil are discussed below.

Changes in the Brazilian Judiciary

The willingness and capacity of the judiciary to participate in environmental cases are best understood in the context of the large changes in the Brazilian judiciary that accompanied redemocratization and the enactment of the 1988 Constitution. Two important ideas shaped these changes. First, there was a consensus that the judiciary should exercise its power to review the constitutionality of legislative and executive acts, thus acting as a guarantor of the Constitution and the rule of law generally. Based on this idea, the Brazilian judiciary was transformed from a typical civil law judiciary into an independent and powerful branch of government.[19]

Second, there was consensus that a new set of collective rights existed that required judicial protection. The establishment and consolidation of collective rights represented a significant change in legal culture, implying a shift away from the liberal legal order in which individual rights are paramount. With access to the courts through the Public Civil Action Law of 1985 and other instruments discussed below, collective rights claims were brought to courts, and Brazilian judges gained the opportunity to pass judgment in a set of cases with clear social and political significance. Édis Milaré, the first environmental prosecutor in São Paulo, concludes that the "introduction of the public civil action into our procedural system was the most spectacular instrument for calling on the courts to make [environmental] rights truly effective" (Milaré 2001: 273).

Like the United States, Brazil has both a federal and a state court system. The state courts generally have two tiers—the lower courts of general jurisdiction and the appeals court. The federal courts have four tiers—the Federal Lower Courts (Vara Federal), the Federal Regional Courts (Tribunal Regional Federal; TRF),[20] the Superior Court of Justice (Superior Tribunal de Justiça; STJ),[21] and the Federal Supreme Court (Supremo Tribunal Federal; STF).[22] The state courts hear the bulk of cases, as the lower and regional federal courts are reserved for disputes that involve the federal government or a federal official. The Superior Court of Justice hears appeals from both state and federal courts when the case involves an issue of federal law.[23] The Federal Supreme Court, in turn, hears such appeals when a constitutional issue is involved.[24] Aside from these courts, the federal judiciary also includes a system of specialized courts for labor law (Justiça do Trabalho), electoral law (Justiça Eleitoral), and military law (Justiça Militar).[25]

However, like judiciaries in other civil law countries, the Brazilian judiciary differs significantly from the U.S. judiciary. Like Brazilian prosecutors, Brazilian judges are civil servants, functionaries of the government. Judges enter the profession through a competitive civil service exam and are promoted on the basis of merit and seniority. They generally begin their careers with assignments in smaller, less populated areas or jurisdictions and move up the ranks to progressively larger ones, and eventually to the capital city and possibly to an appeals court. In 2001, there were about 8,000 judges for a population of about 170 million Brazilians—an average of over 20,000 citizens per judge.[26] Of state judiciaries, São Paulo's is the largest with about 1,500 lower court judges and 130 appeals court judges in 2001—almost 20 percent of all state judges in Brazil. The Pará state judiciary, in comparison, had 167 lower court judges and 30 appeals court judges.[27]

Brazilian judges have traditionally played a very limited role in public policy. In the civil law tradition, judges were not vested with lawmaking power. Rather, their role was to mechanically apply the law made by the legislature. Merryman (1985: 36) describes the civil law judge as an "expert clerk" and as the "operator of a machine designed and built by legislators": "[H]is function is merely to find the right legislative provision, couple it with the fact situation, and bless the solution that is more or less automatically produced from the union." In line with the idea that judges do not have lawmaking power, civil law systems do not include the concept of binding precedent.[28]

In the twentieth century, as Latin American executive branches grew in power, the judicial branch generally became another part of the government's bureaucratic apparatus. As explained by Correa Sutil (1999: 257), "It was one more institution for the political powers to control, one more office where they could appoint their partisans in order to reward them, guarantee their loyalty, and make sure no decisions were taken by judges that could damage the interests of the ruling party." During military dictatorships, prevalent in Latin America from the 1960s through the 1980s, the judicial branch was often brought even further under the control of the executive branch.

In Brazil, as in other Latin American countries, the judiciary was characterized by frequent political interference and institutional weakness through most of the twentieth century (Sadek 1995d: 12).[29] A step toward independence of the judiciary was made in the Constitution of 1934, which provided for the competitive civil service exam and gave the judiciary responsibility for its own recruitment (see Sadek 1995d: 15; Werneck Vianna et al. 1997: 90). While this Constitution and several later ones also established job security for judges that might contribute to judicial independence such as lifetime tenure and protection from transfer or demotion, these guarantees were suspended in times such as the military dictatorship when the executive sought more control. Overall, the Brazilian judiciary continued to suffer political interference in the form of legal alterations and budget constraints (Fernandes 1996: 275).

The redemocratization process of the 1980s, however, brought significant changes to the Brazilian judicial branch. As explained by Arantes (1999: 83), "democratization and the return to 'rule of law' [*estado de direito*] pointed to the need for judges and legitimate arbiters to decide eventual disputes between society and the government and between the branches of the government itself." In response, guarantees of independence were established for both the judiciary as an institution and judges as individuals.[30] The judiciary was assured financial and administrative autonomy, with the powers to control its spending and regulate its internal organization (Sadek 1995d: 13). Judges were guaranteed life tenure and protection from relocation, demotion, and salary reductions.

In tandem with this new level of judicial independence, several procedural innovations in the 1988 Constitution expanded the judicial branch's ability to exert control over the other branches of government. While judicial review of the constitutionality of legislative and executive acts had existed in some form since Brazil's first republican constitution passed in 1891, the Constitution of 1988 strengthened these powers.[31] Instruments of judicial review that were newly instituted or strengthened included the *mandado de injunção* (writ of injunction),[32] *ação direta de inconstitucionalidade* (direct action of unconstitutionality),[33] and *mandado de segurança coletivo* (collective writ of security).[34]

The 1988 Constitution also strengthened instruments that allowed the court to hear cases dealing with public interests, expanding the *ação popular* (popular lawsuit) and the *ação civil pública* (public civil action). Originally established in the Constitution of 1934, the popular lawsuit allowed any citizen to contest an act of a public authority that harmed public property or the public treasury.[35] In the 1988 Constitution, it was expanded to include harm to "administrative morality, environment, and historical and cultural monuments."[36] The 1988 Constitution also strengthened public civil action, established by the 1985 Public Civil Action Law, by expanding its use beyond the defense of environmental, consumer, aesthetic, and cultural interests to include "other diffuse or collective interests."[37]

These organizational and legal changes significantly modified the traditional role of Brazilian courts. They placed the judiciary "in a pivotal position to ensure that the Constitution's plans and programs are implemented" (Ballard 1999a: 247). In addition to expanding the judiciary's power to pass judgment on the acts of the other two branches, they made a whole new set of rights—denominated collective rights—defensible in court. As explained by an environmental prosecutor in São Paulo, "Through the public civil action, the individual and private tradition of the national legal culture was broken, considerably expanding the access to justice to innumerable citizens" (Macedo Júnior 1999a: 106–7). Upon taking office in 1995, the president of the Supreme Court of Brazil remarked, "I don't know of any other constitution—including Brazilian constitutions and foreign constitutions—that has placed more trust than our Constitution of 1988 in the judicial resolution of individual and collective rights of all types and has more extensively opened the courts to citizens, organizations, and the Ministério Público as an instrument for all of society" (Milaré 2001: 499, fn. 101).

Under the 1988 Constitution, the Brazilian judiciary grew and changed. Between 1990 and 1999, the number of state court judges increased by almost two-thirds from 4,930 to 8,098.[38] The federal judiciary grew even more quickly. Between 1990 and 2002, the number of federal judges almost quadrupled from 279 to 1,068.[39] With its growth, the Brazilian judiciary became younger and (while still predominantly male) more feminine (Werneck Vianna et al. 1997: 66–77).[40] Since the 1980s, judicial salaries also increased to a level second in the legal professions only to those of the most successful private lawyers (Sadek 1999: 17). Characterized by prestige and respectable salaries, judicial careers became very desirable, and competitive civil service exams became very selective (see Prillaman 2000: 86, 93).

Moreover, many judges adopted a worldview that encouraged a greater role for the judiciary in public policy. In a multistate survey of state and federal judges conducted in 1993, almost three-quarters (73.7 percent) agreed with the statement, "The judge cannot merely apply law, but must be sensitive to social problems."[41] Almost half (48.1 percent) agreed that the majority of the population does not have access to justice, and over a third (37.7 percent) agreed that "[t]he commitment to social justice should take precedence over the strict application of the law" (Sadek 1995a: 22). In another survey conducted in 1995, 83 percent of judges agreed with the statement, "The judiciary is not neutral and the judge should interpret law according to the social context, so as to bring social change" (Werneck Vianna et al. 1997: 259).[42] In the face of perceived social injustice, judges became willing to take a more activist approach in policy-relevant conflicts (Taylor 2008: 2–26; Castro 1997a: 242).

The result was a very independent and active Brazilian judiciary. The Brazilian judiciary's independence is not just a matter of formal constitutional guarantees but also a substantive reality as judges have been willing to exercise their extensive powers (see Brinks 2004). As described by Alston et al. (2005: 18), the Brazilian Federal Supreme Court has ruled against the executive branch in several cases of "extreme importance" to the executive. One empirical study showed that the Supreme Court ruled against governmental interests in 75 percent of the cases in which private interests contested the government.[43] In a study of seventeen Latin American countries, Brazil was the only one in which citizen confidence in the judicial system grew between 1996 and 2003.[44] Moreover, in 2003, Brazilians had the most confidence in their judicial system: over 40 percent of Brazilians expressed confidence as compared with an average of only 20 percent in the other countries.[45] While the question in most Latin American countries is whether the judiciary is sufficiently independent, the debate in Brazil has focused on whether the judiciary has become overly independent (Santiso 2003: 163).[46]

Despite the changes, prosecutors still cite the judiciary as one of the primary barriers in carrying out its work in the defense of environmental and other public interests. A multistate survey of prosecutors conducted in 1996 indicated that about one-third of state and federal prosecutors viewed the judiciary as strongly or somewhat resistant to the Ministério Público's power to defend *interesses difusos e coletivos* (public interests), and about half viewed courts as weakly resistant or not resistant. The survey further found that prosecutors perceive such judicial resistance in environmental cases less often than in consumer rights and political corruption cases, but more often than in cases involving public services (such as education and health), children's rights, and disability rights (Sadek 1997: 55).

In both São Paulo and Pará, prosecutors say that some judges, particularly the older appellate court judges, are biased against environmental public civil actions. As explained by one São Paulo prosecutor: "[The judges] don't know much about environmental law. They don't study it, and they're not interested in studying it. Many see civil law as first and foremost private law—a fight between private parties—so they aren't able to factor in the public interest. And the higher courts are worse—because if the younger judges haven't absorbed this, then it is even more unlikely that the older judges have" (personal interview, 2002). A Pará prosecutor views federal courts as more receptive to public civil actions than state courts. "State courts are very conservative—it is a reason why [Pará state] prosecutors do not file public civil actions. Federal judges are generally younger and have more modern views. The state appeals court is horrible. This is a limiting factor for us" (personal interview, 2000).

Also, the judiciary is not uniformly independent throughout the country. In Pará, the independence of the state judicial branch from the executive branch is often questioned. While Pará state judges have the same formal guarantees of institutional and individual independence as federal judges and judges of São Paulo, there is a sense that the state judiciary is "greatly influenced by the executive branch" (personal interview, 2000).[47] While similar data are not available for Pará, data from the northeastern state of Bahia illustrate the extent to which prosecutorial evaluations of state and federal judicial institutions vary. Sanches Filho (1999: 54) reports that only 12 percent of Bahia prosecutors rated the work of state courts as excellent or good, while 60 percent rated federal courts as excellent or good. A full 77 percent of Bahia prosecutors say there is substantial inappropriate political interference in state courts, whereas in the national sample (of seven states including Bahia) only 19 percent responded in this way.[48]

Part of the bias against public civil actions perceived by prosecutors may reflect institutional discord between the Judiciary and the Ministério Público. As explained by Sadek (1999: 15), the "judge sees the prosecutor as someone who slows down his decision, as someone who has the power to interfere in a case and make his job more difficult, and at the outer limit, someone who is outside the justice system who lacks a sense of responsibility."[49] This dislike of the Ministério Público and of the public civil action is revealed in survey results. Only 37.2 percent of judges give a positive rating to the "expansion of the powers of the Ministério Público" in the 1988 Constitution.[50] Evaluating the work of federal prosecutors, 42.6 percent of judges cited their work in the criminal area as excellent or good while only 35.4 percent cited their work of investigating and filing public civil actions on behalf of public interests as excellent or good (Sadek 1995e: 20).[51] As explained by one São Paulo state judge, many judges see prosecutors as trying to show off their new powers. She called them "a bit adolescent and immature" and said the Ministério Público "suffers from an identity crisis and is still trying to figure out its proper role" (personal interview, 2002).

Judicial Delay

The Brazilian judicial system presents an interesting riddle: its "impact" has grown tremendously, but its "functionality" has remained low (Taylor 2005). The most common complaint is that Brazilian courts are inefficient and their decisions are prone to considerable delay. In a 1995 survey, 90 percent of Brazilians complained that justice was "too slow" (Prillaman 2000: 75). The "high number of appeals" allowed in the Brazilian legal system is most often cited— by 73.2 percent of judges—to explain judicial delay (Sadek 1995a: 19).[52]

Statistical data show a marked increase in litigation after the passage of the 1988 Constitution. Throughout the Brazilian judicial system, state and federal, the number of cases filed and decided increased significantly in the 1990s and early 2000s. In 1990, the state appeals courts in all Brazilian states received a total of 125,388 cases and decided 114,237; in 2003, they received 863,173 cases and decided 679,832.[53] In the state courts of general jurisdiction throughout Brazil, the trends were similar: the number of cases filed and decided increased by a factor of three to four.[54] Similar increases were observed in the federal courts at both the lower level and the appeals level.[55]

The growth in the number of cases entering Brazilian courts translated into case delays and backlogs. While courts greatly increased the number of cases decided, they were generally not able to keep up with the increase in new filings. In 2003, for example, Brazil's courts of general jurisdiction received 11.9 million new cases but decided only 8.2 million cases.[56] Data provided by Buscaglia (1998: 20) show a 39.1 percent increase in the average delay for the resolution of judicial cases and a 19.7 percent increase in the backlog of cases in federal commercial and civil courts between 1983 and 1993. Prillaman (2000: 76) cites a backlog of over thirty thousand cases in the Supreme Court in 1997.[57]

It is important to note that only a very small percentage of judicial cases in Brazil are public civil actions. In 1995, for example, 652 public civil action cases were filed in the São Paulo State Appeals Court, constituting about 0.7 percent of all cases filed that year (Lima Lopes 1999: 568). However, as public civil actions tend to be more complex cases than most civil suits, they may take even longer than the average case to be decided by the court. In her study of environmental public civil actions in the city of Rio de Janeiro, Araujo (2001: 248) found that it took, on average, four years for environmental public civil actions to be decided, and the lawsuits that had not yet been decided had been under judicial consideration for periods ranging from one to twelve years.[58] Moreover, once decided by the lower court, public civil actions are often appealed.

The delay in judicial resolution tends to undermine the access to justice provided formally by Brazilian law. As stated by Prillaman (2000: 75), "The backlog of cases clogging the court system increased by a factor of ten in just over a decade, and trial delays increased so dramatically—more than doubling—that access for everyone resulted, paradoxically, in access for no one." An environmental agency lawyer cites the delay inherent in judicial resolution as a major barrier to the effectiveness of public civil actions. "A public civil action is a process that takes a long time. It is not effective. In general, our administrative instruments are more effective than lawsuits" (personal interview, 2002). While Brazilian law offered access, the "weakness and extraordinary slowness" of the courts made litigation unattractive (Ames and Keck 1997: 9).

As the Ministério Público ultimately depends on the judiciary for its power, the lack of a responsive judiciary undermines its authority and bargaining power. Its strength in the negotiation of a conduct adjustment agreement is related to the perceived willingness of the courts to rule favorably in public civil actions filed by the Ministério Público. To the extent such lawsuits are rarely filed or are lost in the courts, the Ministério Público's bargaining power and overall effectiveness may decline. As stated by a prosecutor in Pará, the Ministério Público "can have a lot of its activity limited if judges are not prepared to hear and decide the cases they receive" (Moraes and Castro 1998: 7). The same applies if the judiciary is so slow that judicial action is not perceived as a meaningful threat.

The Judicialization of Politics

With the expansion of access to justice for environmental and other public interests, scholars observe an increasing "judicialization of politics" in Brazil, wherein disputes that were formerly considered to be of a political nature are increasingly brought to the courts. It is questioned whether the judiciary is an appropriate or efficient venue for the resolution of such disputes, whether the political involvement of judicial institutions threatens "governability," and whether judicial institutions are being increasingly politicized as a result.

The frequency with which environmental and other public interests are addressed by legal institutions in Brazil has led to concerns about the "judicialization of politics." Courts are now able and willing to involve themselves in issues previously dealt with exclusively in the political sphere by the legislative and executive branches. A trend toward the expansion of judicial power and the judicialization of politics has been observed not just in Brazil but in many countries, and its consequences are widely debated (see Tate and Vallinder 1995). In many ways, the judicialization of politics represents the spread of an American style of politics in which the judicial branch plays a prominent role (see Atiyah and Summers 1987: 270; McCann 1986: 107).

The various public interests defended by the Brazilian Ministério Público, including environmental interests, are closely related to public policies and often depend on government action to become effective. The Public Civil Action Law made it possible for these conflicts to come under judicial consideration. Arantes (2002; 1999) has most fully developed the linkage between the Ministério Público and the judicialization of politics in Brazil. He finds that "the Ministério Público has been the most important agent in the legal defense of collective rights and, given that conflicts relating to such rights are generally of a political nature, it can also be said to have driven a larger process of the judicialization of political conflicts and, inversely, the politicization of the judicial system" (Arantes 1999: 83). He observes that the combination of a zealous Ministério Público, the breadth of constitutional rights, and the obligation of the state to provide public services under penalty of being accused of unconstitutionality by omission sums to the "possibility of an extensive judicialization of political conflicts in the name of seeking to make constitutional rights effective" (ibid.: 97).

A São Paulo prosecutor, Ronaldo Macedo, identifies two political facets of the institution's new role. First, the activity of the Ministério Público "assumed a markedly political character" insofar as it directly and indirectly affected the "institutional risks and operational difficulties" faced by political leaders and large businesses (Macedo Júnior 1999b: 255). Second, and perhaps even more important, "the new responsibilities of the the Ministério Público began to orient or directly affect a variety of state policies." Observing that public civil actions are frequently filed against the government to demand the implementation of public policies in areas such as child welfare, education, and environmental and consumer protection, Macedo asserts that the Brazilian Ministério Público became "one of the principal mechanisms in the implementation of social rights," which inherently involve questions of public policy (ibid.: 256).

The Ministério Público's work also played a role in making the judiciary a significant political actor. In deciding cases involving public interests, judges very frequently find themselves sitting in judgment of the actions and omissions of the executive branch. As stated by a São Paulo prosecutor, "the judiciary . . . at the beginning received the novelty [of the public civil action] with a certain reserve. Today, however, it seems to perceive that the public civil action allows it to truly affirm itself as a branch of the government. It gives the judiciary the opportunity to determine the law related to some of the most sensitive national issues" (Ferraz 2001: 85, fn. 1). Ferreira Filho (1995: 37) observes that the judicial branch can impose its will on administrators through its rulings in public civil actions and concludes that the judiciary has "the ability to impede," which is "intrinsically political."

Given their ability to affect public policies, the Ministério Público and judiciary may act as a "substitute" for executive and legislative institutions that are not perceived by the public or by prosecutors as fulfilling their missions. Kerche (1999: 62) explored the extent to which the work of the Ministério Público and administrative agencies may overlap: "This breadth [of the Ministério Público's mandate to protect the public interest] combined with the absence of regulation permits the Ministério Público to act in questions traditionally reserved to political agents. In other words, there is, or there could be . . . a sort of 'substitution' of elected representatives by the prosecutors of the Ministério Público, legitimated by means other than elections" (see also Arantes 2002: 132–36).

Prosecutors and agency officials comment upon this substitutional quality of the Ministério Público's work. Édis Milaré, who was the first environmental prosecutor in São Paulo, links the deficiencies of administrative agencies and the increasing involvement by the Ministério Público and the courts: "Brazilians have learned to look toward the courts for environmental protection. I don't know how it is in the United States, but people look to our courts because our administrative agencies are failing. If our environmental agencies were effective, our courts would not interfere so much and the Ministério Público would not have so much work in this area" (personal interview, 2001). A former agency official similarly observed that the Ministério Público's role in environmental enforcement arose out of "a lack of technical competence in the environmental agencies" in combination with the demands of citizen environmental groups.[59]

This transfer of disputes that were traditionally confined to the political sphere into the judicial sphere is potentially problematic for several reasons. First, environmental policy choices are polycentric and judges lack the institutional capacity to solve them. As explained by Lima Lopes (1999: 571–74), the multipolar nature of such issues calls for a distributive solution best reached by negotiation or mediation rather than the winner-takes-all solution typical of traditional litigation. Moreover, cases involving distributive conflicts tend to "require decisions about what to do in the future," rather than a more typically judicial sort of decision regarding whether a past action was right or wrong (ibid.: 574). Similar arguments have been made against the involvement of courts in regulatory policy and enforcement in other countries (see Melnick 1983; Rosenberg 1991; DuBois 1996; Horowitz 1977).

Some Brazilian prosecutors recognize that judicial resolution may be inappropriate and ultimately unsuccessful in cases involving complex environmental problems with multiple and conflicting interests. Speaking of an example of the homeless invading protected lands near urban reservoirs, one environmental prosecutor explains: "We have cases where the judge determined that there had been an illegal invasion and ordered that the families remove themselves; the people file an appeal so that the judgment can't be executed, and the appeals court recognizes that on the merits the families should have to leave, but given the situation, they are allowed to stay" (personal interview, 2000). In such a case, the environmental prosecutor may win the case in court but lose it in reality.

An issue of governability also arises as traditionally political disputes are increasingly brought into the courts. Arantes (2000: 335) posits that the judiciary's control of the constitutionality of executive and legislative acts under the 1988 Constitution led to a "governability crisis." Having become a "powerful resource for vetoing majority decisions made in the political sphere," the Brazilian judiciary contributes "in a decisive manner to aggravating political and economic instability" (ibid.: 346–47; see also Sadek 1995b: 161).[60] The issue of governability is particularly evident in the Ministério Público's environmental work when environmental prosecutors challenge large infrastructure and other economic development projects in the courts. Prosecutors have in some cases obtained judicial injunctions that paralyzed projects considered priorities for economic development by state and federal governments. Yet the balancing of economic development and environmental protection objectives is generally better suited to political deliberation than judicial deliberation (Kagan 2001: 224–29).

Finally, Brazilian scholars have noted a connection between the "judicialization of politics" and the "politicization of judicial institutions" (Arantes 2002, 2000, 1999; Ferreira Filho 1995). Ferreira Filho (1995: 38) finds that judges increasingly leak information to the press and consider public opinion in arriving at their decisions. Arantes (1999: 98) observes that judges are more willing to take a stand in political disputes and that prosecutors have adopted ideological positions regarding the reduction of social inequalities and the strengthening of citizen rights. As they become political actors, judicial institutions are then further politicized as they are subject to attempts by the legislative and executive branches to bring them under greater control. Their ability to present themselves as independent and neutral forums for the resolution of conflicts is thereby eroded.

Not all observers, however, view the judicialization of politics as a negative or inevitable phenomenon. In their work, Werneck Vianna et al. (1999) observe the same judicialization but interpret it positively as an expansion of the judiciary's capacity and willingness to respond to the needs of the masses. In its greater involvement with social issues, the judiciary is progressively abandoning decades of legal positivism and becoming an institution central to democracy (ibid.: 9). In their view, the judiciary has begun to "migrate toward being an active guardian of the Constitution and fundamental human rights" (ibid.: 53). Others assert that the judiciary may act as a sufficient control on the Ministério Público and on itself. There is some indication that, despite provocation by the Ministério Público and others, the judiciary remains essentially conservative and reticent to interfere in political decisions (see Castro 1997a). And despite the Ministério Público's efforts to narrow administrative discretion, described in detail in Chapter 5, the separation of powers doctrine has continued to hold sway in the courts (Sadek and Cavalcanti 2003: 222; Arantes 2002: 134).

Conclusion

The prosecutorial mode of enforcement involved an increase in access to justice for environmental interests. This access had both extrajudicial and judicial aspects. In the extrajudicial realm, the Ministério Público assumed the role of being the lawyer and negotiator of society's environmental interests. Environmental organizations and concerned citizens became accustomed to bringing concerns and complaints to prosecutors. Through its investigations and conduct adjustment agreements, the Ministério Público became, in essence, a new forum in which people could mobilize the law to advance their interests.

The prosecutorial mode of enforcement also led to a greater degree of access to the judiciary for environmental interests. The Ministério Público's use of the public civil action, along with other changes in the Brazilian judiciary that accompanied redemocratization in the 1980s, led to an expanded role for courts in resolving environmental problems. As Brazilian scholars have noted, there has been a resulting "judicialization of politics," in which political issues are increasingly being considered and resolved by the courts. In this context, judicial delay has become a large concern for those who seek judicial resolutions to environmental problems.

Differences between the cases of São Paulo and Pará point to several lessons regarding how the Ministério Público's impact on access to justice and the courts generally may vary. The São Paulo Ministério Público became much more engaged in environmental problems than its state counterpart in Pará, and access to justice for environmental interests is accordingly much greater. While delay remained an obstacle in São Paulo courts, judges were more receptive and favorably inclined toward environmental claims than Pará state judges. Like the state Ministério Público, the Pará state judiciary appears to lack political independence relative to its sister institution in São Paulo.

7 Effective Enforcement: Brazil and Beyond

WITH A FOCUS on the environmental enforcement work of the Brazilian Ministério Público, this book addresses a fundamental question about the interaction between law and social change: under what circumstances is law effective in changing human behavior? The simple enactment of environmental laws and policies does not guarantee that any significant changes in environmental protection will occur. Studies of environmental policy in many developing countries make it clear that seemingly strong environmental laws often remain unimplemented and unenforced. Indeed, the Brazilian case is of interest precisely because it appears to be different—through the Brazilian Ministério Público's work, environmental laws are being transformed from mere words on paper into action, and they are affecting the behaviors and practices of polluters, agency officials, and environmental advocacy groups.

The Brazilian model of prosecutorial enforcement illustrates how the involvement of legal actors can significantly strengthen environmental enforcement in countries that lack strong administrative enforcement. Administrative enforcement is often weak because environmental agencies are weak. The pervasive tension between environmental and economic development goals in the political realm tends to translate into a lack of institutional capacity in environmental agencies. Moreover, they suffer from encroachment, wherein more powerful governmental agencies intrude upon the proper authority of the environmental agency, and corruption, wherein agency officials obtain unlawful advantages for themselves. The model of prosecutorial enforcement that emerged in Brazil effectively counteracted these tendencies that weaken enforcement.

Studies based on the experience of advanced industrialized countries generally have not found a positive relationship between the involvement of legal institutions and effective environmental enforcement. Rather, there is considerable evidence that the involvement of lawyers and the judiciary in the American regulatory system increases the cost and adversarial character of the regulatory process while failing to achieve a greater degree of compliance (Gunningham, Kagan, and Thornton 2003; Kagan and Axelrad 2000). In Brazil, in contrast, the inefficiencies of involving prosecutors and courts are strongly outweighed by the gains in effective enforcement and the rule of law.

The success of prosecutorial enforcement in Brazil has depended on having prosecutors with a relatively high level of political independence from the executive branch. In São Paulo, where state prosecutors are highly independent, environmental enforcement has become a significant area of prosecutorial work. In Pará, where the independence of state prosecutors is not well established, environmental enforcement activities remained low. Yet this same independence leads to two important challenges for the Brazilian prosecutorial enforcement model. First, the Ministério Público's work is weakened by the lack of institutionalized forms of cooperation and coordination with other enforcement actors, particularly environmental agencies. Second, the Ministério Público lacks mechanisms of accountability. Prosecutors are not adequately "answerable" and "sanctionable" for unlawful actions or omissions. After a discussion of the effectiveness of prosecutorial enforcement, the issues of prosecutorial independence, coordination challenges, and prosecutorial accountability are considered below. The chapter concludes by examining whether the Brazilian model can be "diffused" or "transplanted" to other developing countries.

Effective Enforcement and the Rule of Law

Effective regulatory enforcement is enforcement that achieves the concrete gains intended by a regulatory scheme (see Kagan 1994). Seeking to resolve long-standing debates about the relative merits of legalistic and cooperative enforcement strategies, Ayres and Braithwaite (1992) set forth the concept of the "enforcement pyramid." With an operative enforcement pyramid, regulatory agencies have a wide range of enforcement tools at their disposal such that "every escalation of noncompliance by the firm can be matched with a corresponding escalation in punitiveness by the state." In these circumstances, defection from cooperation will be less attractive to the regulated entity and more of the work of regulation can be done through persuasion. The enforcement pyramid captures the insight that a mix of regulatory styles or a "sophisticated balance" of persuasion and punishment leads to the most favorable outcomes in terms of both effectiveness and efficiency (see Ayres and Braithwaite 1992; Bardach and Kagan 1982; Scholz 1984).

In advanced industrialized countries the enforcement pyramid tends to be better constructed than in developing countries. Even in the United States, where a legalistic strategy is more embedded in the enforcement process than in many European countries, most of the work of regulatory enforcement is done by persuasion, and prosecution is relatively rare. Regulatory officials have a graduated array of sanctions at their disposal, and they are able to escalate their responses in relation to the degree of noncompliance. Moreover, many norms upon which regulation is based have been internalized, and the majority of regulated entities is committed to complying with the law (Thornton, Gunningham, and Kagan 2005; Vandenbergh 2003).

In Brazil, environmental agencies do not have such a multistoried or well-designed enforcement pyramid. Stronger environmental agencies such as CETESB have an established practice of issuing warnings and fines, and its officials are able to accomplish quite a bit through using persuasion backed up by administrative sanctions. CETESB, in particular, has a history of technical competence and organizational strength that has translated into the development of many compliance-inducing enforcement relationships between agency officials and regulated entities. Weaker environmental agencies such as SECTAM have a more limited practice of enforcement in terms of both the length and quality of enforcement relationships and the capacity to issue administrative sanctions. They are also more susceptible to corruption. Yet while worlds apart in many ways, the enforcement practices of both CETESB and SECTAM share some basic structural weaknesses in their enforcement pyramids. The most severe administrative sanction, the immediate closure of a facility operating in violation of the law, is often politically untenable in both agencies. And neither CETESB nor SECTAM had a practice of using or threatening to use civil or criminal enforcement processes, even though they were provided for by law.

The Brazilian Ministério Público's involvement in environmental enforcement adds several layers to the enforcement pyramid. In addition to being subject to persuasion by agency officials, polluters are now also subject to persuasion by prosecutors, and sometimes by agency officials and prosecutors together. Prosecutors may escalate by proposing conduct adjustment agreements, and ultimately by threatening and using civil and criminal lawsuits. Prosecutorial institutions in Brazil have a long-standing reputation for legal expertise and public service, and prosecutors are generally respected and admired. In addition, they are accustomed to threatening legal penalties and enforcing the law against offenders. In sum, they have a lot of institutional capital in the enforcement realm. The reputation of the Ministério Público for energetic enforcement makes tough legal sanctions credible. The enforcement pyramid in Brazil—incorporating the instruments and processes of administrative, civil, and criminal enforcement—is consequently more imposing.

Also comporting with the concept of the enforcement pyramid, prosecutorial enforcement is most effective when prosecutors use a mix of extrajudicial and judicial resolution. Many cases can be resolved extrajudicially while judicial enforcement is held in reserve for the most serious violations or intractable cases. An appropriate mix of judicial and extrajudicial means of resolution is most likely to emerge when the prosecutor has sufficient bargaining power to convince the investigated parties to settle most cases. Having sufficient bargaining power depends, in turn, on the prosecutor's willingness and ability to use judicial means when extrajudicial means are unsuccessful. To the extent that Brazilian courts are unwilling or unavailable to rule favorably on environmental cases, however, the new enforcement pyramid is not as strong as it otherwise could be.

These contributions that prosecutors make to the effectiveness of enforcement are situated in the larger contributions that Brazilian prosecutorial enforcement makes to the rule of law. The involvement of public prosecutors reshaped environmental enforcement in Brazil because it changed how relevant actors in environmental enforcement regard the law. With prosecutors acting independently from environmental agencies and taking the lead in civil and criminal enforcement of environmental laws, people take the law more seriously. They move toward the belief that the law should and actually does guide the behavior of most members of society. As a strong and generally respected institution, the Ministério Público confers strength and respectability on environmental law. Environmental law becomes, to a greater degree, law that matters. In this way, prosecutorial enforcement contributes to the cultural foundation of the rule of law, understood to mean that "people should be able to rely on the law when they act" (Krygier 1997: 47).

Prosecutorial enforcement is a powerful form of communication about the importance of environmental law. First, it communicates that environmental laws are being enforced. With prosecutorial enforcement, the regulated community and the general public often hear about civil and criminal lawsuits on behalf of environmental interests in the press. They see environmental enforcement in action, even against powerful and wealthy members of society. Prosecutorial enforcement helps change the commonly held notion that environmental law can be violated with impunity.

Prosecutorial enforcement also communicates that environmental agencies are being overseen. Environmental agency officials are legally accountable to prosecutors. They, too, experience the communicative impact of prosecutorial enforcement and tend to both fear and respect environmental prosecutors. While they may be personally inconvenienced or intimidated by prosecutors, agency officials say the Ministério Público's work is "important" because it changes how agency officials, the regulated community, and the general public view environmental law.

Finally, prosecutorial enforcement communicates that citizens have access to legal recourse for environmental problems. The law becomes an instrument of concerned citizens and civil society organizations to further their interests. When they take their complaints to the Ministério Público, they "mobilize" the law. Their concerns and problems have access to prosecutors and ultimately, in some cases, to the courts. Environmental laws are instruments not just in the hands of government officials, but also in the hands of private citizens.

Most broadly, prosecutorial enforcement enriches and thickens the practice of environmental law in Brazil. Krygier (1997: 50) explains that before the law is enforced it must be known and understood by relevant actors. There must be "a thick culture of supplementation and interpretation held in common by them." There must be widespread mutual understanding of the practices that are acceptable and unacceptable. Beginning in the early 1980s, the activity of Brazilian prosecutors helped build the body of knowledge about environmental law. Through writing about it and using it, prosecutors helped create solid normative understandings of environmental law in Brazil.[1] As stated by Selznick (1992: 232), "Institutions are established, not by decree alone, but as a result of being bound into the fabric of social life." In the case of environmental law in Brazil, prosecutorial enforcement contributes to this process.

The claim herein set forth is not that the Ministério Público and its prosecutors can establish "rule of law" in Brazil. But the activities of the institution and its prosecutors can in some contexts raise the bar of what is expected in terms of legal fidelity and compliance. As written in an editorial in a Brazilian newspaper: "Corruption and crime won't and will never end because of action taken by prosecutors. Nevertheless, a certain sense of impunity has been broken. The imprisonment of a banker and the stripping of a rich and powerful senator's legislative mandate acts as an Olympic benchmark. They serve to establish a new parameter of morality . . . which society, little by little, begins to think it possible to attain."[2] The work of prosecutors stands as an important symbol conveying the idea that the ruled and the rulers obey the same rules.

Prosecutorial Independence

The rule of law implications of prosecutorial enforcement are not in evidence throughout Brazil to the same degree. Rather, there is variation in the extent to which prosecutorial enforcement makes people listen to environmental law. Some prosecutorial institutions have developed a rich practice of environmental enforcement while others have not. In the case of São Paulo state prosecutors and Pará federal prosecutors, the effects were shown to be strong. There, political independence of their respective institutions enabled the development of a strong prosecutorial mode of enforcement. Pará state prosecutors, in contrast, were constrained in their environmental enforcement activity. The variation is best explained by observing that the model of the Ministério Público as politically independent from the three traditional branches of government that developed in São Paulo is not a reality throughout Brazil (Sadek and Cavalcanti 2003: 211).[3] A greater degree of political independence was observed in the State Ministério Público of São Paulo and in the Federal Ministério Público in Pará than in the Pará State Ministério Público. This degree of political independence was correlated with the extent to which prosecutors were active in environmental enforcement.

São Paulo state prosecutors and Pará federal prosecutors often expressed their sense of the political independence of their institutions. They also felt that they had the individual autonomy to pursue cases in the manner they deemed appropriate. While they sometimes viewed their attorney generals as being susceptible to influence by the executive branch because of the appointment process, they affirmed that individual prosecutors were largely free from such influence. In Pará, state prosecutors were much less assertive of their institution's political independence and their own autonomy. In addition to viewing the attorney general as influenced by the governor, they viewed individual prosecutors as subject to the influence of the attorney general.

This sense of political independence was the most important determinant of the degree of development of the prosecutorial mode of environmental enforcement in the cases studied. The independence felt by state prosecutors in São Paulo and federal prosecutors in Pará allowed them to pursue environmental cases against powerful political and economic actors, as discussed in Chapter 4. It also allowed them to develop the means to oversee environmental agencies, as described in Chapter 5, and the ability to legally represent environmentally concerned citizens and civil society organizations, as shown in Chapter 6. State prosecutors in Pará, in contrast, had a much less developed mode of prosecutorial environmental enforcement. The institution did not encourage such work, and the levels of prosecutorial activity in this area were notably lower. There, both the Ministério Público itself and the state judiciary lacked a reputation for political independence from the executive branch.

In many ways, the "political independence" of the Ministério Público can be understood as a certain type of "political support" for the institution. For the prosecutorial mode of enforcement to thrive, other political actors must respect the independence of prosecutors and, in some fashion, perceive the institution's work as a valuable and legitimate part of the political and social order. At various points in its establishment and development, the prosecutorial mode of enforcement has depended on the support of those with political power in Brazil. At the national level, political support was manifested in the variety of laws that were passed expanding the powers of the institution, as described in Chapter 3. In the state of São Paulo, political support was crucial in enabling the institution to grow and specialize in the late 1980s and early 1990s. In this period, the leaders of the São Paulo Ministério Público maintained close political ties with state governors that facilitated the budgetary resources for the institution's expansion and restructuring (Silva 2000: 5).[4]

Yet political support may be difficult to maintain, as illustrated by recent political efforts to curb the Brazilian Ministério Público described below. As pointed out by Sarat (1981) in his critique of attorneys general acting as spokespersons for underrepresented interests, there are reasons to "doubt the willingness and ability of the state to tolerate internal challenges to its authority." He asserts that to the extent that such "public advocates" enforce rights vigorously or in a meaningful way, government support will be withdrawn. This tendency is observed in Brazil by a São Paulo environmental prosecutor: "There is a quite efficient articulation in [the national capital] to neutralize the activities of the Ministério Público. Today we worry about how far we will be able to force the implementation of environmental laws without causing this sort of reaction" (personal interview, 2000). While the Ministério Público has been successful in defending itself against reform efforts, prosecutors increasingly perceive a decline in support among political elites.

Coordination Challenges

In the context of environmental enforcement, the Brazilian prosecutor often plays the role of the "lone ranger," who "cleans up a town" in the service of the public interest (Garth, Nagel, and Plager 1988: 396). This is the image of the politically independent prosecutor—free of the influence of other governmental actors and able to follow his or her own conscience in pursuing justice. Yet in its most effective emanations, prosecutorial enforcement involves coordination and cooperation among enforcement actors, both among prosecutors themselves as well as among prosecutors and environmental agencies. Precisely because of the importance placed on independence, such coordination and cooperation is a challenge in the prosecutorial mode of enforcement.[5]

In the case of the São Paulo Ministério Público, the effectiveness of prosecutorial enforcement was hobbled by a lack of coordination among prosecutors. With a large number of state prosecutors working in environmental enforcement, one in each of São Paulo's 225 judicial districts and several in the most populated districts, coordination problems among prosecutors became apparent. Prosecutors' treatment of environmental cases lacked consistency. Without an overall understanding of environmental problems in the state, prosecutors were limited in their abilities to prioritize cases. Efforts by some prosecutors to improve or institute mechanisms to encourage consistency and prioritization, such as the institutional plans discussed in Chapter 4, encountered resistance from other prosecutors as threats to their independence.

The São Paulo Ministério Público's effectiveness was also limited by lack of coordination between prosecutors and environmental agencies. Given the relatively high level of capability of the São Paulo environmental agency, one might expect that prosecutors would develop a greater degree of coordination and partnership. Yet some of the most active environmental prosecutors, referred to as "hardliners" in Chapter 5, viewed the environmental agency as "the enemy" and alienated agency officials. And while agency officials dutifully responded to prosecutorial requests for information, they often resented the burden represented by this workload. São Paulo prosecutors and environmental agency officials had not, on the whole, developed relationships that mutually assisted each other in their respective realms of enforcement. In many cases, the premium that prosecutors placed on political independence prevented them from viewing agency officials as their allies.

The Federal Ministério Público in Pará furnished the best example of a well-coordinated mode of prosecutorial enforcement. Because only a few prosecutors work in environmental enforcement in the state and they are in close communication, their actions are often coordinated. Moreover, federal prosecutors were able to forge a cooperative relationship with the state director of the federal environmental agency. After two predecessors had been implicated in corruption scandals that federal prosecutors played a role in investigating and prosecuting, a new director was selected to head IBAMA/PA who was considered by federal prosecutors to be technically knowledgeable and trustworthy. The new state director took an approach of communication and transparency with the prosecutors, and the prosecutors reciprocated. With this relationship, the two institutions were able to reinforce each other's enforcement capabilities. Prosecutors backed up the state director's efforts to confront and change practices of corruption within IBAMA, and IBAMA provided prosecutors with the information necessary to ramp up their criminal enforcement of forestry laws.

To address the coordination challenges evident in a large prosecutorial institution such as the São Paulo Ministério Público, mechanisms that encourage the consistent handling of cases are needed. However, to the extent that such mechanisms appear as constraints or rules about how to handle cases, prosecutors tend to view them as a threat to their functional independence. An innovation from the Ministério Público of the state of Rio Grande do Sul, located in southern Brazil and also very active in environmental enforcement, offers a potential solution. In 2000, the Rio Grande do Sul State Ministério Público created an environmental council (Conselho de Defesa do Meio Ambiente; CONMAM) consisting of all state prosecutors who have responsibility for environmental prosecution.[6] The council's objectives are to establish nonbinding guidelines that further the harmonization of prosecutorial activity and to promote meetings of environmental prosecutors in the various regions of the state. As explained by one of the prosecutors who attends CONMAM meetings regularly, the council discusses what the priority issues are and how to handle particularly difficult cases or situations (personal interview, 2002). A primary activity of the council has been to organize training workshops for state environmental prosecutors on priority issues such as forest protection, noise pollution, mining, solid waste, and subdivision development.[7]

Another way to improve the effectiveness of prosecutorial enforcement is to establish greater cooperation between prosecutors and agency officials. In São Paulo, where environmental agencies are plagued more by lack of resources than by corruption, there is large potential for cooperation. Agency officials and prosecutors in São Paulo have similar visions of how the relationship might be improved and the benefits that would accrue. As stated by an agency official, "CETESB has what the Ministério Público needs and the Ministério Público has what CETESB needs . . . if the Ministério Público works together with CETESB, it can achieve a much better outcome" (personal interview, 2000). Another agency official explains, "Either their [Ministério Público and CETESB] actions are synergistic and the institutions strengthen each other, or it is the opposite—there is conflict and they work against each other" (personal interview, 2002). He advocates that the Ministério Público change its overall strategy with respect to the agency, seeking to play the role of partner rather than adversary. A São Paulo environmental prosecutor echoes the agency official when he explains that what is needed is an institutional policy forged at the highest levels that makes it the policy of the institution to work in partnership with CETESB (personal interview, 2002). Under such a policy, prosecutors could be strongly encouraged to meet regularly with agency officials to discuss how to help each other resolve priority cases. Dialogue would encourage prosecutors to learn about and respect agency priorities and create a basis for greater cooperation in specific cases.

Although the São Paulo Ministério Público's coordination with state environmental agencies could be improved, São Paulo prosecutors benefited from the substantial degree of interaction and support that did exist. In contrast, Pará state prosecutors had not been able to enlist the technical support of agency officials from their state environmental agency. This inability to tap into the resources of a competent environmental agency contributed to the lack of effectiveness of state environmental prosecutors in Pará.

Making Prosecutors Accountable

Rule of law is enhanced by the accountability that prosecutors provide for environmental agency officials. However, rule of law may be undermined by illegal or improper acts committed by prosecutors themselves. This is the problem of holding institutions of accountability accountable, or that of "second-order" accountability. The problem is particularly acute when the institutions of accountability are "specialized, nonelective, autonomous state organizations" like the Brazilian Ministério Público (Schedler 1999: 25–26).

The lack of prosecutorial accountability has been a key source of criticism of the Brazilian Ministério Público since it gained new powers in the Federal Constitution of 1988. President Fernando Henrique Cardoso, for example, criticized techniques used by prosecutors in their investigation of his former Central Bank director as an "invasion" and a "return to arbitrary rule" (Sadek and Cavalcanti 2003: 210). In cases like this, prosecutors have been accused of pursuing political figures based on unfounded accusations in order to appear in the media and make a name for themselves. The Ministério Público is also criticized for paralyzing public decision making and inappropriately intervening in decisions made by publicly elected officials. While a popular image abounds of the prosecutor as the "people's true defender," there is another widespread image of the prosecutor as the "irresponsible exhibitionist" (ibid.: 221).

Indeed, the Brazilian prosecutorial mode of enforcement has very weak vertical and horizontal accountability. As discussed in Chapter 5, vertical accountability refers to ways in which government officials must answer to the public, principally through democratic elections, while horizontal accountability refers to ways in which governmental officials answer to other governmental officials (O'Donnell 1999a). Prosecutors are not vertically accountable because they are selected through competitive civil service exams rather than popular election. Recruiting through civil service exams has served the Ministério Público well because it selects based on competence and it limits nepotism and political influence. Studies have shown that prosecutorial careers have become increasingly open to candidates that do not have familial connections and to candidates from lower socioeconomic backgrounds (Sadek and Cavalcanti 2003: 218). Despite these advantages, this form of selection does not provide vertical accountability. Only the media's coverage contributes a dimension of vertical accountability as the role of the Ministério Público, and the actions of individual prosecutors have become the subject of media attention and public debate.[8]

The executive branch's power to appoint the attorney general provides some horizontal accountability, but it is limited in two significant ways (see Kerche 2003: 68–70). First, a sitting attorney general is relatively protected from removal because the 1988 Constitution requires a majority vote in the legislature. This constraint constitutes an "exception in Brazilian politics relative to both other appointed positions and previous constitutions" (ibid.: 68).

Second, the attorney general has relatively little control over the actions of other prosecutors. The constitution guarantees "functional" independence, meaning that prosecutors independently determine how to conduct the investigations and lawsuits in their jurisdiction. Constitutionally protected from dismissal, demotion, and involuntary transfer, prosecutors are not required to follow guidelines established by the attorney general concerning the conduct of cases (Sadek and Cavalcanti 2003: 220). Moreover, the attorney general often cannot exercise control through the promotion process. Other institutional leaders are involved in promotion decisions, and in some states such as São Paulo, promotions are based primarily on duration of service (see Kerche 2003: 102, 108–9).

The Constitution provides that prosecutors may be involuntarily removed from their positions only through a judicial process. The attorney general may file a civil action to remove a tenured prosecutor after the prosecutor has been convicted of a crime that is incompatible with the exercise of his or her duties; upon discovery that the prosecutor is practicing as a lawyer; or after a prosecutor has abandoned his or her position for more than thirty continuous days (Mazzilli 1997: 40).[9] Prosecutors may only be involuntarily transferred to another position when it is "in the public interest," as determined by a majority vote of the Superior Council (Conselho Superior), a body that includes the attorney general and other institutional leaders.[10]

Perhaps the most important agent of horizontal accountability for the Ministério Público is the Brazilian judiciary. Prosecutors require a judge's approval to obtain a search warrant, and one study showed that judges have denied such requests in about 40 percent of the cases (Sadek and Cavalcanti 2003: 220–22). Moreover, the judge rather than the prosecutor ultimately decides the case and imposes the sanction. In some types of cases, particularly prosecutorial challenges of administrative discretion, judges have tended to rule in favor of public administrators.[11]

Given the importance of the judiciary's role in providing a check on prosecutorial power, accountability problems are particularly present in the Ministério Público's heavy reliance on extrajudicial resolution. As described in Chapter 4, the large majority of cases are resolved without judicial involvement. While the Superior Council does routinely oversee prosecutorial decisions to close an investigation, it does not generally have mechanisms in place to constrain an overzealous prosecutor or identify inadequacies or illegalities in a conduct adjustment agreement.[12]

An inquisitorial instrument, the prosecutorial investigation does not guarantee the investigated party's right to be heard. As explained by Antunes (2001: 665), "The investigation is a powerful instrument that, without doubt, when opened against a person or company, exerts enormous pressure. It cannot be forgotten that sometimes the opening of an investigation might be arbitrary and imply real harm to the investigated party." The São Paulo Ministério Público's Superior Council has the power to suspend an investigation in response to an appeal by the investigated party, but it is rarely used. The Superior Council appears more concerned with the possibility of a failure to zealously investigate and prosecute than the possibility of prosecutorial abuse or overreaching (see Arantes 2002: 260).

Nor is there much institutional or public oversight of the conduct adjustment agreements negotiated by prosecutors. While such agreements are submitted to the Superior Council of the Ministério Público for review, few standards have been established and the agreements are almost always approved. Yet the possibility of duress and abuse exists as the prosecutor can threaten civil or criminal charges if the defendant does not settle. Arantes (2002: 260) points out that many cases are resolved during the investigative phase through a conduct adjustment agreement, "thanks to the pressure that the prosecutor can place on the investigated party before filing a public civil action." In addition to potential abuses of power in the negotiation of an agreement, questions have been raised about the consistency of such agreements. Depending on the prosecutor, two similarly situated parties may be subject to very different requirements. Finally, there is no requirement that conduct adjustment agreements be approved by the complainant or otherwise publicized.

Conduct adjustment agreements might also be abused in the other direction. The agreements may not be stringent enough. They may allow for partial or incomplete handling of environmental degradation by a private party. Prosecutors might be actively corrupt, receiving bribes in exchange for writing an agreement that fails to remedy the environmental harm. Prosecutors might also be lax in verifying that conduct adjustment agreements are actually fulfilled. The Superior Council generally does not monitor the content and performance of conduct adjustment agreements to guard against such abuses.[13]

Comparing prosecutorial institutions in various countries, Kerche (2003: 157) discerns an inverse relationship between the discretionary power and the accountability of legal actors. Where prosecutors exercise discretion in deciding whether to file charges, as in the United States, the political system provides a strong accountability mechanism such as democratic elections. Where strong accountability mechanisms are absent, as in Brazil and Italy, prosecutors formally abide by the "principle of obligation" that implies less discretionary power. Brazilian prosecutors, however, actually exercise a great deal of discretion in areas such as political corruption and environmental enforcement because they decide which cases of the many potential cases to investigate and how rigorously to pursue them. Kerche (2003: 82) calls this combination of discretion and weak accountability "a strange formula for the democratic process."

Critics of the Ministério Público have sought constitutional and statutory reforms. One measure considered by the legislature, referred to by prosecutors as the "muzzle law," would have imposed restraints on prosecutors' communications with the press about investigations (see Arantes 2002: 256–60; Ferraz 1995). Other proposed reforms include allowing the executive to choose an attorney general who is not a member of the institution; allowing the attorney general to make promotions without regard for the traditional criteria of years of service; and allowing only the attorney general to file charges against mayors (Sadek and Cavalcanti 2003: 225).

The calls for reform can be viewed as a signal that the Ministério Público is having a significant impact on the political status quo (see ibid.). This sentiment is echoed in the statement of an environmental prosecutor: "The Ministério Público . . . does very little of what needs to be done, but the little that it does makes sectors of society that have never been held accountable very uncomfortable—the government, the large businesses, the large political forces that were totally forgotten by the system and always did whatever they wanted" (personal interview, 2000). Many prosecutors viewed the muzzle law in particular as an effort by political elites to weaken the Ministério Público's ability to pursue corruption cases.

Reformers within the Ministério Público have also set forth proposals to enhance institutional accountability, particularly with respect to the public. A group led by members of the São Paulo Ministério Público that is concerned with the efficiency and effectiveness of the institution has proposed that prosecutors should be held accountable for achieving certain goals established in relation to the most important social problems in their jurisdictions (Ferraz 2003: 101–3, 111–15). These goals would be set with the input of civil society in a "transparent and public" planning process, and promotions would be used to create incentives for prosecutors to meet their goals.[14]

Internal reformers have also proposed that the institution measure and publicize the substantive outcomes of its environmental enforcement work. While Brazilian prosecutorial institutions tend to collect some information from prosecutors about their activities on a periodic basis, these reporting mechanisms are not geared toward portraying the substantive outcomes of their work. In São Paulo, for example, prosecutors are required to file monthly reports specifying information such as the number of investigations opened, conduct adjustment agreements signed, and public civil actions filed. The format does not permit evaluation of the institution's work in a particular substantive area such as environmental protection because data are reported for several or all public interest areas together. Even more important, no effort is made to get beyond the number of investigations, agreements, and lawsuits to assess their actual environmental impact. As explained by Macedo (1995: 48–49), the future of the institution depends on its effectiveness: "The continued legitimacy and expansion of its functions, powers, and prerogatives will directly depend on . . . its success in achieving its goals." An effort to measure such success would facilitate the institution's ability to communicate this success to the public and others, enabling it to fend off threats to its political independence and power.

In 2004, a constitutional amendment on judicial reform was passed that partially responds to the Ministério Público's critics. Most important, the amendment established a National Council of the Ministério Público (Conselho Nacional do Ministério Público; CNMP) with authority to oversee certain aspects of the institution's work. The council consists of fourteen members, including eight prosecutors from the federal and state Ministérios Públicos, two judges, two lawyers chosen by the bar association, and two societal representatives chosen by the legislature. The Council's function is to oversee the administrative and financial activities of prosecutorial institutions as well as the legality of prosecutorial actions. The Council may receive complaints about prosecutors, conduct disciplinary proceedings, and apply administrative sanctions.[15] The Ministério Público has been successful in avoiding more significant reforms with the arguments that such reforms would destroy prosecutorial independence, violate the public right to information, and grant impunity to corrupt politicians.

The question for the Brazilian Ministério Público is how to preserve the institutional and functional independence that has served the institution in terms of promoting rule of law while ensuring that prosecutors themselves are accountable. What is needed is the "right balance" among "independence, efficiency, efficacy, and responsibility" (Sadek and Cavalcanti 2003: 224). To the extent that the institution takes its own steps to enhance its vertical and horizontal accountability, it becomes less vulnerable to attacks by political actors that seek to reduce the Ministério Público's power to increase its own.

The Diffusion of Prosecutorial Enforcement

Many developing countries have substantial legal frameworks for environmental protection that are not adequately enforced. Their environmental agencies typically lack the resources to effectively implement and enforce environmental laws. In this context of strong laws and weak agencies, the mode of prosecutorial enforcement wherein prosecutors energetically enforce environmental laws, oversee environmental agencies, and legally represent environmental interests flourished in Brazil. The question thus arises of whether prosecutorial enforcement could develop and lead to similar outcomes in other countries.

There is a large literature on the "diffusion of law" that is relevant to this question. As observed by Twining (2004: 5), the study of the diffusion of law has proceeded under many labels, including "reception, transplants, spread, expansion, transfer, exports and imports, imposition, circulation, transmigration, transposition, and transfrontier mobility of law." Over many years beginning in the 1970s, Alan Watson (1993: 95) argued that "transplanting" legal rules was both extremely common and "socially easy."[16] He contended that "successful borrowing could be made from a very different legal system" and "could be achieved even when nothing was known of the political, social or economic context of the foreign law" (Watson 1976: 79).

In response, scholars argued that the success of legal transplants depends greatly on the social and political context (see Kahn-Freund 1974). While some features of a particular legal system may be too culturally specific for viable transplant, others may be able to thrive in many diverse countries. The institution of the ombudsman and the constitutional courts seem to be examples of the latter (Friedman 1978: 30–31; Krygier 1999: 83). Taking an even more critical position, Legrand (1997) argues that legal transplants are "impossible" under any conditions because, while a legal rule might be copied from one legal system into another, the cultural meaning of the rule that constitutes its essence cannot be transferred.

Twining usefully identifies and describes a "naïve model of diffusion" that has predominated in the comparative law literature. The naïve model involves "a *bipolar* relationship between *two countries* involving a *direct one-way* transfer of *legal rules or institutions* through the agency of *governments* including *formal enactment or adoption* at a particular moment of time (*a reception date*) *without major change*" (emphasis in original; Twining 2004: 15).[17] Twining advocates a more complex and varied conception of legal diffusion that includes, for example, transfers that involve substate or nonstate actors; transfers of legal phenomena and ideas beyond legal rules and institutions; and transfers that involve transformation.

Brazilian prosecutorial enforcement is a product of legal diffusion, and the story of its development illustrates the complexity that Twining suggests. As described in Chapter 3, the Brazilian prosecutors who drafted the Public Civil Action Law built upon an initiative of Brazilian legal scholars and judges who were, in turn, inspired by the writings of Italian legal scholars, particularly Mauro Cappelletti. Cappelletti and his coauthors in the Florence Access to Justice project of the 1970s viewed collective or diffuse interests such as the interests of consumers and environmentalists as a new category of social rights that had emerged in the modern state and required legal protection to become effective. Cappelletti observed that such representation was occurring in the United States through class actions and private attorney general actions. He considered the *Ministère Public* as one of the most "promising institutions" for litigating to protect modern social rights in civil law countries.[18] In essence, Cappelletti sought to diffuse the type of public interest legal advocacy that was occurring in the United States to Italy and other countries.

Brazilian legal scholars were influenced by Cappelletti's writings in the waning years of the military dictatorship to consider the legal representation of public interests in Brazil. After legal scholars drafted a bill that emphasized the role of civil society groups in filing public interest legal actions, the prosecutors of the Ministério Público of São Paulo drafted a competing bill that gave greater powers to the Ministério Público. In the context of a political environment that favored democratization and with the political skill of the institution's leaders in presenting the legal representation of diffuse and collective interests as essential to democracy, the Ministério Público's bill was passed into law in 1985. This story shows how pathways of diffusion may be "complex and indirect," with a variety of "agents of diffusion" (Twining 2004: 19–22).

The Brazilian Ministério Público in many ways exceeded Cappelletti's vision of what a *Ministère Public* could accomplish in terms of representing and defending "diffuse and collective" interests. Cappelletti recognized the possibility that the *Ministère Public* might play this role but ultimately argued that it was incapable. He saw major obstacles in both the institution's dependence on the executive branch and its unspecialized bureaucratic structure. He concluded that the "*Ministère Public* thus appears inherently unsuited to becoming the forceful promoter of the type of group, class, and public-interest actions that are most important in modern societies" (Cappelletti 1978: 785).

In Brazil, Cappelletti's ideas were transformed in ways that made prosecutors more capable of promoting environmental interests. The Brazilian Ministério Público was made largely independent of the executive branch, constituting a sort of fourth branch of government, and prosecutors were granted individual autonomy and job security equivalent to judges. The Brazilian Ministério Público was also able to build specialized capacity in the area of environmental enforcement.

As evident in the comparison between the São Paulo and the Pará state Ministérios Públicos, however, the prosecutorial mode of enforcement has not been fully diffused throughout Brazil. Under the Constitution and relevant federal statutes, the Ministério Público is responsible for environmental protection in all Brazilian states. Yet, in Pará and several other northern states, the Ministério Público is not as active in environmental protection as in São Paulo and other southern states. In many northern states, the executive branch has managed to maintain a larger degree of influence over the budgets and activities of the institution, and the institution has been unable to sufficiently specialize.

The story of the diffusion of prosecutorial enforcement within Brazil furnishes insight about how a similiar kind of enforcement might be diffused to other developing countries. Prosecutorial enforcement developed within the legal culture and tradition of Brazil, a country similar in many ways to other Latin American countries. Indeed, most Latin American countries have a Ministério Público with traditional functions resembling those of the Brazilian Ministério Público, and several have formally established "collective and diffuse interests" in law (Grinover 2000: 147). Moreover, in most Latin American countries, the Ministério Público is formally independent from other branches of government.[19] Latin American countries with similar legal-cultural and political characteristics are likely to provide the most "fertile" ground for transplant (see Friedman 1978: 32).

Moreover, in many Latin American countries, democratization and governmental accountability remain high on the political agenda. In this context, prosecutors and civil society organizations might lobby for changes to the Ministério Público similar to those made in Brazil, and their proposals might reach a receptive legislative audience. In other words, the combination of the institution's political skill and a favorable political context that enabled the Brazilian Ministério Público to gain new enforcement powers may also be found in other countries. As occurred in Brazil, transport of the idea of prosecutorial environmental enforcement to other legal systems would likely involve indirect pathways of diffusion and considerable transformation.

Conclusion

Environmental law suffers from "rule of law" problems that make it ineffective in many developing countries. These problems include the impunity enjoyed by powerful economic and political actors; the lack of accountability of regulatory agencies; and the inability of citizens and citizen groups to vindicate environmental rights. Environmental law is not part of the "psychological economy" of daily life, and it is not effective in changing behavior. This book has argued that the prosecutorial mode of enforcement, as it developed in Brazil, contributes to making environmental law more effective. The work of legal institutions on behalf of environmental interests changes the behavior of polluters, agency officials, and the public generally as the law is put into action and made visible.

Brazilian prosecutorial enforcement is, in many ways, a homegrown rule of law institution. As legal reformers consider how to further the rule of law in developing countries, they would do well to look at what makes the Brazilian Ministério Público successful. In comparison to many rule of law reforms that form part of a "global prescription," the prosecutorial mode of enforcement is a culturally and politically sensitive candidate for legal transplant (Dezalay and Garth 2002). In countries with substantial but underenforced legal frameworks for environmental protection, the diffusion of the Brazilian model of prosecutorial enforcement holds potential for making environmental law matter.

Reference Matter

Notes

Chapter 1

1. This definition of regulation is the "narrowest and simplest" of three outlined by Jordana and Levi-Faur (2004: 2–4), following Baldwin, Scott, and Hood (1998). (In the narrow sense, "regulation refers to the promulgation of an authoritative set of rules, accompanied by some mechanism, typically a public agency, for monitoring and promoting compliance with these rules.")

2. The term "developing" is used with reservation because of its implication that there is a single path of economic and political change upon which all countries may be located, the end of which resembles the political and economic conditions of the United States. For a critique of prevailing ideas of development, see Escobar (1995); Norgaard (1994); Sachs (1992). It is used in this work for lack of a better word to refer to the large group of countries that are generally capitalist and democratic, but that are not in the small group of advanced industrialized countries.

3. The term "capacity" is used here in the same sense as "state capacity" in sociology, which refers to the state's ability to implement its policies (Skocpol 1985: 10, 17).

4. In the United States, the closest analog at the federal level is the Office of the Attorney General. As specified by Voigt (2006: 4), the following criteria define a procuracy: "(i) it has the competence to gather information on the behavior of criminal suspects, or to instruct the police to gather more information; (ii) on the basis of the information, it has the competence to indict a suspect; [and] (iii) during a trial, it represents the interests of the public."

5. In Brazilian law, "diffuse interests" are interests held by an indeterminable number of people or society as a whole, while "collective interests" refer to those of an identifiable group of people. The term "public interests" has a different connotation in Brazil than in the United States, referring to the interests of the state rather than

society. In this work, the term "public interests" (and sometimes, "societal interests") is used to denote both diffuse and collective interests. For further explanation, see Chapter 3.

6. The Brazilian Ministério Público is composed of the twenty-six state Ministérios Públicos and the Ministério Público of the Union, which in turn consists of the Federal Ministério Público, the Military Ministério Público, the Labor Ministério Público, and the Ministério Público of the Federal District and Territories. While each Ministério Público is governed in terms of organization and functions by the 1988 Constitution, they are autonomous institutions. Each state Ministério Público is headquartered in its state capital and has one or more state prosecutor in each *comarca* (judicial district). This book focuses on the state Ministérios Públicos in São Paulo and Pará, as well as the Federal Ministério Público, which is headquartered in the national capital, Brasilia, and has federal prosecutors in each state.

7. See Chapter 3 for further discussion on the absence of prosecutorial discretion.

8. The Brazilian Ministério Público also plays a very significant role in fighting corruption. See especially Arantes (2004) and Taylor and Buranelli (2007).

9. Environmental provisions are included in the constitutions of Argentina, Chile, Colombia, Costa Rica, Ecuador, El Salvador, Honduras, Nicaragua, Paraguay, Uruguay, and Venezuela. "Derecho del ciudadano: Análisis comparativo de constituciones de los regimenes presidenciales." *Base de datos políticos de las Americas* (1998). Washington, DC: Georgetown University y Organización de Estados Americanos. Available at http://pdba.georgetown.edu/Comp/Ambiente/derecho.html (last visited Dec. 12, 2007).

10. See "Atribuciones del Ministério Público: Análisis comparativo de constituciones de los regimenes presidenciales." *Base de datos politicos de las Americas* (1998). Washington, DC: Georgetown University y Organización de Estados Americanos. Available at http://pdba.georgetown.edu/Comp/Control/Publico/atribuciones.html (last visited Dec. 12, 2007); and Agatiello (1995: 263).

11. See Chapter 6 for further discussion of the judicialization of politics in Brazil.

12. São Paulo accounts for 35 percent of the national income, and its per capita income is 63 percent greater than the national average. Brazilian Institute of Geography and Statistics (IBGE), Project Cidades@. Available at http://www.ibge.gov.br/ (last visited Dec. 12, 2007).

13. State Government of Pará, SECTAM (Dec. 1996; on file with author); Brito and Barreto (2006: 38).

14. A recent example is the murder of the American nun Dorothy Stang in 2005 (Hochstetler and Keck 2007: 1).

15. For a similar list of the characteristics of the rule of law, see Fuller (1969: 38–39).

16. Legal culture is best defined as the understandings and meanings of law that are held by people in a society (Friedman 1985: 31; Silbey 2002: 8623).

17. See Domingo (2005: 23–28) for a discussion of the relationship between the judicialization of politics and rule of law construction. Domingo finds that, in Mexico, the former contributes to the latter but that this connection will depend on "the form that the judicialization of politics takes and the specific characteristics in particular political, institutional, and social contexts" (ibid.: 23). The positive relationship between prosecutorial enforcement and the construction of rule of law in environmental matters will depend on such factors as well.

18. In a narrower and more pejorative sense, legalism may also refer to a "rigid adherence to rules, without regard to their purpose or to the fairness of the outcome" (Kagan 2001: 255, n. 1). See Chapter 5 for a discussion of how prosecutorial enforcement can lead to this type of legalism.

19. On how different actors in the enforcement process may understand "compliance" differently, see Hutter (1997) and DiMento (1986: 25–27).

20. As described by Ayres and Braithwaite (1992: 37), regulatory agencies are most effective when they have a wide range of enforcement tools at their disposal such that "every escalation of noncompliance by the firm can be matched with a corresponding escalation in punitiveness by the state." In these circumstances, defection from cooperation will be less attractive to the regulated entity, and more of the work of regulation can be done through persuasion (ibid.: 19, 36).

Chapter 2

1. Aragão and Bunker (1998: 478) call this the "environmental legislation paradox."

2. "Half-Measures to Protect the Amazon." Editorial Desk. *New York Times* (Feb. 2, 1998, Late Edition), p. A22, col. 1.

3. The most common translations are *implementação da lei*, *aplicação da lei*, and *fazer cumprir a lei*. *Fiscalização* and *controle* are also used, particularly in the administrative sphere. Given the lack of a clear equivalent, the English word has come into usage in Portuguese. See Ferraz and Ferraz (1997).

4. Even in the area of pollution control, federal regulations and guidelines influence how states administer their permitting systems. See especially CONAMA resolution 01/86 of Jan. 23, 1986, and resolution 237/97 of Dec. 19, 1997. Also, the 1981 National Environmental Policy Act sets forth the national framework for environmental policy. Federal law no. 6,938 of Aug. 31, 1981.

5. As argued by Drummond and Barros-Platiau (2006: 84), a "developmentalist" model characterized by a "deep and lasting social consensus in favor of economic growth, at any and all costs" endured in Brazil from the 1930s through the 1980s.

6. Federal decree no. 73,030 of Oct. 30, 1973; see Findley (1988).

7. Federal law no. 6,938 of Aug. 31, 1981, reprinted in Benjamin (1999b: 83–90).

8. Ibid., art. 9.

9. Ibid., art. 6. Neves (2006) investigates the legal duties and powers of Brazilian

municipalities and the resources available to them. She concludes that municipalities do quite a bit in the area of environmental policy, but much less than they could do with available resources and much less than the Brazilian constitution requires.

10. CONAMA consists of 108 members. In addition to the Minister of the Environment and the Minister's executive secretary, CONAMA includes 37 members from the federal government; 27 members from state governments; 8 members from municipal governments; 8 members from industry; 22 members from professional societies, environmental organizations, and labor organizations; 1 honorary member; and 3 members who have the power to speak but not to vote—one from the Federal Ministério Público, one from a state Ministério Público, and one from the congressional committee concerned with environment issues. See http://www.mma.gov.br/port/conama/estr.cfm (last visited Dec. 12, 2007).

11. CONAMA resolution 02/85 of Mar. 5, 1985.

12. Maglio (2000: 24) asserts that the councils distinguish the Brazilian environmental system from that of many other countries. "The Environmental Councils give the environmental system a greater ability to deal with pressures and allow the sharing of visions presented by direct representatives of important segments of society, thus creating a process of permeability and societal negotiation."

13. CONAMA resolution 01/86 of Jan. 23, 1986, reprinted in Benjamin (1999b: 327–31). See Biller (2003: 119, Table 6.2) for a translation of the list of activities subject to environmental permitting under the resolution.

14. CONAMA resolution 237/97 of Dec. 19, 1997, reprinted in ibid.: 377–87). See Biller (2003: 119–20, Table 6.3) for a translation of the main provisions of this resolution.

15. 1988 Const. art. 225.

16. Ibid., § 1.

17. Ibid., §§ 2–4.

18. The National Constituent Assembly charged with writing the new constitution consisted of the combined Chamber of Deputies and Senate (the lower and upper houses of the federal congress, respectively) elected in 1986 (Hochstetler and Keck 2007: 46).

19. Federal law no. 7,735 of Feb. 22, 1989.

20. The total workforce numbered 6,230, with 183 transferred from the Rubber Bureau, 384 from SEMA, 2,111 from the Fishing Bureau, and 3,553 from the Brazilian Institute of Forestry Development. See "Relatório de Atividades do IBAMA 2001" and associated spreadsheets (on file with author).

21. SEMAM was created by provisional measure no. 150 of Mar. 15, 1990; IBAMA, formally subordinated to the Ministry of the Interior, was linked to SEMAM by federal law no. 8,028 of Apr. 12, 1990, art. 36. For institutional history, see "Histórico Institucional," available at http://www.mma.gov.br/ (last visited Dec. 12, 2007). See also Santos and Paul (1995: 133).

22. The Ministry of the Environment was established in federal law no. 8,490 of Nov. 19, 1992, art. 2. Its name and responsibilities changed several times in the 1990s. It was changed to the "Ministry of the Environment and the Amazon" in 1993 (by federal law no. 8,746 of Dec. 9, 1993); to the "Ministry of the Environment, Water Resources, and the Amazon" in 1995 (by art. 16 of provisional Meas. no. 813 of Jan. 1, 1995); and to the "Ministry of the Environment" in 1999 (by provisional meas. no. 1,795 of Jan. 1, 1999). See MMA, "Histórico Institucional," available at http://www.mma.gov.br/ (last visited Dec. 12, 2007).

23. Federal law no. 9,605 of Feb. 12, 1998, and federal decree no. 3,179 of Sept. 21, 1999. Both are reprinted in Benjamin (1999b). Also, see Chapter 4 for more information on criminal enforcement powers.

24. Federal law no. 9,605, art. 75. In 1998 Brazilian currency (reais), these fines were roughly equivalent to the same amount in U.S. dollars.

25. Federal law no. 9,605 of Feb. 12, 1998.

26. Ibid., arts. 66 and 67.

27. Federal decree no. 3,179 of Sept. 21, 1999, reprinted in Benjamin (1999b: 309). For a more complete review of the Brazilian Environmental Crimes Law, see Edesio Fernandes, "Punishing environmental crimes in Brazil" (on file with author).

28. State decree no. 50,079 of July 24, 1968.

29. State law no. 997 of May 31, 1976, with further regulation provided by state decree no. 8,468 of Sept. 8, 1976.

30. See Government of São Paulo, "CETESB Profile" (on file with author). See also Dias and Sanchez (2001).

31. Maglio (2000: 113), quoting CETESB, "Relatório Cetesb—25 anos" (1993). For more information on the Cubatão case, see Lemos (1998) and Ferreira (1993).

32. Maglio (2000: 28–29); Filho (1993: 59).

33. Like the national council, the state council is composed of representatives of the public and private sectors. CONSEMA currently has 35 members. The Secretary of the Environment presides over the council, and members include three representatives of the Environmental Secretariat; 14 members of other São Paulo state secretariats; a representative of the Ministério Público; and 17 representatives of civil society organization, including both industry associations and environmental groups (Dias and Sanchez 2001: 170).

34. São Paulo state decree no. 24,932 of Mar. 23, 1986, as altered by São Paulo state decree no. 2,642 of Apr. 1, 1987, and São Paulo state decree no. 30,555 of Oct. 3, 1989, which further restructured and reorganized SMA.

35. See State of São Paulo / SMA (1998). The organizational structure of SMA is also available at http://www.ambiente.sp.gov.br/sobreasecretaria/organo.htm (last visited Dec. 12, 2007).

36. CETESB was linked to SMA by state decree no. 26,942 of Apr. 1, 1987.

37. See "Relatório de Atividades do IBAMA 2001" and associated spreadsheets (on file with author). See also the interview of Wilson Almeida Lima, executive director of IBAMA in São Paulo, published in *Revista de Serviços: Uma Publicação da Federação de Serviços do Estado de São Paulo* (FESESP), Year 5, no. 13 (Aug. 2001), pp. 24–27.

38. While not the focus of this examination of environmental policy in Brazil, the problems of institutional conflict and the lack of clear jurisdictional boundaries among agencies at various levels of government as well as within a specific level of government are often cited as contributing factors to weak environmental management in Brazil. See Findley (1988: 9–15); Filho (1993: 58–59); Guimarães, MacDowell, and Demajorovic (1996: 38).

39. "The Amazon's major threat: Illegal logging," Greenpeace press briefing (July 2000). Available at http://archive.greenpeace.org/forests/forests_new/html/content/reports/press_amazonthreats.pdf (last visited Dec. 12, 2007).

40. The three states that had not created an agency were Acre, Amapá, and Roraima, all in the northern Amazonian region of Brazil (Maglio 2000: 28–29).

41. Governo do Estado do Pará, Secretaria de Estado de Ciência, Tecnologia e Meio Ambiente, "Relatório de Atividades, 1995–1998" (on file with author).

42. Ibid.

43. Pará state law no. 5,887 of May 9, 1995.

44. As explained earlier, IBAMA incorporated the Brazilian Institute of Forestry Development (IBDF) and thus had a strong historical presence in the forestry sector in the Amazon region. IBAMA has not played a major role in pollution control issues even though the Pará state environmental agency has also been weak in this area.

45. This figure includes SECTAM employees in the director's office, environmental division, administrative and financial offices, and supporting offices such as information technology, the library, and laboratories.

46. Pers. comm., IBAMA (May 31, 2002); "SECTAM Staff List (May 2002)" (on file with author).

47. Governo do Estado do Pará, Secretaria de Estado de Ciência, Tecnologia e Meio Ambiente, *Relatório de Atividades, 1995–1998*.

48. Toward this end, Pará passed a new forestry law and regulations in 2002. See Pará state law no. 6,462 of July 4, 2002, and Pará state decree no. 5,565 of Oct. 11, 2002. In March 2006, federal law no. 11,284 amended the federal Forestry Code (federal law no. 4,471 of 1965) to transfer jurisdiction for forestry management from the federal government to state and municipal governments. In September 2006, new forestry management plans began to be submitted to SECTAM rather than IBAMA. See Greenpeace, "A descentralização da gestão florestal na Amazônia Brasileira" (Dec. 2006). Available at http://www.greenpeace.org.br/amazonia/pdf/briefing_descentralizacao.pdf (last visited Dec. 12, 2007).

49. Since the late 1980s, the Brazilian government and international development

agencies have identified the institutional weakness of environmental agencies as a problem and have devoted resources toward strengthening institutional capacity at both the state and federal levels. In 1987, the National Environmental Program (Programa Nacional do Meio Ambiente) was developed by the Brazilian government in collaboration with the United Nations Environment Program. It was financed in 1989 with a loan of the World Bank and a donation of the German Reconstruction Bank at a level of US$193 million. The program continued through 1996. One of its primary goals was the strengthening of institutions and the legislative and normative legal structure for the environment. MMA, *Relatório de Atividades 1991/96* (1997). Available at http://www.mma.gov.br/port/se/pnma (last visited Dec. 12, 2007).

50. Pers. comm., CETESB Human Resources Dept.

51. State of São Paulo/SMA (1992b); *Diário Oficial do Estado de São Paulo* 109(86)—supp.; 111(93)—supp.

52. Pers. comm., CETESB Human Resources Dept. (Feb. 5, 2002).

53. Complaints of funding shortages were also common in the early 1990s. As stated in an environmental profile of São Paulo prepared in preparation for the UNCED in Rio de Janeiro in 1992, environmental protection in São Paulo "has been greatly encumbered by that perennial bugaboo, shortage of funding" (State of São Paulo/SMA 1992b: 75). Another profile that discusses the southeastern region as a whole states: "The analysis of the budgets of environmental agencies reveals the insufficiency of financial resources for carrying out their obligations" (State of São Paulo/SMA 1992a: 113).

54. CETESB, Diretoria Administrativa e Financeira, pers. comm. (Mar. 4, 2002); graph of data available in CETESB (2001: 28).

55. In 1995, 45 percent of the motor vehicle fleet was out of compliance with the regulation against *fumaça preta* (dirty emissions). By December 2000, this percentage had declined to 8 percent. See CETESB (2001: 13).

56. Governo de Estado de São Paulo, Secretaria de Economia e Planejamento, *Orçamento do Estado*, Years 1992 to 2001.

57. Currency conversions were computed using the July 1, 2002, exchange rate of R$1 = US$0.3541. The average CETESB salary was about ten times the national minimum wage of R$200/month (US$71). For comparison with prosecutors' salaries, see Chapter 3.

58. See World Bank (1996a). See also Maglio (2000) and Cappelli (2000).

59. See Programa Nacional do Meio Ambiente (PNMA; 1998), "Implantação da nova estrutura do IBAMA," *Relatório das Atividades, 1991/96*. Available at http://www .mma.gov.br/port/se/pnma/dese21.html (last visited Dec. 12, 2007).

60. Ibid.

61. The TCU is a branch of the Brazilian National Congress that conducts audits of governmental agencies and state-owned enterprises to oversee their "legality, legitimacy, efficiency and effectiveness." It is analogous to the General Accountability Office

(GAO) in the United States. See "Audit profile: The Brazilian Court of Accounts," *International Journal of Government Auditing* (July 1996). Available at http://findarticles .com/p/articles/mi_qa3662/is_199607/ai_n8745587/pg_1 (last visited Dec. 12, 2007).

62. Tribunal de Contas da União process no. 930.263/1998–7, as cited and discussed in Brito and Barreto (2006: 37). For further information, see "Decisão 651/1999— Plenário," available at https://contas.tcu.gov.br/portaltextual/MostraDocumento?lnk =(Decisao+COM+651/1999+COM+Plenario)%5Bidtd%5D (last visited Dec. 12, 2007).

63. "Mais da metade da madeira extraída na Amazônia é desperdiçada," *Estado de São Paulo* (Feb. 4, 2006), as cited and discussed by Brito and Barreto (2006:37, fn. 9).

64. IBAMA, official announcement of the *concurso público* (civil service exam), on file with author.

65. Ibid.

66. Ibid.

67. Pers. comm., SECTAM (May 2002). Including the science and technology directorate, researchers affiliated with SECTAM financed by the federal research center CNPq, and SECTAM employees on loan to other government institutions, SECTAM had a total staff of 343. "SECTAM Staff List, May 2002" (on file with author).

68. Based on a comparison of data in Dourado (1993: 124) and data obtained from SECTAM in May 2002.

69. Notably, a total of 42 percent of the state's land area is in federally designated protected areas: 21.7 percent is designated as indigenous territories (Terras Indígenas), 14.6 percent as Sustainable Use Conservation Areas (Unidades de Conservação de Uso Sustantável), and 5.6 percent as Full Protection Conservation Areas (Unidades de Conservação de Proteção Integral) (Veríssimo et al. 2006: 16).

70. SECTAM's efforts to promote decentralization have been promoted and funded as part of the "Pilot Program to Conserve the Brazilian Rain Forest." As of March 2002, the program had received funding amounting to US$346 million primarily from donations by Germany, the European Union, the United Kingdom, and the United States, along with counterpart contributions from the Brazilian government. About US$83 million has gone toward strengthening environmental agencies in Brazil, with over $8 million toward programs in the state of Pará.

71. See Maglio (2000: 229). Studying the states of São Paulo, Minas Gerais, and Sergipe, Maglio found decentralization of environmental management responsibility to the municipalities to be occurring in a "scattered way" and that systematically designed programs aimed toward strengthening municipal environmental institutions did not exist.

72. As an example, the mayor of Paragominas, a municipality of Pará, has been identified as part of a group responsible for a large portion of the illegal extraction of mahogany in the state (personal interview, 2002).

73. The study included the states of Acre, Amapá, Amazonas, Pará, Rondônia, Roraima, and Tocantins.

74. ABEMA study cited in Gustavo Hees de Negreiros, Marli Maria de Mattos, Cassio Alves Pereira, and Daniel Curtis Nepstad, "Mineração x sociedade civil: O caulim do Rio Capim e o futuro da atividade mineral na Amazônia," Instituto de Pesquisa Ambiental (Belém) and The Woods Hole Research Center (circa 1995).

75. One exception is Bunker (1985), who explores the problem of corruption among federal officials responsible for land settlement projects in the Brazilian state of Pará. Comparing two different projects, Bunker links the difference in the extent of corruption to a difference in the personal relationships between the staffs of the two federal agencies involved in the land resettlement projects. Where the staffs of the two agencies had extensive personal contact, corruption was prevalent. Where they did not, the staff of each served as a check on corruption in the staff of the other.

76. See Chapter 5 for more detailed discussion of IBAMA corruption cases in Pará.

77. Maurício Hashizume, "Operação Ananias: PF e Ibama desmontam esquemas de fraude e corrupção no Pará," Carta Maior (Feb. 7, 2007). Available at http://www.rel-uita.org/internacional/operacao_ananias.htm (last visited Dec. 12, 2007).

78. See "Brazil fells massive Amazon timber fraud ring," Environmental News Service (ENS) (June 6, 2005). Available at http://www.ens-newswire.com/ens/jun2005/2005-06-06-03.asp (last visited Dec. 12, 2007).

79. In the tradition of the Federal Police, major operations are given unique names. Those targeting environmental crimes between 2003 and 2007 include Setembro Negro, Faroeste, Curupira I and II, Ouro Verde, Rio Pardo, Terra-Limpa, Trinca-Ferro, Terra do Meio, Cerrado, Novo Empate, Isaías, Euterpe, Daniel, Kayabi, Passagem, Renascer, Cedro-Maracá, and Ananias. See http://www.dpf.gov.br/DCS/operacoes/indexop.html (last visited Dec. 12, 2007).

80. For a detailed description of an operation, see "Brazilian government press release on the actions taken by the Ministry on Environment to dismantle gang acting in Mato Grosso for 14 years" (June 2, 2005), Consulate General of Brazil, San Francisco. Available at http://www.brazilsf.org/brazil_press6.htm (last visited Dec. 12, 2007).

81. http://www.ambienteemfoco.com.br/?p=3831 (last visited Dec. 12, 2007).

82. See Hashizume, supra note 77.

83. Roberta Pennafort, Bruno Lousada, and Clarissa Thomé, Agência Estado, "24 fiscais do Ibama são presos acusados de corrupção; Funcionários presos são acusados de extorquir empresários, amenizar multas e vender autorização para construções em áreas de reserva ambiental" (Aug. 30, 2006).

84. A total of 348 out of 2,026 employees in January 2000 held commissioned positions. Pers. comm., CETESB Human Resources Dept. (Informações Gerenciais, Depto. Recursos Humanos; Jan. 2002). Since the State Secretariat of the Environment is

unable to hire, its employees generally come from other agencies, including CETESB. In January 2000, 391 employees who form part of CETESB's permanent staff actually served in the Secretariat (with 157 of them in commissioned positions).

85. Pers. comm., CETESB Human Resources Dept. (data from Jan. 2000). The average salary of a commissioned position, including the directors of CETESB, was R$4,298/month (US$2,362). The average salary of agency employees with college degrees was R$2,635/month (US$1,449). The average salary of all CETESB employees was R$1,890/month (US$1,039). Currency conversions were computed using the January 1, 2000, exchange rate of R$1 = US$0.55.

86. While this occurs in U.S. environmental agencies as well, many argue that it does not have a significant impact on regulatory policy or enforcement rates (see Wood and Waterman 1991). While comparative data are not available, it seems unlikely that the percentage of appointees in U.S. environmental agencies is as high as in Brazilian agencies (about 17 percent in CETESB). Moreover, in the United States, there is a larger political constituency for environmental protection, narrowing the range of politically acceptable changes that newly elected leaders may institute.

87. Similarly, of the 255 employees in the agency who work in all areas related to environmental protection, 96 (38 percent) have full job security.

88. Job titles include *servidor temporario* and *prestador de serviço*.

89. In some states, the operating permit is called the *licença de funcionamento* (operating permit). Federal decree no. 99,274 of June 6, 1990, is the primary legal reference setting forth these three phases of the permitting process (art. 19).

90. São Paulo state law no. 997 of May 31, 1976.

91. CONAMA resolution no. 01/86 of Jan. 23, 1986.

92. 1988 Const. art. 225, § 1, IV.

93. CONAMA resolution no. 237/97 of Dec. 19, 1997.

94. In projects with less significant impact, a Preliminary Environmental Report (Relatório Ambiental Preliminar; RAP) may serve as a substitute for a full environmental impact study. São Paulo SMA resolution 42/94 governs the use of the RAP in São Paulo.

95. CETESB, Diretoria de Controle de Poluição Ambiental, "Plano de Ação 2001/2002" (Jan. 21, 2002).

96. The number of employees in the pollution control division fell from 901 in 1992 to 677 in 1998, and then rose to 707 in 2001. Pers. comm., CETESB Human Resources Dept.

97. Data concerning the number of preliminary, installation, and operating permits issued by SMA for the years 1995 through 2001 are on file with the author. The data show an increase from a total of 39 permits issued in 1995 to 122 in 2001. Pers. comm., SMA (Feb. 2002).

98. São Paulo state law no. 997 of May 31, 1976, art. 5.

99. Federal law no. 9,605 of Feb. 12, 1998, arts. 2 and 60. These provisions of the Environmental Crimes Law are described at greater length in Chapter 5.

100. Data for 1990 to 1994 from SIPOL, "Total Documents per Year," pers. comm., CETESB Pollution Control Division (Nov. 2001); data for 1995 to 2001 from "Total Activities 1995–2001," pers. comm., CETESB Pollution Control Division (Jan. 2002); data for 2002 from "Total Activities 2002–2006," pers. comm., CETESB Pollution Control Division (Apr. 2007).

101. Data on public complaints are included in "Total Activities 1995–2001," pers. comm., CETESB Pollution Control Division (Jan. 2002) and "Total Activities 2002–2006," pers. comm., CETESB Pollution Control Division (Apr. 2007).

102. The increase was likely due to an aggressive enforcement approach under the leadership of Édis Milaré, who was secretary of the Environment in São Paulo from July 1992 through December 1994. As described in Chapter 3, Milaré had previously served as the first environmental prosecutor in the São Paulo Ministério Público.

103. Because CETESB was initially established as a private legal entity (*pessoalidade de direito privado*) rather than as part of the public administration, it could not directly collect fines. DAE was a shareholder in CETESB.

104. An arrangement was being negotiated under which the state government's lawyers (Procuradoria Geral do Estado) would collect the fines. Officials in the legal department were hopeful that this would improve the effectiveness of agency fines.

105. An official in the legal department referred to three types of legal claims commonly filed against the agency: suits to annul an administrative act; suits to suspend the effects of an administrative act; and suits challenging the constitutionality of an administrative act.

106. It is worth noting that the fees associated with environmental permitting are received directly by the agency and can be used to support agency work. This has served as an incentive for agencies to increase their permitting activities (personal interview, 2000).

107. While this assertion cannot be verified, the low number of inspections, detailed below, further suggests that the agency does not impose and verify compliance with project-specific conditions before issuing the operating permit.

108. Data are from State of Pará / SECTAM (2002).

109. IBAMA has generally remained responsible for permitting forestry activities in the Amazon region known as "Amazônia Legal," which included the states of Acre, Amapá, Amazonas, Mato Grosso, Pará, Rondônia, Roraima, Tocantins, and part of Maranhão.

110. The fines in all 55 cases totaled R$1.494 million (about US$500,000 in 2003) (Brito and Barreto 2006: 48, fig. 3).

111. Inscription of the violator's name in the government's registry of accounts receivable prevents the violator from obtaining government contracts or loans. Also,

inscription is required to initiate a judicial debt collection action (Brito and Barreto 2006: 41–42).

112. The case age refers to the time from the issuance of the fine to case closure or, alternatively, until June 2004, when the data were collected. The study calculates a median of 806 work days, which is roughly equivalent to three years (Brito and Barreto 2006: 44, 49).

113. At least one IBAMA lawyer, however, responded by citing the slowness and lack of effectiveness of judicial enforcement (Brito and Barreto 2006: 58).

114. Carlos Mendes, "Ibama aplica R$60 mi em multas no Pará," *Estado de São Paulo* (July 13, 2006). Available at http://clipping.planejamento.gov.br/Noticias.asp ?NOTCod=282453 (last visited Dec. 12, 2007).

115. In equivalent 2001 and 2004 U.S. dollars, the increase was from $94 million to $198 million.

Chapter 3

1. In Brazil, the term *interesses difusos e coletivos* (diffuse and collective interests) is preferred to *interesses público* (public interest) in referring to those interests commonly grouped together as the public interest in the American legal context. Traditionally, "public interest" has been used in Brazil to refer to interests of the state or government. "Diffuse interests," in contrast, are those of society as a whole, defined in Brazilian law as interests that are transindividual, indivisible by nature, and held by an indeterminate number of people linked by a factual situation. See Consumer Defense Code (Código de Defesa do Consumidor) of 1990, federal law no. 8,078 of Sept. 11, 1990, art. 81. The interest in conserving forests and many other environmental interests are examples of diffuse interests. *Interesses coletivos* (collective interests) are transindividual, indivisible interests held by a determinable number of people of a particular group, class, or category who are united through a basic legal relationship. An example would be the protection of the lands of a certain indigenous group. Brazilian law further distinguishes *interesses individuais homogeneous* (homogenous individual interests), which refers to collective interests that are divisible, such as the recovery of damages by purchasers of an automobile with a manufacturing defect. It is also important to note that the term "diffuse and collective interests" is used interchangeably with "diffuse and collective rights" (*direitos difusos e coletivos*). For a complete definition of these terms, see Mazzilli (2001: 41). See also Silva (2001: 40–41).

2. As such, the members of the Ministério Público are herein referred to as "prosecutors," although readers from common law countries must not forget that the use of this English term does not signify that the roles of civil law and common law prosecutors are identical.

3. The attorney general may also be descended from the French *Ministère Public,*

thus explaining the similarity of its formal mandate (Cappelletti 1978: 807). In common law countries, however, matters of political and legal culture relating to the distrust of the executive branch have led to a reduced role for the institution in civil matters (see Cappelletti 1978: 807–8; Langer 1988: 302).

4. The same can be said of the judicial branch itself. The Brazilian executive branch has historically dominated the other branches of government, though not as completely as in many other Latin American countries (see Meili 1998: 494–97; Fernandes 1996: 275; Ungar 2002: 119–68; Prillaman 2000: 77–78).

5. Brazilian states had created separate institutions, generally called the Procuradoria do Estado, to defend the state government in civil lawsuits.

6. States varied in their treatments of the Ministério Público. The São Paulo constitution of 1947 guaranteed prosecutorial salaries equivalent to judicial salaries (Mazzilli 1997: 6).

7. Since 1881 in Belgium, 1914 in France, and 1942 in Italy, the *Ministère Public* has had the power to initiate or intervene in civil cases involving the *ordre public*—a vague term that may mean the interests of the state's leaders or may, in contrast, denote the interests of society or the public generally (Cappelletti 1979: 526).

8. Code of Civil Procedure of 1973, art. 82, cited by Macedo Júnior (1995: 41).

9. The Ministério Público argued that diffuse interests were similar in nature to the interests traditionally represented by the *Ministère Public*. See Arantes (2002: 60–61).

10. Federal law no. 6,938 of Aug. 31, 1981, art. 14, chap. IV, §1, reprinted in Benjamin (1999b: 83).

11. While modeled after procedural instruments of other countries, the Brazilian public civil action went beyond many of those instruments in the breadth of interests that can be represented and its liberal standing requirements. See Arantes (1999: 101, fn. 27).

12. 1988 Const. art. 127.

13. Ibid., art. 129, I–III.

14. Ibid., art. 129, V and VII.

15. Federal law no. 7,853 (Os Direitos das Pessoas Portadoras de Deficiência) of Oct. 24, 1989.

16. Federal law no. 8,069 (*Estatuto da Criança e do Adolescente*) of July 13, 1990.

17. Federal law no. 8,078 (Código de Defesa do Consumidor) of Sept. 11, 1990.

18. Federal law no. 8,429 (Lei de Improbidade Administrativa) of July 2, 1992.

19. Federal law no. 8,884 (Lei de Livre Concorrência) of June 11, 1994.

20. See infra note 47 and associated text of the Consumer Defense Code (Código de Defesa do Consumidor) of 1990.

21. The terms "independence" and "political independence" are used throughout this work to refer to the relationship between the Ministério Público and other

branches of government, particularly the executive branch. This use is consistent with many discussions of judicial independence (see Santiso 2003: 162; Brinks 2004: 596).

22. Several authors have noted the divergence between de jure and de facto independence of legal institutions. An empirical study of procuracies by Voigt (2006: 18–19) finds a negative correlation between the two concepts, and Brinks (2004: 597) notes that formal judicial independence often correlates poorly or even negatively with actual independent behavior.

23. State and federal Budget Guidelines Laws are passed each year to set guidelines for the passage of the Annual Budget Law (Lei Orçamentária Anual). Typically, the Budget Guidelines Law specifies a certain percentage of the annual budget that is destined for the Ministério Público. See art. 12, Paraná state law no. 13,235 of July 25, 2001, art. 12 (wherein the state of Paraná's annual budget for 2002 specifies 3.3 percent of annual treasury receipts for the state Ministério Público).

24. The 1993 National Organic Law of the Ministério Público of the States (Lei Orgânica Nacional do Ministério Público dos Estados) further specifies the financial autonomy of the institution. According to this law, for example, the Ministério Público manages its own financial resources, determines its salaries, independently makes hiring and promotion decisions, directly acquires goods and contract services, and independently organizes the work of the institution. Federal law no. 8,625 of Feb. 12, 1993, art. 3.

25. The executive branch has greater powers to determine the composition of the upper echelon of the judicial branch, such as the judges of the higher federal courts. Supreme Court judges, for example, are only required to be citizens of appropriate age, legal knowledge, and reputation, nominated by the president, with approval by the Senate. Unlike in the United States, they do not have life tenure. See 1988 Const. art. 104.

26. Ibid., art. 128, II, § 4. The National Organic Law of the Ministério Público of the States further determines that this list shall be generated by a vote by all the members of the institution. Federal law no. 8,625 of Feb. 12, 1993, art. 9, § 1.

27. 1988 Const. art. 128, II, § 1.

28. Ibid., § 4.

29. Ibid., § 2.

30. Ibid., § 5, I.

31. This leadership body is generally the Colégio de Procuradores de Justiça, consisting of prosecutors who have been promoted from *promotor* to *procurador*, meaning that they work at the appeals court level rather than the trial court level. On the responsibilities of the Colégio de Procuradores de Justiça, see Kerche (2003: 101–2).

32. But see Kerche (2003: 110–11), who closely examines the internal dynamics of the Brazilian Ministério Público and discusses several mechanisms by which the attorney general can exert some influence.

33. 1988 Const. art. 128, II, § 5, II.

34. This argument is the central thesis of Arantes (2002). On "political skill," see Levin and Ferman (1985); Bardach (1972); Kagan (1994).

35. The study by Arantes is one of several by Brazilian scholars on the Ministério Público's institutional reconstruction in the 1980s. Others include Sadek (1997), Wiecko V. de Castilho and Sadek (1998), Kerche (1997), Silva (2001), and Bonelli (2001). This section draws from the work of these scholars in addition to data collected in the author's research.

36. Federal law no. 6,938 of Aug. 31, 1981, art. 14, chap. IV, § 1. Reprinted in Benjamin (1999b: 83).

37. Machado consulted primarily with the president of the Members Association of the Ministério Público of São Paulo (Associação Paulista do Ministério Público), a private organization of São Paulo prosecutors with the mission of furthering their corporatist interests. Throughout the 1980s and 1990s, the association helped facilitate and promote the legal and institutional changes that strengthened the Ministério Público.

38. Explaining this victory, Nogueira-Neto opined that concerns about environmental protection and conservation "transcended the political sphere" (Costa 2003: 77).

39. Federal decree no. 88,351 of June 1, 1983, revoked by federal decree no. 99,274 of June 6, 1990.

40. A copy of the lawsuit is available in Ferraz, Milaré, and Nery Júnior (1984: 89).

41. A 1982 state law had provided for the attorney general's designation of a prosecutor responsible for environmental protection in each of the state's judicial districts. In less populated judicial districts with only one prosecutor, that prosecutor simply gained another new official responsibility. Lei Complementar Estadual de São Paulo, São Paulo state law no. 304 of Dec. 28, 1982, art. 32, I, 34 (a) and (c).

42. Another early lawsuit, filed in August 1984 and referred to as the *Passarinhada de Embú* (Birdfest of Embú), sought to make the mayor of Embú, São Paulo, liable for the harm to wildlife that he caused by hosting a party in which about five thousand wild birds were served. A copy of the lawsuit is available in Milaré (2001: 561–63).

43. Other Italian scholars who also influenced Brazilian doctrine include Vittorio Denti and Andréa Proto Pisani (Arantes 2002: 54).

44. Federal bill no. 3,034/84, written by Ada P. Grinover, Candido Dinamarco, Kazuo Watanabe, and Waldemar Mariz de Oliveira Júnior and introduced by Congressman Flávio Bierrenbach (Arantes 2002: 58).

45. The provision of the bill stating that the public civil action could be used to defend "any other diffuse interest" was vetoed by the president. However, this provision was reinserted in amendments made to the law in the Consumer Defense Code, federal law 8,078 of Sept. 11, 1990 (Mancuso 1999: 37–39).

46. Federal bill no. 4,984 / 85 in the Câmara dos Deputados; federal bill no. 20 / 85 in the Senado Federal (see Milaré 1995: 483–93, appendices 3 and 4).

47. As described below, the law was amended by the Consumer Defense Code of 1990 to reincorporate the phrase "and other diffuse and collective interests." Other areas in which the instrument came to be used frequently include anticorruption, children's rights, urban and housing issues, and disability rights.

48. Federal law no. 7,347 of June 24, 1985. The term "cultural patrimony" is used here as shorthand for "artistic, aesthetic, historical, touristic, and scenic values," which is the wording of the law.

49. Later in 1986, Fabio Feldmann was elected as representative of São Paulo to the federal Congress. He is best known for his leadership as a Constitutional Assembly member in the passage of the environmental provisions. The lawsuit text is available in Milaré (2001: 579–83).

50. Arantes (2002: 39–44) describes how the military dictatorship used the Ministério Público to enforce federal laws against states and insulate the regime from legal challenge. He also argues that the Ministério Público was able to strengthen its image in the areas of law enforcement and the oversight of government agencies during the military dictatorship in a way that benefited the institution afterwards.

51. See 1988 Const. art. 128, par. 5, II (e), qualifying this restriction by the statement "except as provided by law."

52. See above for a description of these articles.

53. The number of environmental groups grew from about forty in 1980 to about seven hundred in 1989 (Peritore 1999).

54. See Arantes (2002) discussing the paradox that the Ministério Público, a state institution, was able to expand its role in this new area despite the strong "anti-state" sentiment of the new social movements emergent during the redemocratization. As he explains, "the paradoxical ascension of the Ministério Público in a context marked by anti-state ideologies was able to occur only because during the redemocratization, the Ministério Público fought to disassociate itself from the executive branch and to construct the image of itself as an agent of society capable of overseeing the state, despite its being a part of the state" (Arantes 2002: 24).

55. The National Constitutional Assembly (Assembléia Nacional Constituinte) consisted of the group of 559 popularly elected representatives and senators who held office in the years from 1986 to 1988 and were associated with thirteen different political parties. The work of the assembly took one year and eight months and included the preparation of eight drafts as well as the final constitutional text. There was significant public participation in the process, and more than sixty-five thousand amendments were offered (Kerche 1997: 5, 57–60).

56. "Lista de Antigüidade," published yearly in the São Paulo Ministério Público's journal, *Justitia.*

57. "Lista de Antigüidade." Available at http://www.mp.sp.gov.br/portal/page?_pageid=288,716084&_dad=portal&_schema=PORTAL (last visited Dec. 12, 2007).

58. There were 220 prosecutors in the year 2000. Pers. comm., Pará State Ministério Público (Apr. 2002). New prosecutors were hired in 2002, 2003, and 2006. See "Lista de Antigüidade," published in resolução no. 001/2007/MP/CSMP of Jan. 11, 2007. Available at http://www.mp.pa.gov.br/csmp/CSMP-Resoluca02007-001.doc (last visited Dec. 12, 2007).

59. The 1985 data are from "Procuradoria Geral da República, Ministério Público Federal, Relatório de Atividades do MPF no período de Junho/81 a Março/85," Brasilia (on file with author). The 2001 data are from the "Lista de Antigüidade" (Dec. 31, 2001), Conselho Superior de Ministério Público Federal, resolução no. 67 of July 3, 2002, published in the *Diário da Justiça*, sec. 1, pp. 875–82 (Aug. 2, 2002). The 2006 data are from ibid., resolução no. 89 of Apr. 17, 2007, published in the *Diário da Justiça*, sec. 1, pp. 785–94 (Apr. 25, 2007).

60. See Pozzo (1993: 173), showing a 103 percent real increase in the São Paulo Ministério Público's budget between 1990 and 1991. See also Fabbrini (2002: 49), showing another 100 percent real increase in the São Paulo Ministério Público's budget between 1994 and 1995.

61. It is worth noting that many of these were contract employees who do not have the job security traditionally associated with government service.

62. The Brazilian law degree, as in other civil law countries, is an undergraduate degree. Generally, law students begin their legal studies at age 18 and conclude at age 22 (Werneck Vianna et al. 1997: 170).

63. In 1990 and 1991, two hiring processes were conducted each year. Information from both hiring processes is included in the data for the year.

64. Pers. comm. (electronic mail; June 11, 2004).

65. Currency conversion is based on the July 1, 2001, exchange rate of R$1 = US$0.4329.

66. Data on Ministério Público salaries were acquired from the General Directorate (Diretoria Geral), São Paulo Ministério Público. Data on other salaries are from the 2001 RAIS (*Relação Anual de Informações Sociais*), published annually by the Ministry of Labor and Employment (Ministério do Trabalho e Emprego). The minimum salary was R$180/month (US$84) from April 2001 to March 2002, after which it increased to R$200/month (US$90). Currency conversions use the April 2001 and April 2002 exchange rates of R$1 = US$0.4647 and R$1 = US$0.4482, respectively.

67. About one-eighth of São Paulo prosecutors were in this category in 2001. Data are from the Diretoria Geral (Nov. 2001).

68. This number is a conservative estimate based on the fact that there were 2,378 judicial districts in Brazil, with at least one (and usually only one) state prosecutor responsible for environmental protection in each judicial district. Instituto Brasileiro

de Geografia e Estatística (IBGE), Censo de 2000, Tribunais de Justiça. In addition, some federal prosecutors have environmental protection among their responsibilities. The number of specialized environmental prosecutors was estimated based on the author's research.

69. The career track of federal prosecutors (*procuradores da república*) is similar. They begin as generalists in the state offices of the Federal Ministério Público, and they are promoted to more specialized positions and eventually to the country's capital, Brasilia. Ultimately, they may be promoted to work in the federal appeals courts (*subprocurador da república*).

70. Pers. comm. (shared internal data), Diretoria Geral, Ministério Público of São Paulo (Nov. 2001). There were 37 million people, 645 municipalities, and 225 *comarcas* in São Paulo in 2000, Instituto Brasileiro de Geografia e Estatística (IBGE), Censo de 2000, Tribunais de Justiça.

71. This reform was instituted by federal law no. 8,625 of Feb. 12, 1993, art. 33.

72. In Pará in 2000, there were about 6.2 million people, 143 municipalities, and 103 *comarcas*. Instituto Brasileiro de Geografia e Estatística (IBGE), Censo de 2000, Tribunais de Justiça.

73. Other participants included Antonio Herman Benjamin, another member of the São Paulo Ministério Público; Fábio Feldmann, an environmentalist and Constitutional Assembly member from São Paulo who coordinated the Constitution's environmental protection chapter; several prosecutors with environmental experience from other states; and several environmentalists from Pará.

74. Pers. comm. (electronic mail; May 20, 2002).

75. Portaria no. 408/88 of Oct. 19, 1988, of Attorney General Arthur Cláudio Mello.

76. In contrast to São Paulo and most other states, the Pará State Ministério Público did not establish a prosecution support center to support environmental work.

77. The survey was conducted by the Institute of Economic, Social, and Political Studies of São Paulo (Instituto de Estudos Econômicos, Sociais e Políticos de São Paulo; IDESP). It included 51 members of the Federal Ministério Público and 712 members of state Ministérios Públicos comprising 20 percent of all members of the Ministério Público of each of seven states: Goias, Sergipe, Bahia, São Paulo, Rio de Janeiro, Paraná, and Rio Grande do Sul. Results of the survey are published in Sadek (1997) and discussed in Arantes (1999).

78. The institution's role in criminal proceedings did not change in the 1980s as much as its role in civil proceedings.

79. Calculated from data in the listing of prosecutors ("Lista de Antigüidade") of December 1997, published in the January 1998 issue of the São Paulo Ministério Público's journal, *Justitia*.

80. Ibid.

Chapter 4

1. Prosecutorial enforcement also sends a message about the Ministério Público as an institution, showing the public that the institution is actively using its powers to defend public interests. This expressive action builds the legitimacy of the Ministério Público (see Hawkins 2002: 209; Edelman 1964).

2. See Milaré (2001: 253–54), citing article 225, §3 of the 1988 Constitution: "Conduct and activities considered harmful to the environment will subject violators . . . to penal and administrative sanctions, independently of the obligation to repair the harm caused."

3. Environmental agencies are also authorized to file public civil actions under the Public Civil Action Law, but in fact they rarely do.

4. Unlike in the American system, such motivation would often not be related to a goal of being elected to political office. Brazilian prosecutors who entered the Ministério Público after the passage of the 1988 Constitution are prohibited from seeking elected political office unless they resign from the Ministério Público. See 1988 Const. art. 128, II, § 5, II, (e). See also Kerche (2003: 115).

5. Civil investigations are provided for by law in federal law no. 7,347, art. 8, and in 1988 Const. art. 129, III, § 1. The Brazilian police, rather than the Ministério Público, are primarily responsible for conducting an *inquérito policial* (criminal investigation).

6. See Silva (2001: 84), stating "The prosecutor customarily has continuous contact with the people in his district, especially in rural areas. Attending to the public is one of the oldest responsibilities of the Ministério Público, through which prosecutors orient and inform themselves, send off information, and receive accusations and complaints."

7. Federal law no. 7,347, art. 6.

8. Ibid., art. 8, § 1.

9. Ibid., art. 10.

10. Federal Law no. 7,347, art. 5, II, § 6 states: "The public institutions with jurisdiction can negotiate agreements to bring conduct into accord with legal requirements, with fines in case of noncompliance, that will be considered judicially enforceable agreements."

11. Rudolfo de Camargo Mancuso, in a speech at the Ministério Público's Environmental Conference, Campos do Jordão, São Paulo, Nov. 2001.

12. See Mazzilli (2001: 275–76). Other prosecutors argue that prosecutors should exercise discretion so as to be able to dedicate greater resources to larger or more important cases. See Proença (2001: 156). This debate is discussed further in Chapter 6.

13. Federal Law no. 7,347, arts. 3 and 13.

14. Ibid., art. 5.

15. The question of whether the Brazilian Ministério Público has the power to conduct criminal investigations was widely debated. In 2003, a panel of the Federal Supreme Court ruled that it did not. See Recurso Ordinário en Habeas Corpus

81.326–7, Distrito Federal, as discussed by Arantes (2004: 26). In 2007, the same question was before the full court in two other cases, a habeas corpus case and a direct action of unconstitutionality. See "A grande polêmica: Poder investigatório do Ministério Público" (June 12, 2007), available at http://www.wiki-iuspedia.com.br/article. php?story=20070612133003534 (last visited Mar. 12, 2008).

16. See Kerche (2003: 77–78). The principle of obligation stands in contrast to the model of discretionary prosecution that characterizes the U.S. legal system.

17. As explained by Fionda (1995: 9), "Under this principle, prosecution of all offences where sufficient evidence exists of the guilt of the defendant is compulsory, and public interest criteria are irrelevant in the prosecutor's decision-making."

18. Art. 2, Criminal Procedure Code (Código Procesal Penal) of Peru. See Christian Salas Beteta, Principio de Oportunidad y Reforma Judicial. Available at http://ofdnews.com/imprimible/1411_0_1_0/ (last visited Dec. 12, 2007).

19. In order to terminate and archive an investigation, the prosecutor must obtain final approval from the institution's leadership body, the Superior Council (Conselho Superior). Its members are elected from among those who have been promoted to the position of *procurador*, the highest promotion level. This approval process is considered a form of oversight of prosecutors to ensure that investigations are not terminated for improper reasons. See Mazzilli (2001: 328–34); Milaré (2001: 492–94).

20. For the contrasting view of one São Paulo environmental prosecutor, see Proença (2001 no. 625: 150).

21. Paulo Affonso Leme Machado, a retired member of the São Paulo Ministério Público, is known as the father of Brazilian environmental law. Antonio Herman Benjamin was appointed to Brazil's Federal Supreme Court in August 2006.

22. The term "environmental prosecutor" is used in this work to refer to any prosecutor who does environmental work, and is not limited to those prosecutors who solely or primarily do environmental work.

23. Data were acquired from the São Paulo Ministério Público's Environmental Prosecution Support Center. Prosecutors are required to notify the support center of all investigations opened and lawsuits filed relating to environmental protection. The center maintains two databases with this information, one covering the years from 1985 to 1997 and the other beginning in 1998. The databases are not assumed to be complete, as some prosecutors may neglect to notify the center. Rather they represent the minimum number of investigations and lawsuits undertaken by state prosecutors.

24. For explanation of these prosecutorial instruments and others referred to in this section, see Chapter 3.

25. In 2003, the Environmental Prosecution Support Center was merged with the Housing and Urban Life Prosecution Support Center (Centro de Apoio Operacional das Promotorias de Justiça de Habitação e Urbanismo). The new center is called the Environmental and Urban Life Prosecution Support Center (Centro de Apoio Operacional de Urbanismo e Meio Ambiente).

26. Regarding Table 4.1 and Figure 4.1, data for the years 1985 to 1997 were compiled from the author's analysis of a database covering this period from the Environmental Prosecution Support Center. Data for the years 1998 to 2001 were acquired directly from the support center.

27. Amendments to federal law no. 7,347 were made by the Consumer Defense Code, federal law no. 8,078 of 1990.

28. Pers. comm., Superior Council (Conselho Superior) of the Ministério Público of São Paulo (Dec. 2002). This number, however, does not include conduct adjustment agreements signed after a public civil action has been filed. Such agreements are approved by the court rather than the Superior Council. An experienced environmental prosecutor estimated that 30 percent of agreements are signed after a public civil action has been filed. Pers. comm. (electronic mail; Apr. 11, 2002).

29. The Public Civil Action Law authorizes judges to grant injunctive relief. Federal law no. 7,347 of 1985, art. 12. For a more complete description of the use of the injunction in environmental public civil actions, see Araujo (2001: 54–56).

30. Author's analysis of the database of São Paulo Ministério Público's Environmental Prosecution Support Center.

31. See Forestry Code (Código Florestal), federal law no. 4,771 of Sept. 15, 1965, and Atlantic Coastal Rainforest Law, federal decree no. 750 of Feb. 10, 1993, in Benjamin (1999b: 41, 289).

32. The Environmental Police, a division of the São Paulo Military Police, has over two thousand police statewide and is the frontline in the administrative enforcement of forestry-related laws in São Paulo. Until changed by state decree no. 46,263 of Nov. 9, 2001, it was called the Forestry and Watershed Police (Comando de Policiamento Florestal e de Mananciais).

33. In a study of environmental public interests filed by the State Ministério Público of Rio de Janeiro between 1985 and 1991, Fuks (1999: 68), finds a similar breakdown in the topics of cases. The five most prevalent problems were deforestation (25 percent), noise levels (12 percent), water pollution (10 percent), mineral extraction (9 percent), and air pollution (7 percent).

34. See Chapter 5 for more information about the volume and nature of these information requests.

35. "Justiça deixa maiores poluidores impunes," *Folha de São Paulo* (Oct. 14, 2001), p. C1.

36. In some states, including Rio Grande do Sul, specialized environmental prosecutors can also file criminal charges.

37. Data were unavailable for federal prosecutors working in other parts of the state who are not specialized in environmental prosecution but who may have some environmental cases.

38. Pers. comm. (telephone; June 2, 2002).

39. The Pará State Ministério Público also created an Environmental Nucleus (Núcleo do Meio Ambiente) in 1996 that forms part of the institution's Prosecution Support Center for Community Defense and Citizen Rights (Centro de Apoio Operacional de Defesa Comunitaria e da Cidadania). The Environmental Nucleus, however, has not been directly involved in environmental prosecution. Rather, as described below, it has focused on the implementation of the "Pilot Program to Conserve the Brazilian Rain Forest."

40. Data were obtained from the Environmental Prosecution Office, State Ministério Público of Pará.

41. Author's analysis of data, ibid.

42. "MPF promete ação severa contra devastação," *Liberal* (Belém; Apr. 28, 2002), painel, p. 7.

43. Ibid.

44. Between 1999 and 2002, IBAMA/PA sent 1,244 notifications of environmental crimes to the Federal Ministério Público in Pará (Brito, Barreto, and Rothman 2005: 7).

45. *Estado de São Paulo* (Oct. 6, 2002), as quoted in the Greenpeace news article, "Our role in stopping the illegal Brazilian mahogany trade" (Oct. 15, 2003). Available at http://www.greenpeace.org/usa/news/our-role-in-stopping-the-illeg (last visited Dec. 12, 2007).

46. For further discussion of deforestation in Pará as a criminal activity, see Greenpeace, "Partners in mahogany crime: Amazon at the mercy of 'gentlemen's agreements,'" (Oct. 2001). Available at http://archive.greenpeace.org/forests/reports/Mahoganyweb. pdf (last visited Dec. 12, 2007).

47. The concept of prosecutorial independence, like judicial independence is complex and subject to many interpretations. Brinks (2004: 599–600) separates judicial independence into two aspects: preference independence and decisional independence. Rios-Figueroa and Taylor (2006: 743) set forth the structure of judicial independence as including autonomy (the relation between the judiciary as an institution and the elected branches of government); the external independence of Supreme Court justices (their relation with elected branches of government); and the internal independence of lower court judges (their relation with high court judges). Such distinctions are similar in nature to the one made here between political independence and functional autonomy.

48. Ronaldo Brasiliense, "Não vão nos impedir de governar." Interview of the Governor of Pará, Almir Gabriel, *Amazon Press* (Nov. 11, 2000).

49. Ibid.

50. In São Paulo, in contrast, governors have had a very different relationship with the state Ministério Público. Most notably, the governor from 1990 to 1994, Luiz Antônio Fleury, came from the state Ministério Público, and the institution generally grew in terms of resources and political independence in these years. However, pros-

ecutors accuse the then attorney general, Antônio Araldo Ferraz Dal Pozzo, of being too closely allied with the governor and inappropriately proposing a law that limited the investigation and prosecution of public officials to the attorney general. See Silva (2001: 60–62).

51. While in some ways similar to the support center of the São Paulo Ministério Público, the environmental nucleus of the Pará Ministério Público has not focused on supporting and encouraging environmental enforcement work throughout the state.

52. Ministério Público do Pará, "Anais of I Congresso Estadual do Ministério Público do Pará" (Dec. 5–7, 2000, Belém, Pará), p. 145.

53. Kerche (2003: 110–11) sets forth six powers that state attorneys general have that enable them to "reward their allies and construct a network of prosecutors aligned with their interests." These include their powers to appoint a prosecutor as a temporary substitute in a position that is vacant; to appoint prosecutors to higher-paying "election prosecutor" positions; to assign positions to prosecutors who work in the capital city who do not have fixed positions; to appoint trial court prosecutors to temporarily substitute for appeals court prosecutors when a vacancy arises; to select prosecutors as assistants; and to select prosecutors to work in the prosecution support centers.

54. 1988 Const. art 129, II.

55. See Chapter 5.

56. In São Paulo, 499 of 2,197 (23 percent) of the São Paulo Ministério Público's environmental public civil actions filed from 1985 to 1997 named a governmental entity as a defendant. The municipality was a defendant in 87 percent of these cases, and the state was a defendant in 20 percent of these cases. Note that the total sums to more than 100 percent because in some cases, both the municipality and the state were named as defendants.

57. See Chapter 3.

58. "Ação ambiental tem 'efeito educativo' para empresas," *Folha de São Paulo* (Oct. 21, 1995), p. 3–2.

59. "Caso tramita há 15 anos na Justiça de SP," *Folha de São Paulo* (Oct. 14, 2001), p. C2.

60. On the broader tension between allowing discretion and establishing rules, see Davis (1969: 42–44).

61. São Paulo State Complementary Law (Lei Complementar Estadual) no. 734/93.

62. Ibid., arts. 97–102.

63. On the experience of a regional procuracy established to protect the São Francisco River basin in the state of Minas Gerais, see Soares Júnior (2003).

64. The natural prosecutor principle is interpreted as being implied in the guarantee of "immovability" in art. 128 of the Federal Constitution of 1988. See Chapter 3.

65. As Kerche (2003: 96) discusses, the principle may also be a disadvantage to the institution as it limits the leadership's ability to create institutional policies.

66. Changes in the administration of the São Paulo government and the Ministério Público also contributed to the lack of the full implementation of Pozzo's institutional vision. Pozzo's administration was discredited by a close association with the state governor, and an opposition party within the São Paulo Ministério Público was selected to leadership. While not inherently contrary to the idea of institutional planning, this new administration did not focus on implementing the reforms articulated and sought by Pozzo.

67. For more specific examples of such cases, see Chapter 5.

Chapter 5

1. This oversight role is not specific to environmental agencies, but extends generally from its role as *fiscal da lei* of overseeing the application of the law. This role was reinforced in article 129 of the Constitution, which provides that one of the Ministério Público's institutional functions is to "ensure that the government and other entities of public relevance respect constitutional rights." As they became active in environmental enforcement, prosecutors increasingly used the article's powers to oversee environmental agencies. See Alberton (1985); Ackel Filho (1990); Topan (1994).

2. For a discussion of the Brazilian Ministério Público as an agent of accountability beyond the environmental sphere, see Sadek and Cavalcanti (2003) and Taylor and Buranelli (2007: 63), stating that the Federal Ministério Público is "arguably the most important institution of accountability at the federal level in Brazil."

3. Vertical accountability refers to democratic elections and other ways in which governments are made to answer to citizens in a democratic political system (O'Donnell 1999a: 30).

4. As described by Diamond, Plattner, and Schedler (1999: 3) the locus classicus of horizontal accountability involves the checks and balances among the judicial, executive, and legislative branches of government. However, as the division of powers within the modern state has become more complex, agents of horizontal accountability have expanded to include new institutions such as election commissions, auditing agencies, anticorruption bodies, ombudsmen, administrative courts, human rights commissions, and central banks. These new agents of accountability tend to be independent, nonelective, and specialized, and they may form part of any of the three traditional branches.

5. In a comparative study of sixty-five countries, Voigt (2006), finds a correlation between de facto prosecutorial independence and lower perceptions of corruption. The author concludes that the structure of the legal institutions of a country can be an important determinant of the amount of corruption.

6. Federal law no. 7,347 of July 24, 1985.

7. National Organic Law of the Ministério Público (Lei Orgânica Nacional do Ministério Público), federal law no. 8,625 of Feb. 12, 1993, art. 27, § IV.

8. The Federal Ministério Público increasingly uses recommendations in its environmental work. Lists of its recommendations for each year since 2003 are available at http://ccr4.pgr.mpf.gov.br/atuacao-do-mpf/recomendacoes/ (last visited Dec. 12, 2007).

9. Federal law no. 8,429 of June 2, 1992; text available in Benjamin (1999b: 121–28). The law was established pursuant to the Federal Constitution of 1988, art. 37, § 4, which states: "Acts of administrative improbity will result in the suspension of political rights, the loss of the public job, the return of any illegal gains, and repayment to public coffers, in the manner and severity provided by law, without barring the possibility of criminal prosecution."

10. On the quasi-criminal nature of sanctions under the Administrative Improbity Act, see Arantes (2002: 102).

11. The Law of Administrative Improbity has been widely used by the Brazilian Ministério Público to investigate and prosecute public officials generally, not just those in the environmental sphere. Indeed, the institution has gained extensive national and even international press coverage for its anticorruption work. See Flamínio Fantini, "Corrupção mata," Veja (July 12, 2000), pp. 11–15; Larry Rohter, "Crusading prosecutor delights and amazes many," New York Times (Sept. 7, 2000), p. A4.

12. Federal law 8,429 of June 2, 1992, art. 11, § I.

13. Federal law 9,605 of Feb. 12, 1998.

14. While prosecutors oversee agencies through investigations, their main purpose in sending information requests to agencies is to get technical information that they need to resolve their environmental cases. A 1996 survey of federal prosecutors and state prosecutors from seven states found the lack of technical help (cited by 92 percent of prosecutors), difficulty in getting expert opinions (91 percent), difficulty in collecting evidence (88 percent), and lack of specialization in specific problems such as pollution, public finance, and interest rates (82 percent) to be the largest obstacles to the institution's work in defending environmental and other public interests (Sadek 1997: 56, Table 15).

15. These annual reports were internal CETESB documents to which the author had access through CETESB's Enforcement Division. Each of the regional offices prepared a report for the year 2001 detailing its activities over the year, including the managers' estimates of how much staff time was dedicated to various enforcement-related tasks. Where possible, the percentage of time spent on dealing with requests from the Ministério Público was calculated by the author based on this data.

16. Data are from a table of departmental activities given to the author by an agency official. The 2001 figure includes requests received through November 2001. While the data include requests sent by the Ministério Público as well as the courts

and possibly other governmental legal entities, agency officials estimate that the great majority comes from the Ministério Público.

17. Notably, the twelve requests came from a series of different prosecutors. As prosecutors get promoted or change positions, their caseloads pass to other prosecutors.

18. A 1996 World Bank report focusing on the Rio de Janeiro state environmental agency, FEEMA, made a similar observation: "Major changes are required in the way in which environmental agencies conduct their business. In the presence of legal requirements to respond to numerous nonpriority requests by the judicial branch and other entities that undermine any effort for setting priorities, the agencies are attempting to do too much without achieving much progress in any field" (World Bank 1996a).

19. 2001 Annual Report of Regional CETESB Office in Baurú, São Paulo.

20. Akaoui (1999) writes, for example, that a resolution passed by the São Paulo State Secretariat of the Environment in 1994 (resolução no. 42/94) is unconstitutional because the Constitution requires that an EIA be prepared for all activities that potentially cause significant harm, whereas the resolution gives the Secretariat the discretionary authority to approve a project without a full EIA after a Preliminary Environmental Report (Relatório Ambiental Preliminar) is prepared.

21. As described in Chapter 2, article 225 of the 1988 Constitution imposes a duty on the government to require an environmental impact study when proposed projects or activities potentially cause significant environmental degradation.

22. CONAMA resolution no. 001/86 of Jan. 23, 1986.

23. Ação civil pública (public civil action) no. 506/96, filed in the 3rd Vara Civil in São Carlos, São Paulo, by prosecutor Osvaldo Bianchini Veronez Filho on Apr. 26, 1996.

24. "Volks inaugura fabrica em S. Carlos," Folha de São Paulo (Oct. 11, 1996), p. 2–2.

25. Judicial decision of the 3rd Vara Civil of São Carlos in favor of Ministério Público on January 13, 2000 (on file with author).

26. Ministério Público do Estado de São Paulo v. Stela Goldenstein et al., filed July 14, 1998, in São Paulo, SP (12th Vara da Fazenda Pública) by prosecutor Sérgio Turra Sobrane (on file with author).

27. At least two additional cases were brought by the Ministério Público against agency officials in São Paulo: Ministério Público do Estado de São Paulo v. Osmar Rebizzi, et al., filed August 30, 1999, in Cubatão, SP, by prosecutor Daniel Isaac Friedmann (on file with author); and Ministério Público do Estado de São Paulo v. Fabio Feldmann et al., filed July 10, 2000, in Guaruja, SP, by prosecutor Adriana Cerqueira de Souza Pina (on file with author).

28. Federal law no. 8,429 of June 2, 1992, art. 11, § I.

29. Decision of the 12th Vara da Fazenda Pública, Proc. no. 1, 047/98–1, signed July 30, 1999, by Judge João Andre de Vincenzo (on file with author).

30. Apelação Cível no. 170.902–5/1, São Paulo, SP, Relator Desembargador Clímaco de Godoy, voto no. 13.622 (on file with author).

31. The title "regional manager" is herein used to denote either a *gerente da agencia*, an agency official in charge of a regional office of the state environmental agency, or a *gerente regional*, an agency official who oversees one or more managers of regional offices.

32. CONAMA resolution 01/86 of Jan. 23, 1986. For more information on CONAMA (Conselho Nacional do Meio Ambiente), see Chapter 2.

33. See SMA resolution no. 42/94 of Dec. 29, 1994.

34. As described in Chapter 2, IBAMA has retained jurisdiction for implementing and enforcing forestry laws in Pará.

35. Federal decree no. 1,282 of Oct. 19, 1994; IBAMA portaria no. 48 of July 10, 1995.

36. IBAMA portaria no. 48.

37. Cited in Marcelo Marquesini and Gavin Edwards, Greenpeace Amazon, "The Santarem five and illegal logging: A case study" (Oct. 2001; on file with author).

38. Greenpeace Brasil played a significant role in providing information to federal prosecutors about illegal practices in the Pará logging industry. See Greenpeace, "Partners in mahogany crime" (Oct. 2001; on file with author).

39. *Ministério Público Federal, Procuradoria da República no Municipio de Marabá/PA v. Moíses Carvalho Pereira et al.*, filed Feb. 4, 1998, by Neide M. C. Cardoso de Oliveira and José Roberto F. Santoro, case no. 1998.39.01.000117–3 (on file with author).

40. *Ministério Público Federal, Procuradoria da República no Municipio de Santarem/PA v. Paulo Mayo Koury de Figueireido et al.*, filed Dec. 15, 1999, by federal prosecutor Felício Pontes Jr., case no. 1999.39.02.001318–9 (on file with author).

41. Carlos Mendes, "Ibama investiga funcionarios envolvidos na aprovação de projeto irregular no Pará," *Estado de São Paulo* (Feb. 21, 2000).

42. The charges were based on acts committed before the passage of the 1998 Environmental Crimes Law and were thus premised on articles 317 and 319 of the Código Penal, decree-law no. 2,848 of Dec. 7, 1940.

43. CNN Environmental News Network, "Amazon timber stewards busted for bribes" (October 11, 2000). Available at http://www.cnn.com/2000/NATURE/10/11/logging.bribes.enn/ (last visited Dec. 12, 2007). See also Agencia Folha, "Ex-superintendente do Ibama consegue habeas corpus," *Folha Online* (June 8, 2000). Available at http://www1.folha.uol.com.br/fol/pol/ult08062000280.htm (last visited Dec. 12, 2007).

44. Currency conversion based on the May 31, 2000, exchange rate of R$1 = US$.5467.

45. Ministério da Justiça, Agência de Noticias, "Operação da PF combate corrupção ligada a crimes ambientais." June 2, 2005.

46. The project involved construction of a 32-kilometer canal that would join two rivers on the Island of Marajó, shortening the length of the trip between Belém and Macapá from 580 to 432 kilometers.

47. Technically, the lawsuit filed was a civil action to annul a contract (*pedido de declaração da nulidade do contrato*) rather than a public civil action.

48. "Atraso na Hidrovia do Marajó irrita governador," *Provincia do Pará* (Apr. 24, 1999), p. 6.

49. The Pará state governor, Almir José de Oliveira Gabriel, was openly critical of the Ministério Público for litigating this action, saying that the Ministério Público was defending "snake holes." Also, the attorney general that served from 1995 through 1998, Manoel Santino Nascimento Júnior, was perceived to have disapproved of the state prosecutors' decision to join the lawsuit. As explained by a Pará state prosecutor, the Pará State Ministério Público was generally afraid to take a position against the state government (personal interview, 2002).

50. See Chapter 4 for further discussion on this point.

51. Agency officials tend to be older than prosecutors, as environmental agencies experienced hiring freezes while prosecutorial institutions quickly grew in the 1990s. See Chapters 2 and 3.

52. *Discricionariedade administrativa* (administrative discretion) is a traditional principle within Brazilian administrative law that has been defined as the "margin of freedom left to the administrator as a result of indeterminacy as to the concrete means to fulfill, in each case, the result desired by law" or the "administrator's liberty to choose how to exercise his police power based on opportunity and convenience" (Meirelles 2000: 127; Mello 1984: 214; Benjamin 1992). Brazilian legal doctrine distinguishes between *atos discricionarios* (discretionary acts), which entail such freedom, and *atos vinculados* (nondiscretionary acts), for which the law establishes the conditions and requirements for the administrative action (Meirelles 2000: 157–58). Nondiscretionary acts are fully reviewable by the courts, whereas discretionary acts are subject only to a limited review focusing on whether the administrator abused his or her power by acting outside the confines of the law (Meirelles 2000: 156–61).

53. According to Sadek (1997: 57), 47 percent of state and federal prosecutors surveyed agreed fully with this statement.

54. Carlos Mendes, "Selma fecha torneira da corrupção no IBAMA," *Liberal* (Belém, Pará; 2001, exact date unknown).

55. See Chapter 3 for further information about conduct adjustment agreements.

56. This phrase is from Selznick, Nonet, and Vollmer (1969) and cited by Kagan (1994: 385) in a discussion of the tradeoffs between legal fidelity and administrative efficacy.

Chapter 6

1. The term "public interests" refers to what Brazilian legal scholars call "diffuse and collective interests." Briefly, "diffuse interests" refer to those that are of society as a whole (such as air quality), and "collective interests" are those of an identifiable group (such as consumers of a certain product). See Chapter 3 for further explanation.

2. Access to courts is also implied in Dicey's (1959) definition of the rule of law, which states, "the general principles of the [C]onstitution [are] the result of judicial decisions determining the rights of private persons in particular cases brought before the courts."

3. On the concept of the ombudsman generally, see Gellhorn (1966); Rowat (1965).

4. See Chapter 4 for further discussion of the principle of obligation.

5. Both studies made special note of the relatively low percentage of cases opened on the basis of a provocation by nongovernmental environmental groups. In the São Paulo study, such groups constituted only 5 percent of all identified complainants (Maciel 2002: 83). In the Rio de Janeiro study, 9 percent of the complainants were environmental groups (Fuks 1999: 65). The authors of both studies attribute these low percentages to the organizational weakness of environmental groups and their preference for activities directed at legislative and executive branch decisions (Maciel 2002: 85–86; Fuks 1999: 66).

6. The response to this question was not available for the entire sample of state and federal prosecutors together.

7. The term "environmental groups" or "environmental organizations" as used here includes community-based organizations (an association or a mobilized group within a particular community focused on local place-based issues); social movement organizations (translocal organizations that may be formed by the aggregation or linkage of many community-based organizations dedicated to similar issues); and nongovernmental organizations (those with a higher degree of institutionalization, visible in their employment of professionals, fund-raising capabilities, and potential linkages with international networks) (Evans 2002; Keck and Sikkink 1998).

8. Brazil's environmental movement is characterized as incorporating social concerns to a greater extent than advanced industrialized countries. See Viola and Nickel (1994: 175); Ames and Keck (1997). Many of these groups are associated with urban popular movements that, as described by Mainwaring (1987), focus on demands related to the sphere of reproduction. They "attempt to improve urban living conditions, usually through demands on the state for public services including sewers, paved roads, better transportation facilities, better medical facilities, running water, and electricity" (Mainwaring 1987: 133). See also Viola and Nickel (1994: 177); Keck (2002); Hochstetler (1997: 205).

9. See Chapter 5 for discussion of specific cases in São Paulo and Pará, including more description of the Belo Monte case.

10. See Amazon Watch, "Brazil, Belo Monte Dam." Available at http://www.amazon watch.org/amazon/BR/bmd/index.php?page_number=99 (last visited Dec. 12, 2007).

11. Description of the facts and arguments in this case is based on Moraes (2005).

12. The forty-one organizations employed a total of 294 people. Thirty groups had no employees; eight had 10 or fewer employees; two had between 10 and 50 employees,

and one had more than 100 employees (Instituto Brasileiro de Geografia e Estatística 2004).

13. For a more detailed discussion of conduct adjustment agreements, see Chapter 4.

14. On the tradeoff between responsiveness and prioritization in regulatory enforcement generally, see Bardach and Kagan (1982: 166–72); Scholz (1994); Hutter (1997: 132–33).

15. Note that available data described above suggest that about 75 percent of investigations are opened because of external provocations.

16. See Chapter 4 for a full description of the types of cases.

17. One hectare is equivalent to 2.47 acres. Percentages are based on the number of database entries for deforestation cases whose description included the area or number of trees affected. Sixty-one percent of the deforestation case descriptions included such information.

18. As suggested by an anonymous reviewer, public civil actions might also be used more in these cases precisely because they are "easy" cases. The facts of the harm and its causation and remedy are straightforward, and prosecutors are more likely to succeed in such cases than in more complicated ones.

19. An increase in judicial prominence and power has been observed in many countries (Tate and Vallinder 1995; Correa Sutil 1999).

20. There are five TRFs, each with between 15 and 27 judges (referred to as *desembargadores*). Under the 1988 Constitution, one-fifth of judges in the TRFs is selected from among lawyers and prosecutors (referred to as the *quinto constitucional,* or "constitutional fifth") while the rest are promoted into the position from lower federal courts, based on merit and years of service. 1988 Const. art. 107.

21. The Superior Court of Justice consists of 33 *ministros* (judges): one-third from the TRFs, one-third from the state appeals courts, and one-third from among lawyers and prosecutors, in equal parts. In the case of those selected from lower courts, the court votes for a list of three judges to be candidates, from which the president must choose. In the case of lawyers and prosecutors, their respective organizations (the Bar Association and the Ministério Público) vote for a list of six candidates for the president to choose from. Presidential nominations are confirmed by the Senate. 1988 Const. art. 104.

22. The Federal Supreme Court is composed of eleven judges (*ministros*), selected by the president among Brazilian citizens from 35 to 65 years of age possessing "notable legal knowledge and unblemished reputation, and confirmed by the Senate. 1988 Const. art. 101.

23. Article 105 of the 1988 Constitution fully describes the jurisdiction of the STJ.

24. Article 102 of the 1988 Constitution fully describes the jurisdiction of the STF.

25. For more information on the structure of Brazilian courts, see Lima Lopes (1999); Ballard (1999a).

26. The ratio of Brazilian judges per person has thus increased since 1985, when it stood at about one judge for every twenty-five thousand citizens. However, it remains much lower than the Organization for Economic Co-operation and Development (OECD) average of one judge for every three thousand citizens (Prillaman 2000: 93).

27. Supremo Tribunal Federal, National Judicial Database (Banco Nacional dos Dados do Poder Judiciário; BNDJP). In all Brazilian states combined, there were about 7,200 lower court judges and 900 appeals court judges.

28. In 2004, a form of binding precedent (*súmula vinculante*) was established in Brazil through an amendment to the 1988 Constitution. Const. amend. no. 45 of Dec. 8, 2004. *Súmulas* are "capsulized legal rules, usually one sentence in length, summarizing the holding of the court" that are generally established only after the case law has become firm on a certain point (Rosenn 1998: 26). Under the amendment, the Federal Supreme Court can approve a *súmula* that is binding on lower courts with a two-thirds vote of its members.

29. It is important to note, however, that the Brazilian judiciary has a stronger historical reputation for independence from the executive branch than many other Latin American judiciaries (Meili 1998: 508; Prillaman 2000: 77–78). Sadek (1995d: 14) explains that the Brazilian judiciary became progressively stronger throughout the twentieth century and "did not entirely" bend to the government's will under the military dictatorship. See Ballard (1999a: 239–44) on conflicts between the executive and judicial branches during the military dictatorship.

30. The institutional and individual guarantees of the judiciary are basically the same as those of the Ministério Público. Indeed, the Ministério Público's constitutional lobby made the successful argument that it should have equivalent constitutional guarantees to the judicial branch (Mazzilli 1991: 39).

31. As described by Arantes (2000), Brazil has a "hybrid system" of judicial review, combining elements of both the "diffuse" system used in the United States in which all courts may declare a law or act unconstitutional and the "centralized" model relied on in many European countries in which the power to declare unconstitutionality is held by a single constitutional court. The first Brazilian Republican Constitution, written in 1891 and strongly influenced by the U.S. Constitution, provided for judicial review of the constitutionality of laws by all courts (Arantes 2000: 342). Alterations, however, were made in the constitutions of 1934, 1937, and 1946 as well as after the military coup of 1964 that tended toward a more centralized system of judicial review, in which only the Supreme Court could declare a law unconstitutional and a limited number of actors were given jurisdiction to challenge a law's constitutionality (ibid.). The 1988 Constitution incorporated elements of both the diffuse system and the centralized system. Courts retained the general authority, characteristic of a diffuse judicial review system to enforce constitutional rights that are self-executing. However, following the model of European constitutional courts, the responsibilities of the

Federal Supreme Court became predominantly constitutional. The Superior Court of Justice was created under the Federal Supreme Court to be primarily responsible for deciding appeals from the regional courts (TRFs) and state courts that involved an issue of federal law (Sadek 1995b: 163). Five TRFs were created in the place of what had been a single federal appeals court (Tribunal Federal dos Recursos), an organizational change expected to ease caseload congestion. These changes are generally interpreted by scholars as advances toward the democratization and growing accessibility of the courts (see Arantes 2000: 345; Sadek 1995d; Rosenn 2000).

32. The writ of injunction (*mandado de injunção*) allows a legal challenge to the government's failure to enact regulations to bring a constitutional provision that is not self-executing into force. 1988 Const. art. 5, LXXI.

33. The direct action of unconstitutionality (*ação direta de inconstitucionalidade*) is a legal challenge to the constitutionality of an executive or legislative branch that is filed directly with the Brazilian Supreme Court. Until 1988, only the federal attorney general could file such an action. After 1988, potential plaintiffs were expanded to also include the president; the chairs of the federal Senate and House of Representatives; the chairs of state legislatures; state governors; the federal council of the Brazilian bar association; political parties represented in Congress; and national trade unions and professional associations. 1988 Const. art. 103, par. 1 (see also Sadek 1995b: 161). The new constitution also made it possible to challenge the constitutionality of a legislative or executive omission. 1988 Const. art. 103, par. 2. For more information on such actions, see Werneck Vianna (1999); Ferreira Filho (1995); Prillaman (2000); Taylor (2005: 424).

34. The *mandado de segurança* (writ of security) allows an individual to challenge the constitutionality of an official act. Using the collective writ of security, instituted in the 1988 Constitution, a political party, union, or organization may collectively defend the constitutional rights of its members. 1988 Const. art. 5, LXX.

35. 1934 Const. art. 113, no. 38.

36. 1988 Const. art. 5, LXXIII. See also Fernandes (1995: 120).

37. 1988 Const. art. 129, III.

38. The 1990 datum is from Sadek (1995b: 164). The 1999 datum is the sum of the number of judges in the lower courts and appeals courts, as reported in Supremo Tribunal Federal, National Judicial Database (Banco Nacional de Dados do Poder Judiciário; BNDPJ), "Justiça comum de 1º grau, percentual do número de juízes/juízas em relação aos cargos providos, percentual de vacância e demonstrativo de juízes em relação à população no ano de 1999" and "Justiça comum—Tribunais de Justiça, Número de desembargadores e percentual de vacância no ano de 1999."

39. The 1990 datum is from Junqueira (2003: 83). The 2002 datum is the sum of the number of judges in the lower federal courts and regional federal courts, as reported in Supremo Tribunal Federal, National Judicial Database (Banco Nacional de Dados

do Poder Judiciário; BNDPJ): "Justiça federal de 1º grau: Processos distribuídos e julgados em relação aos cargos providos de juízes em 2002," and "Tribunais Regionais Federais: Processos distribuídos e julgados em relação aos cargos providos de juízes em 2002."

40. In two states, Pará and Sergipe, more than half of all lower court judges were female. In thirteen other states, more than a quarter of all lower court judges were female. See Supremo Tribunal Federal, National Judicial Database (Banco Nacional de Dados do Poder Judiciário; BNDPJ), "Justiça comum de 1º grau: Percentual do número de juízes/juízas em relação aos cargos providos, percentual de vacância e demonstrativo de juízes em relação à população no ano de 1999."

41. The survey was conducted by the Institute of Economic, Social, and Political Studies of São Paulo (Instituto de Estudos Econômicos, Sociais e Políticos de São Paulo; IDESP). It included 41 members of the federal judiciary and 529 members of the state judiciaries, comprising 20 percent of federal judges and 20 percent of state judges in five states: Goias, Paraná, Pernambuco, Rio Grande do Sul, and São Paulo. Results of the survey are published in Sadek (1995a; 1995c: 67–70).

42. Survey results were obtained by sending out 12,847 questionnaires to state and federal judges in 1995. Of these, 3,927 (30 percent) responded in roughly equal percentages from the various regions of the country (north, southeast, northeast, central west, and south) and types of courts (state judiciary, federal judiciary, labor, and military). See Werneck Vianna (1997: 325–29) for a full description of the research.

43. Castro (1997b) as cited and discussed by Alston et al. (2005: 19), noting that most of the private victories involved tax issues and that the court ruled in favor of the private interests in 23 percent of non-tax cases.

44. The number of respondents expressing confidence grew from about 41 percent to about 43 percent. See Centro de Estudios de Justicia de las Americas (CEJA), "Informe comparativo, opinión pública, grafico 20: Indice de confianza en el sistema de justicia, Latinobarometro." Available at http://www.cejamericas.org/reporte/muestra_seccion.php?idioma=espanol&capitulo=ACJU-030&tipreport=REPORTE 2&seccion=INST_261 (last visited Dec. 12, 2007).

45. Ibid.

46. Judicial reform debates in the 1990s and 2000s were fueled by the view that the Brazilian judiciary had become overly accessible and willing to interfere in political and governmental issues. See Prillaman (2000: 75); Ballard (1999b: 29). In 2004, constitutional amendment no. 45 established the National Judicial Council (Conselho Nacional de Justiça; CNJ) to exercise external oversight over judicial administrative decisions (such as budget and promotion decisions) and instituted a form of binding precedent (súmula vinculante) in which a vote of 8 of the 11 STF judges makes a ruling binding on other courts (See Taylor 2007: Table 2.2). On the judicial reform debate preceding this amendment, see Falcão (1996); Ballard (1999a, 1999b); Rosenn (1998);

Prillaman (2000). General sources on judicial reform in Latin America include Dakolias (1995); Buscaglia (1997); Correa Sutil (1999); Santos (2000); Jarquín Calderón and Carrillo Flórez (1998); Domingo and Sieder (2001).

47. But see Frota (1995: 315), rejecting the idea that judges are less independent in northern Brazil than in southern Brazil.

48. Sanches Filho (1999: 54) attributes the differences between the results of the Bahia sample and the national sample to interference by a particularly powerful politician, Antonio Carlos Magalhães.

49. On institutional conflict between judges and prosecutors, see also Bonelli (1999).

50. Sadek (1995e: 19–20) explains that, particularly since the 1988 Constitution, judges view prosecutors as "competitors" and that their negative evaluations of prosecutors can be viewed as a corporatist response.

51. The survey also revealed, however, that judges considered the Ministério Público's work significantly more positive than that of executive or legislative branch institutions: the federal and state Ministério Público's approval ratings (38.2 percent and 37 percent, respectively) were higher than those of the federal government (22.6 percent), state governments (4.6 percent), and national Congress (3.3 percent) (Sadek 1995e: 21).

52. On the relationship between appeals and judicial delay in Brazil, see also Brinks (2004: 613) and Taylor (2006, 2008). Other factors considered important by judges included the "private interests of the lawyers" (cited by 58.4 percent); "private interests of the parties" (53.5 percent); "slowness in the appeals courts" (49.1 percent); and "private interests of the government" (48.2 percent). Only 35.6 percent cited the slowness of judges themselves as an important cause of delay. See Sadek (1995a: 19).

53. Supremo Tribunal Federal, National Judicial Database (Banco Nacional de Dados de Poder Judiciário; BNDJP). On the volume and types of cases in Brazilian courts, see Taylor (2008: chapter 2).

54. Supremo Tribunal Federal, National Judicial Database (Banco Nacional de Dados de Poder Judiciário; BNDJP).

55. Supremo Tribunal Federal, National Judicial Database (Banco Nacional de Dados de Poder Judiciário; BNDJP).

56. Supremo Tribunal Federal, National Judicial Database (Banco Nacional de Dados de Poder Judiciário; BNDJP).

57. The problem of increasing case delay and backlogs is not unique to Brazil but is present throughout the region. In Argentina and Venezuela, for example, average delay and backlogs both increased between 1983 and 1993 by about 50 percent. In Chile, average delay increased by 11.1 percent and backlog increased by 29.4 percent (Buscaglia 1998: 20).

58. The author studied a sample of 52 lawsuits, of which 12 had been decided and 40 had not (Araujo 2001).

59. Statement of Carlos Celso de Amaral e Silva, reported in "Uma lei que mudou o Brasil" in *Ambiente Legal* 1, no. 4 (Dec. 2001 / Jan. 2002 / Feb. 2002), a newsletter published by the Brazilian law firm Pinheiro Pedro Advogados. Available at http://www .pinheiropedro.com.br/biblioteca/boletim_amb_legal/01a08/amblegal0004/umalei .htm (last visited Dec. 12, 2007).

60. Ballard (1999a) and Castro (1997a) describe several concrete cases with significant political ramifications. See also Rosenn (1998: 22–23) on how Brazilian courts are caught in the middle of conflicts between the executive and legislative branches and must choose between handing down decisions that might throw the country into a state of "legal paralysis" and not enforcing the Constitution.

Chapter 7

1. The most highly regarded scholars of environmental law in Brazil have generally been members of the Ministério Público. Paulo Affonso Leme Machado, Antonio Herman Benjamin, and Édis Milaré are three prominent examples, all former or present members of the São Paulo Ministério Público.

2. *Folha de São Paulo* (July 9, 2000), quoted in Sadek and Cavalcanti (2003: 210).

3. Sadek and Cavalcanti (2003: 212) hypothesize that the variability in the Ministério Público's political independence across Brazilian states may be explained by the relative degree of political pluralism. "The probability that prosecutors will be more 'independent' should increase in states that have a more diversified political and electoral base (i.e. more pluralist), or in states where any elite political faction does not hold a quasi-monopoly on political power within the state." They note that the degree of political pluralism does not necessarily coincide with the degree of economic development.

4. In 1990, a São Paulo state prosecutor, Luiz Antonio Fleury, was elected state governor. His administration included sixteen other state prosecutors in appointed positions and was popularly dubbed the "republic of the prosecutors" (Arantes 2002: 289–91). The proximity of the Ministério Público to the executive branch led to accusations that the institution was under the control of the governor, and more particularly that the attorney general had interfered in individual prosecutors' efforts to investigate the governor and his political associates (Silva 2000: 6). This controversy led in turn to the emergence of an opposition leadership group in the São Paulo Ministério Público that distanced itself from the old leadership. An opposition candidate was chosen as attorney general in 1996 (Arantes 2002: 281, 289–92; Bonelli 2002; Silva 2000: 6).

5. Similarly, Taylor and Buranelli (2007: 63–65) suggest that the Federal Ministério Público is the most important institution of accountability at the federal level in Brazil, but that it is undermined by its lack of interaction with other institutions.

6. There are approximately ninety-five environmental prosecutors in the state

(personal interview, 2002). CONMAM was officially established by provimento no. 09 / 2000, issued by Attorney General Claudio Barros Silva.

7. In a similar vein, for several years in the late 1990s, the São Paulo Ministério Público's support center sponsored the meetings of thematic work groups (*grupos especiais*) in which prosecutors discussed approaches to specific environmental problems. See Maciel (2002: 117, fn. 32) and Proença (2001: 149, fn. 10).

8. On how the media fits into definitions of vertical accountability, see O'Donnell (1999a: 30) and Schedler (1999: 25).

9. To file a civil action to remove a tenured prosecutor, the attorney general must also get the authorization of the institution's leadership body (Colégio de Procuradores de Justiça), generally consisting of all prosecutors who have been promoted to work in the courts of appeal.

10. Before the passage of the judicial reform amendment (Const. amendment no. 45 of Dec. 8, 2004), approval by three-quarters of the members of the Superior Council was required.

11. Kerche (2003: 67) observes that another problem with relying on courts to curb prosecutorial overreaching is that courts take a long time to resolve cases and the simple filing of charges may do great damage to the accused.

12. This legal power of the Superior Council is granted by complementary state law no. 734 of Nov. 26, 1993, art. 108. However, this grant of power has been disputed by São Paulo prosecutors as an unconstitutional infringement on their functional independence since its establishment (Arantes 2002: 260–63).

13. Akaoui (2004: 96–97) writes that in cases where a conduct adjustment agreement is inadequate or illegal, an interested party could file a civil public action against the responsible party and judicially seek invalidation of the agreement.

14. Some prosecutors have suggested that civil society groups be directly involved in setting goals and priorities for the Ministério Público (see Goulart 1998: 116). For other discussions of how the Ministério Público should strengthen its political base by increasing its connections to civil society, see Silva (2000: 11); Ferraz (1993: 14); Macedo Júnior (1999a: 113); and Proença (2001: 150–51).

15. See CNMP homepage, "Sobre o CNMP." Available at http://www.cnmp.gov.br (last visited Dec. 12, 2007).

16. Watson (1993) defines a "legal transplant" as the adoption of a particular legal or institutional feature from one legal system into another.

17. In another article on legal diffusion, Twining (2005) points out that comparative law scholars have virtually ignored a large social science literature on the diffusion of innovations that might help them move past the naïve model of diffusion.

18. See Cappelletti and Garth (1978: 36–37, 40–41).

19. Duce and Riego (2006) surveyed thirteen countries in the region and found that the Ministério Público is formally autonomous from the other branches of

government in nine countries; affiliated with the judicial branch but functionally autonomous in three countries; and part of the judicial branch in one country. In Mexico and Uruguay, two countries not included in their survey, the Ministério Público is part of the executive branch. See Centro de Estudios de Justicia de las Americas (CEJA), "Informe comparativo: Organismo a cargo de la persecución penal." Available at http://www.cejamericas.org/reporte/muestra_seccion.php?idioma =espanol&capitulo=ACJU-030&tipreport=REPORTE2&seccion=MINPUBLI (last visited Dec. 12, 2007).

Bibliography

Abrams, Norman. 1971. Internal policy: Guiding the exercise of prosecutorial discretion. *UCLA Law Review* 19:1–58.

Ackel Filho, Diomar. 1990. Discricionariedade: Administrativa e ação civil pública. *Revista dos Tribunais* 657:51–59.

Agatiello, Osvaldo R. I., ed. 1995. *Environmental law and policy in Latin America*. London: Baker & McKenzie.

Akaoui, Fernando Reverendo Vidal. 1998. Improbidade administrativa em relação à administração ambiental. *Revista de Direito Ambiental* 3 (12):94–99.

———. 1999. Resolução No. 42/94 da Secretaria Estadual do Meio Ambiente de São Paulo: Um texto contaminado pela eiva de inconstitucionalidade. Paper read at the 3rd Environmental Conference of the Ministério Público of São Paulo, November, Ubatuba, SP.

———. 2004. *Compromisso de ajustamento de conduta ambiental*. São Paulo: Editora Revista dos Tribunais.

Alberton, José Galvani. 1985. O Ministério Público e os abusos do poder administrativo. *Justitia* 47 (131-A):113–23.

Albuquerque, Roberto Chacon de. 2000. Legal responses to the fiscal crisis in Brazil. *Saint Louis–Warsaw Transatlantic Law Journal* 2000:163–73.

Alston, Lee J., Marcus André Melo, Bernardo Mueller, and Carlos Pereira. 2005. Political institutions, policymaking processes, and policy outcomes in Brazil. Boulder, CO: Institute of Behavioral Science, Research Program on Environment and Behavior.

Ames, Barry, and Margaret E. Keck. 1997. The politics of sustainable development: Environmental policy making in four Brazilian states. *Journal of Interamerican Studies and World Affairs* 39 (4):1.

Antunes, Paulo de Bessa. 2001. O inquérito civil (considerações críticas). In *Ação civil pública, Lei 7347/1985—15 anos*, edited by É. Milaré. São Paulo: Revista dos Tribunais.

Aragão, Murillo de, and Stephen G. Bunker. 1998. Brazil: Regional inequalities and eco-logical diversity in a federal system. In *Engaging countries: strengthening compliance with international environmental accords*, edited by E. B. Weiss and H. K. Jacobson. Cambridge, MA and London: MIT Press.

Arantes, Rogério Bastos. 1999. Direito e política: O Ministério Público e a defesa dos direitos coletivos. *Revista Brasileira de Ciências Sociais* 14 (39):83–102.

————. 2000. The judiciary, democracy, and economic policy in Brazil. In *Handbook of global legal policy*, edited by S. S. Nagel. New York: Marcel Dekker.

————. 2002. *Ministério Público e política no Brasil*, Série Justiça. São Paulo: EDUC; Editora Sumaré; FAPESP.

————. 2004. The Brazilian "Ministério Público" and political corruption in Brazil. Oxford: University of Oxford Centre for Brazilian Studies.

————. 2005. Constitutionalism, the expansion of justice, and the judicialization of politics. In *The judicialization of politics in Latin America*, edited by R. Sieder, L. Schjolden, and A. Angell. New York: Palgrave Macmillan.

Araujo, Lilian Alves de. 2001. *Ação civil pública ambiental*. Rio de Janeiro: Lúmen Júris.

Atiyah, P. S., and Robert S. Summers. 1987. *Form and substance in Anglo-American law: A comparative study of legal reasoning, legal theory, and legal institutions*. Oxford: Clarendon.

Ayres, Ian, and John Braithwaite. 1992. *Responsive regulation: Transcending the deregula-tion debate*. Oxford Socio-Legal Studies. New York: Oxford University Press.

Badaracco, Joseph. 1985. *Loading the dice: A five-country study of vinyl chloride regulation*. Boston: Harvard Business School Press.

Baldwin, Robert, Colin Scott, and Christopher Hood, eds. 1998. *A reader on regulation*. Oxford: Oxford University Press.

Ballard, Megan J. 1999a. The clash between local courts and global economics: The poli-tics of judicial reform in Brazil. *Berkeley Journal of International Law* 17:230–76.

————. 1999b. Global trends and local strife: The politics of judicial reform in Brazil. *LLM*, University of Wisconsin Law School.

Bankobeza, Sylvia. 2003. Latin American Needs Assessment and Judges and Prosecutors Planning Meeting. Paper read at the Symposium of Judges and Prosecutors of Lat-in America: Environmental Compliance and Enforcement, Sept. 23–24, 2003, Bue-nos Aires.

Bardach, Eugene. 1972. *The skill factor in politics: Repealing the mental commitment laws in California*. Berkeley: University of California Press.

Bardach, Eugene, and Robert A. Kagan. 1982. *Going by the book: The problem of regula-tory unreasonableness*. Philadelphia: Temple University Press.

Bello Filho, Ney de Barros. 2000. Aplicabilidade da lei de improbidade administrati-va à atuação da administração ambiental brasileira. *Revista de Direito Ambiental* 5 (18):57–79.

Benjamin, Antonio Herman. 1992. Os princípios de estudo de impacto ambiental como limites da discricionariedade administrativa. *Revista Forense* 317:25–45.

———. 1998a. Criminal law and the protection of the environment in Brazil. Paper read at the Fifth International Conference on Environmental Compliance and Enforcement, Nov. 16–20, 1998, Monterey, CA.

———. 1998b. Um novo modelo para o Ministério Público na proteção do meio ambiente. *Revista de Direito Ambiental* 3 (10):7–13.

———. 1999a. Introdução ao direito ambiental brasileiro. Paper read at the Third International Conference on Environmental Law: A Proteção Jurídica das Florestas Tropicais / The Legal Protection of Tropical Forests, May 30–June 2, 1999, São Paulo, 75–113.

———, ed. 1999b. *Legislação ambiental.* São Paulo: IMESP.

Bernard, H. Russell. 1995. *Research methods in anthropology: qualitative and quantitative approaches.* 2nd ed. Walnut Creek, CA: AltaMira Press.

Biderman Furriela, Rachel. 2002. *Democracia, cidadania e proteção do meio ambiente.* São Paulo: Annablume; FAPESP.

Biller, Dan. 2003. Environmental impact assessment in Brazil. In *Does environmental policy work? The theory and practice of outcomes assessment,* edited by D. E. Ervin, J. R. Kahn, and M. L. Livingston. Cheltenham, UK: Edward Elgar.

Bonatto, Claudio. 1992. A coordenadoria das promotorias de defesa comunitária: A lei de ação civil pública e os recursos na proteção dos interesses difusos e coletivos. *Revista do Ministério Público, Rio Grande do Sul* 1 (27):183–87.

Bonelli, Maria de Gloria. 1999. As interações dos profissionais do direito em uma comarca do Estado de São Paulo. In *O sistema de justiça,* edited by M. T. Sadek. São Paulo: IDESP, Editora Sumaré.

———. 2001. Ministério Público Paulista: Construção institucional e identidade profissional. Unpublished manuscript. São Paulo.

———. 2002. *Profissionalismo e política no mundo do direito.* São Paulo: Editora da Universidade Federal de São Carlos; Editora Sumaré; FAPESP.

Braithwaite, John. 1985. *To punish or persuade: Enforcement of coal mine safety.* Albany: State University of New York Press.

Bresser Pereira, Luiz Carlos. 1996. *Economic crisis and state reform in Brazil: Toward a new interpretation of Latin America.* Boulder, CO: Lynne Rienner.

Brinks, Daniel. 2004. Judicial reform and independence in Brazil and Argentina: The beginning of a new millenium? *Texas International Law Journal* 40:595–622.

Brito, Brenda, and Paulo Barreto. 2005. Aplicação da lei de crimes ambientais pela Justiça Federal no setor florestal do Pará. *Revista de Direito Ambiental* 10 (37):218–43.

———. 2006. A eficácia da aplicação da lei de crimes ambientais pelo Ibama para proteção de florestas no Pará. *Revista de Direito Ambiental* 11 (43): 35–65.

Brito, Brenda, Paulo Barreto, and John Rothman. 2005. Brazil's new environmental crimes law: An analysis of its effectiveness in protecting the Amazon forests. Belém: IMAZON.

Bunker, Stephen G. 1985. *Underdeveloping the Amazon: Extraction, unequal exchange, and the failure of the modern state.* Urbana: University of Illinois Press.

Buscaglia, Eduardo. 1997. A quantitative assessment of the efficiency of the judicial sector in Latin America. *International Review of Law and Economics* 17:275–91.

————. 1998. Obstacles to judicial reform in Latin America. In *Justice delayed: Judicial reform in Latin America*, edited by E. Jarquín Calderón and F. Carrillo Flórez. Washington, DC, and Baltimore: Inter-American Development Bank; Johns Hopkins University Press.

Cappelletti, Mauro. 1978. Governmental and private advocates for the public interest in civil litigation: A comparative study. In *Access to justice.* Vol. 2: *Promising institutions*, edited by M. Cappelletti and J. Weisner. Amsterdam: Sijthoff and Noordhoff.

————. 1979. Vindicating the public interest through the courts: A comparativist's contribution. In *Access to justice.* Vol. 3: *Emerging issues and perspectives*, edited by M. Cappelletti and B. Garth. Amsterdam: Sijthoff and Noordhoff.

Cappelletti, Mauro, and Bryant Garth. 1978. Access to justice: The worldwide movement to make rights effective—a general report. In *Access to justice.* Vol. 1: *A world survey*, edited by M. Cappelletti and B. Garth. Amsterdam: Sijthoff and Noordhoff.

————. 1981. Access to justice and the welfare state: An introduction. In *Access to justice and the welfare state*, edited by M. Cappelletti. Florence, Italy: European University Institute.

Cappelli, Silvia. 2000. Novos rumos do direito ambiental. In *Temas de direito ambiental: Uma visão interdisciplinar*, edited by E. C. Hausen, O. P. B. Teixeira, and P. B. Alvares. Porto Alegre: AEBA, APESP.

Carter, Leif H. 1974. *The limits of order.* Lexington, MA: Lexington Books.

Castro, Juventino V. 1998. *El Ministerio Público en México: Funciones y disfunciones.* Mexico City: Editorial Porrúa.

Castro, Marcos Faro de. 1997a. The courts, law, and democracy in Brazil. *International Social Science Journal* 49 (152):241–52.

————. 1997b. O Supremo Tribunal Federal e a judicialização da política. *Revista Brasileira de Ciências Sociais* 12(34).

CETESB, São Paulo State. 2001. Relatório Anual da CETESB 2000. São Paulo: CETESB/SMA.

Coles, Catherine M., and George L. Kelling. 1998. Prosecution in the community: A study of emergent strategies. Cambridge, MA: Harvard University Press.

Correa, Jorge, María Angélica Jiménez, Franz Vanderschueren, and Enrique Oviedo. 1995. *Acceso de los pobres a la justicia en países de America Latina.* Santiago: Programa de Gestion Urbana, PNUD, UNCHS, Banco Mundial, Centro de Estudios Sociales y Educación, Ediciones Sur.

Correa Sutil, Jorge. 1999. Judicial reforms in Latin America: Good news for the under-privileged? In *The (un)rule of law and the underprivileged in Latin America*, edited by J. E. Méndez, G. A. O'Donnell, and P. S. d. M. S. Pinheiro. Notre Dame, IN: University of Notre Dame Press.

Costa, Vera Rita da. 2003. Perfil: Paulo Nogueira-Neto: Advogado da natureza. *Ciência Hoje* 33(195).

Dakolias, Maria. 1995. A strategy for judicial reform: The experience in Latin America. *Virginia Journal of International Law* 36:167–231.

David, René. 1978. French Law. In *Comparative law: Western European and Latin American legal systems*, edited by J. H. Merryman and D. S. Clark. Indianapolis, IN: Bobbs-Merrill.

Davis, Kenneth Culp. 1969. *Discretionary justice: A preliminary inquiry.* Baton Rouge: Louisiana State University Press.

Dawalibi, Marcelo. 1999. O poder de policia em matéria ambiental. *Revista de Direito Ambiental* 4 (14):91–102.

Debert, Guita Grin. 2000. Ministério Público no Pará. In *Justiça e cidadania no Brasil*, edited by M. T. Sadek. São Paulo: Editora Sumaré / IDESP.

Dezalay, Yves, and Bryant G. Garth. 2002. *Global prescriptions: The production, exportation, and importation of a new legal orthodoxy.* Ann Arbor: University of Michigan Press.

Diamond, Larry, Marc F. Plattner, and Andreas Schedler. 1999. Introduction. In *The self-restraining state: Power and accountability in new democracies*, edited by A. Schedler, L. Diamond, and M. F. Plattner. Boulder, CO: Lynne Rienner.

Dias, Elvira Gabriela Ciacco da Silva, and Luis Enrique Sanchez. 2001. Deficiências na implementação de projetos submetidos à avaliação de impacto ambiental no estado de São Paulo. *Revista de Direito Ambiental* 6 (23):163–204.

Dicey, Albert Venn. 1959. *Introduction to the study of the law of the constitution.* 10th ed. London and New York: Macmillan, St. Martin's Press.

DiMento, Joseph F. 1986. *Environmental law and American business: Dilemmas of compliance, environment, development, and public policy. Environmental policy and planning.* New York: Plenum Press.

Domingo, Pilar. 2005. Judicialization of politics: The changing political role of the judiciary in Mexico. In *The judicialization of politics in Latin America*, edited by R. Sieder, L. Schjolden, and A. Angell. New York: Palgrave Macmillan.

Domingo, Pilar, and Rachel Sieder. 2001. *Rule of law in Latin America: The international promotion of judicial reform.* London: Institute of Latin American Studies.

Dourado, Maria Cristina Cascaes. 1993. *Meio ambiente no Pará: Fato e norma.* Edited by N. d. m. ambiente, *Universidade e Meio Ambiente.* Belém: Universidade Federal do Pará.

Drummond, José, and Ana Flávia Barros-Platiau. 2006. Brazilian environmental laws and policies, 1934–2002: A critical overview. *Law & Policy* 28 (1):83–108.

DuBois, Francois. 1996. Social justice and the judicial enforcement of environmental rights and duties. In *Human rights approaches to environmental protection*, edited by A. E. Boyle and M. R. Anderson. Oxford: Clarendon.

Duce, Mauricio, and Cristián Riego. 2006. *Desafíos del Ministerio Público Fiscal en América Latina*. Santiago: Centro de Estudios de Justicia de las Américas (CEJA).

Dwyer, John. 1990. The pathology of symbolic legislation. *Ecology Law Quarterly* 17:233–316.

Edelman, Murray J. 1964. *The symbolic uses of politics*. Urbana: University of Illinois Press.

Emerson, Robert M., Rachel I. Fretz, and Linda L. Shaw. 1995. *Writing ethnographic fieldnotes*. Chicago: University of Chicago Press.

Escobar, Arturo. 1995. *Encountering development: The making and unmaking of the Third World, Princeton studies in culture / power / history*. Princeton, NJ: Princeton University Press.

Evans, Peter B. 1997. *State-society synergy: Government and social capital in development*. Berkeley: University of California at Berkeley International and Area Studies.

———, ed. 2002a. *Livable cities? Urban struggles for livelihood and sustainability*. Berkeley: University of California Press.

———. 2002b. Introduction: Looking for agents of urban livability in a globalized political economy. In *Livable cities? Urban struggles for livelihood and sustainability*, edited by P. B. Evans. Berkeley: University of California Press.

Fabbrini, Renato Nascimento, ed. 2002. *O MP e a crise orçamentária*. São Paulo: Associação Paulista do Ministério Público.

Falcão, Joaquim. 1996. Acesso a justiça: Diagnóstico e tratamento. In *Justiça: Promessa e realidade*, edited by Associação dos Magistrados Brasileiros. Rio de Janeiro: Nova Fronteira.

Farber, Daniel A. 2002. Rights as signals. *Journal of Legal Studies* 31:83.

Fearnside, Philip M. 2000. How well does Brazil's environmental law work in practice? Environmental impact assessment and the case of the Itapiranga private sustainable logging plan. *Environmental Management* 23 (3):251–67.

———. 2001. Environmental impacts of Brazil's Tucuruí Dam: Unlearned lessons for hydroelectric development in Amazonia. *Environmental Management* 27 (3):377–96.

———. 2006. Dams in the Amazon: Belo Monte and Brazil's hydroelectric development of the Xingu River basin. *Environmental Management* 38 (1):16–27.

Feldmann, Fabio. 1995. Ação civil pública: Fator de mobilização social. In *Ação civil pública, Lei 7347/85—reminiscências e reflexões apos dez anos de aplicação*, edited by É. Milaré. São Paulo: Revista dos Tribunais.

Fernandes, Edesio. 1995. Collective interests in Brazilian environmental law. In *Public interest perspectives in environmental law*, edited by D. Robinson and J. Dunkley. London: Wiley.

———. 1996. Constitutional environmental rights in Brazil. In *Human rights approaches to environmental protection*, edited by A. E. Boyle and M. R. Anderson. Oxford: Clarendon.

Ferraz, Antonio Augusto Mello de Camargo. 1991. O ombudsman parlamentar e o Ministério Público. *Justitia* 53 (154):98.

———. 1993. O delineamento constitucional de um novo Ministério Público. *Justitia* 55 (161):9–16.

———. 1995. Inquérito civil: Dez anos de um instrumento de cidadania. In *Ação Civil Público, Lei 7347/85—Reminiscências e reflexões apos dez anos de aplicação*, edited by É. Milaré. São Paulo: Revista dos Tribunais.

———. 2001. Ação civil pública, inquérito civil e Ministério Público. In *Ação civil pública, Lei 7347/1985—15 anos*, edited by É. Milaré. São Paulo: Revista dos Tribunais.

———, ed. 2003. *Um novo modelo de gestão para o Ministério Público*. São Paulo: Edições APMP.

Ferraz, Antonio Augusto Mello de Camargo, and Patrícia André de Camargo Ferraz. 1997. Ministério Público e enforcement. In *Ministério Público e afirmação da cidadania*, edited by A. A. M. d. C. Ferraz. São Paulo: author.

Ferraz, Antonio Augusto Mello de Camargo, and João Lopes Guimaraes Júnior. 1999. A necessária elaboração de uma nova doutrina de Ministério Público, compatível com seu atual perfil constitucional. In *Ministério Público: Instituição e processo*, edited by A. A. M. d. C. Ferraz. São Paulo: Atlas.

Ferraz, Antonio Augusto Mello de Camargo, Édis Milaré, and Hugo Nigro Mazzilli. 1986. O Ministério Público e a questão ambiental na constituição. *Revista dos Tribunais* 611:14–24.

Ferraz, Antonio Augusto Mello de Camargo, Édis Milaré, and Nelson Nery Júnior. 1984. *A ação civil público e a tutela jurisdicional dos interesses difusos*. São Paulo: Saraiva.

Ferreira da Costa Passos, Lidia Helena. 2001. Discricionariedade administrativa e justiça ambiental: Novos desafios do poder judiciário nas ações civis públicas. In *Ação civil pública, Lei 7347/1985—15 anos*, edited by É. Milaré. São Paulo: Revista dos Tribunais.

Ferreira Filho, Manoel Gonçalves. 1995. O poder judiciário na Constituição de 1988: Judicialização da política e politização da justiça. *Revista Juridica: Revista da Procuradoria Geral do Município de São Paulo* 1:21–42.

Ferreira, Leila da Costa. 1998. *Os atores e as instituições na definição da política ambiental em São Paulo*. São Paulo: Jinkings.

Ferreira, Lúcia de Costa. 1993. *Os fantasmas do vale: qualidade ambiental e cidadania*. Campinas, São Paulo: Unicamp.

Fetterman, David M. 1998. *Ethnography: Step by step*, Applied Social Research Methods Series, vol. 17. Thousand Oaks, CA: Sage.

Filho, Paulo de Goes. 1993. Institutional Framework of Environmental Policy in Brazil. In *Towards a sustainable urban environment: The Rio de Janeiro study*, edited by A. e. a. Kriemer. Washington, DC: World Bank.

Findley, Roger W. 1988. Pollution control in Brazil. *Ecology Law Quarterly* 15 (1):1–68.

Fink, Daniel Roberto. 2001. Alternativa a ação civil público ambiental (reflexões sobre as vantagens do termo de ajustamento de conduta). In *Ação civil pública, Lei 7347/1985—15 anos*, edited by É. Milaré. São Paulo: Revista dos Tribunais.

Fink, Daniel Roberto, Hamilton Alonso Jr., and Marcelo Dawalibi. 2000. *Aspectos jurídicos do licenciamento ambiental*. Rio de Janeiro: Forense Universitária.

Fionda, Julia. 1995. *Public prosecutors and discretion: A comparative study*. Oxford: Clarendon.

Fleisher, David V. 2002. Corruption in Brazil: Defining, measuring and reducing. Washington, DC: Center for Strategic and International Studies (CSIS).

Friedman, Lawrence M. 1978. Access to justice: Social and historical context. In *Access to justice*. Vol. 2: *Promising institutions*, edited by M. Cappelletti and J. Weisner. Amsterdam: Sijthoff and Noordhoff.

———. 1985. *Total justice*. New York: Russell Sage Foundation.

Frota, Paulo Sérgio. 1995. Organização e processo sobre o meio ambiente na justiça do Estado do Pará. In *Amazônia perante o direito: Problemas ambientais e trabalhistas*, edited by R. A. O. Santos and W. Paul. Belém: Universidade Federal do Pará.

Fuks, Mario. 1999. *Arenas de ação e debate públicos: Os conflitos do meio ambiente enquanto problema social no Rio de Janeiro (1985–1992)*. Estudos Economicos. Rio de Janeiro: Tribunal de Contas, Instituto Serzedello Correa.

Fuller, Lon L. 1969. *The morality of law*, rev. ed. New Haven, CT: Yale University Press.

Garth, Bryant, Ilene H. Nagel, and S. Jay Plager. 1988. The institution of the private attorney general: Perspectives from an empirical study of class action litigation. *Southern California Law Review* 61:353–98.

Gellhorn, Walter. 1966. *Ombudsmen and others: Citizens' protectors in nine countries*. Cambridge, MA: Harvard University Press.

Goulart, Marcelo Pedroso. 1998. *Ministério Público e democracia: Teoria e práxis*. Leme, SP: Editora de Direito Ltda.

Grinover, Ada Pellegrini. 1999. A ação civil pública refém do autoritarismo. Paper read at the 3rd International Environmental Law Conference (3° Congresso Internacional de Direito Ambiental), May 30–June 2, São Paulo.

———. 2000. A defesa do meio ambiente em juízo como conquista da cidadania. *Stvdia Ivridica* (boletim da Faculdade de Direito, Universidade de Coimbra, Portugal) 40 (Colloquia 2):141–48.

Guimaraes Júnior, Renato. 1981. O futuro do Ministério Público como guardião do meio ambiente e a história do direito ecológico. *Justitia* 43 (113):151–92.

Guimarães, Paulo C. Vaz, Silvia F. MacDowell, and Jacques Demajorovic. 1996. Fiscalização em meio ambiente no estado de São Paulo. *Cadernos Fundap: Revista da fundação do desenvolvimento administrativa* 20:35–46.

Gunningham, Neil. 1987. Negotiated non-compliance: A case study of regulatory failure. *Law and Policy* 9 (1):69–95.

Gunningham, Neil, Peter N. Grabosky, and Darren Sinclair. 1998. *Smart regulation: Designing environmental policy*. Oxford Socio-Legal Studies. Oxford: Clarendon.

Gunningham, Neil, Robert A. Kagan, and Dorothy Thornton. 2003. *Shades of green: Regulation, business, environment*. Stanford, CA: Stanford University Press.

Hammergren, Linn. 1998. *Institutional strengthening and justice reform*. U.S. Agency for International Development (USAID) Document no. PN-ACD-20. Washington, DC: USAID Center for Democracy and Governance.

Harrison, Kathryn. 1995. Is cooperation the answer? Canadian environmental enforcement in comparative context. *Journal of Policy Analysis and Management* 14 (2):221–44.

Hawkins, Keith. 1984. *Environment and enforcement: Regulation and the social definition of pollution*. Oxford Socio-Legal Studies. Oxford: Clarendon.

———. 2002. *Law as last resort: Prosecution decision-making in a regulatory agency*. Oxford Socio-Legal Studies. Oxford, NY: Oxford University Press.

Hawkins, Keith, and John M. Thomas. 1984. *Enforcing regulation*. Law in Social Context Series. Boston: Kluwer-Nijhoff.

Hendley, Kathryn. 1996. *Trying to make law matter: Legal reform and labor law in the Soviet Union*. Ann Arbor: University of Michigan Press.

Hochstetler, Kathryn. 1997. The evolution of the Brazilian environmental movement and its political roles. In *The new politics of inequality in Latin America*, edited by D. A. e. a. Chalmers. New York: Oxford University Press.

———. 2002a. After the boomerang: Environmental movements and politics in the La Plata river basin. *Global environmental politics* 2 (4):35–57.

———. 2002b. Brazil. In *Capacity building in national environmental policy: A comparative study of 17 countries*, edited by H. Weidner and M. Jänicke. Berlin and New York: Springer.

Hochstetler, Kathryn, and Margaret E. Keck. 2007. *Greening Brazil: Environmental activism in state and society*. Durham, NC: Duke University Press.

Horowitz, Donald L. 1977. *The courts and social policy*. Washington, DC: Brookings Institution.

Huber, Richard M., Jack Ruitenbeek, and Ronaldo Seroa de Motta. 1998. *Market based instruments for environmental policymaking in Latin America and the Caribbean*. Washington, DC: World Bank.

Hutter, Bridget. 1988. *The reasonable arm of the law? The law enforcement procedures of environmental health officers*. Oxford Socio-Legal Studies. Oxford: Clarendon.

———. 1997. *Compliance: Regulation and environment*, Oxford Socio-Legal Studies. Oxford: Clarendon.

Instituto Brasileiro de Geografia e Estatística (IBGE). 2004. *As Fundações privadas e associações sem fins lucrativos no Brasil 2002.* Rio de Janeiro: IBGE.

Jarquín Calderón, Edmundo, and Fernando Carrillo Flórez. 1998. *Justice delayed: Judicial reform in Latin America.* Washington, DC, and Baltimore: Inter-American Development Bank, Johns Hopkins University Press.

Johnson, David T. 2002. *The Japanese way of justice: Prosecuting crime in Japan,* edited by D. Black. Studies on Law and Social Control. Oxford: Oxford University Press.

Jordana, Jacint, and David Levi-Faur, eds. 2004. *The politics of regulation: Institutions and regulatory reforms for the age of governance.* Cheltenham, UK: Edward Elgar.

Junqueira, Eliane Botelho. 2003. Brazil: The road of conflict bound for total justice. In *Legal culture in the age of globalization: Latin America and Latin Europe,* edited by L. M. Friedman and R. Pérez-Perdomo. Stanford, CA: Stanford University Press.

Kagan, Robert A. 1978. *Regulatory justice: Implementing a wage-price freeze.* New York: Russell Sage Foundation.

———. 1994. Regulatory enforcement. In *Handbook of Regulations and Administrative Law,* edited by D. H. Rosenbloom and R. D. Schwartz. New York: Marcel Dekker.

———. 1997. Should Europe worry about adversarial legalism? *Oxford Journal of Legal Studies* 17 (2):165–85.

———. 1999. Trying to have it both ways: Local discretion, central control, and adversarial legalism in American environmental regulation. *Ecology Law Quarterly* 25 (4):718–32.

———. 2001. *Adversarial legalism: The American way of law.* Cambridge, MA: Harvard University Press.

Kagan, Robert A., and Lee Axelrad. 2000. *Regulatory encounters: Multinational corporations and American adversarial legalism.* Berkeley: University of California Press.

Kahn-Freund, O. 1974. On uses and misuses of comparative law. *Modern Law Review* 37 (1):1–27.

Kapiszewski, Diana, and Matthew M. Taylor. 2006. Doing courts justice? Studying judicial politics in Latin America. Paper read at Annual Meeting of the American Political Science Association, Aug. 31–Sept. 3, 2006, Philadelphia.

Kaufman, Herbert. 1960. *The forest ranger, a study in administrative behavior.* Baltimore: Published for Resources for the Future by Johns Hopkins University Press.

Keck, Margaret E. 2002. "Water, water, everywhere, nor any drop to drink": land use and water policy in São Paulo. In *Livable cities? Urban struggles for livelihood and sustainability,* edited by P. B. Evans. Berkeley: University of California Press.

Keck, Margaret E., and Kathryn Sikkink. 1998. *Activists beyond borders: Advocacy networks in international politics.* Ithaca, NY: Cornell University Press.

Kerche, Fábio. 1997. O Ministério Público e a constituinte de 1987/88. Master's thesis, Political Science, Universidade de São Paulo, São Paulo.

———. 1999. O Ministério Público e a constituinte de 1987/88. In *O sistema de justiça*, edited by M. T. Sadek. São Paulo: IDESP, Editora Sumaré.

———. 2003. O Ministério público no Brasil: Autonomia, organização e atribuições. PhD diss., Political Science, Universidade de São Paulo, São Paulo.

Krygier, Martin. 1997. Virtuous circles: Antipodean reflections on power, institutions, and civil society. *East European Politics and Societies* 11 (1):36–88.

———. 1999. Institutional optimism, cultural pessimism and the rule of law. In *The rule of law after communism: Problems and prospects in east-central Europe*, edited by M. Krygier and A. W. Czarnota. Aldershot, UK: Ashgate.

———. 2002. Rule of law. In *International encyclopedia of the social and behavioral sciences*, edited by N. J. Smelser and P. B. Baltes. Amsterdam and Miamisburg, OH: Elsevier, ScienceDirect online.

LaFave, Wayne R. 1970. The prosecutor's discretion in the United States. *American Journal of Comparative Law* 18:532–48.

Lamounier, Bolivar, and Alkimar Ribeiro Moura. 1990. *De Geisel a Collor: O balanço da transição*. São Paulo: IDESP; Editora Sumaré; MCT / CNPq.

Langer, Vera. 1988. Public interest in civil law, socialist law, and common law systems: The role of the public prosecutor. *American Journal of Comparative Law* 36:279–305.

Legrand, Pierre. 1997. The impossibility of "legal transplants." *Maastrict Journal* 4:111–24.

Lemos, Maria Carmen de Mello. 1998. The politics of pollution control in Brazil: State actors and social movements cleaning up Cubatão. *World Development* 26 (1):75–87.

Levin, Martin A., and Barbara Ferman. 1985. *The political hand: Policy implementation and youth employment programs*. Pergamon Government and Politics Series. New York: Pergamon Press.

Levine, Kay L. 2005. The new prosecution. *Wake Forest Law Review* 40:1125–1214.

Lima Lopes, José Reinaldo de. 1999. Social rights and the courts. In *From dissonance to sense: Welfare state expectations, privatisation and private law*, edited by T. Wilhelmsson and S. Hurri. Aldershot, UK: Ashgate.

Lopes, Syglea Rejane Magalhães. 1999. Uma avaliação do sistema de licenciamento ambiental e das sanções administrativas no estado do Pará. *Movendo Idéias* 4 (6):140–52.

Lynch, Gerard E. 1997. Our administrative system of criminal justice. *Fordham Law Review* 66:2117–50.

Macedo Júnior, Ronaldo Porto. 1995. A evolução institucional do Ministério Público brasileiro. In *Uma introdução ao estudo da justiça*, edited by M. T. Sadek. São Paulo: IDESP, Editora Sumaré.

———. 1999a. Ministério Público brasileiro: Um novo ator político. In *Ministério Público II: Democracia*, edited by J. M. M. Vigliar and R. P. Macedo Júnior. São Paulo: Atlas.

———. 1999b. Quarto poder e o terceiro setor: O Ministério Público e as organizações não governamentais sem fins lucraticos, estratégias para o futuro. In *Ministério Público II: Democracia*, edited by J. M. M. Vigliar and R. P. Macedo Júnior. São Paulo: Atlas.

Machado, Paulo Affonso Leme. 1999. *Direito ambiental brasileiro*. 8th ed. São Paulo: Malheiros.

Maciel, Débora Alves. 2002. Ministério Público e sociedade: A gestão de conflitos ambientais em São Paulo. PhD diss., Sociology, Universidade de São Paulo, São Paulo.

Magalhães Lopes, Syglea Rejane. 2000. *Procedimentos legais para exploração das florestas naturais do bacia* Amazônica. Belém: E.F.S.

Maglio, Ivan Carlos. 2000. A descentralização da gestão ambiental no Brasil: O papel dos órgãos estaduais e as relações com o poder local, 1990/1999. Master's thesis, Environmental Health, Universidade de São Paulo, São Paulo.

Mainwaring, Scott. 1987. Urban popular movements, identity, and democratization in Brazil. *Comparative Political Studies* 20 (2):131–59.

———. 2003. Introduction: Democratic accountability in Latin America. In *Democratic accountability in Latin America*, edited by S. Mainwaring and C. Welna. Oxford and New York: Oxford University Press.

Mancuso, Rudolfo de Camargo. 1999. *Ação civil pública*. 6th ed. São Paulo: Revista dos Tribunais.

May, Peter J., and Soren Winter. 2000. Reconsidering styles of regulatory enforcement: Patterns in Danish agro-environmental inspection. *Law and Policy* 22 (2):143–73.

Mazzilli, Hugo Nigro. 1989. *O Ministério Público na constituição de 1988*. São Paulo: Saraiva.

———. 1991. *Manual do promotor de justiça*. 2nd ed. São Paulo: Saraiva.

———. 1995. *Regime jurídico do Ministério Público*. São Paulo: Saraiva.

———. 1997. *Introdução ao Ministério Público*. São Paulo: Saraiva.

———. 1999. Independência do Ministério Público. In *Ministério Público: Instituição e processo*, edited by A. A. M. d. C. Ferraz. São Paulo: Atlas.

———. 2001. *A defesa dos interesses difusos em juízo*. 13th ed. São Paulo: Saraiva.

McCann, Michael W. 1986. *Taking reform seriously: Perspectives on public interest liberalism*. Ithaca, NY: Cornell University Press.

Meili, Stephen. 1998. Cause lawyers and social movements: A comparative perspective on democratic change in Argentina and Brazil. In *Cause lawyering: Political commitments and professional responsibilities*, edited by A. Sarat and S. A. Scheingold. New York: Oxford University Press.

Meirelles, Hely Lopes. 2000. *Direito administrativa brasileira*. 25th ed. São Paulo: Malheiros.

Mello, Celso Antonio Bandeira. 1984. *Elementos de Direito Administrativo*. São Paulo: Revista dos Tribunais.

Melnick, R. Shep. 1983. *Regulation and the courts: The case of the Clean Air Act*. Washington, DC: Brookings Institution.

———. 1995. Separation of powers and the strategy of rights: The expansion of special education. In *The new politics of public policy*, edited by M. K. Landy and M. A. Levin.

Baltimore: Johns Hopkins University Press.

Merryman, John Henry. 1985. *The civil law tradition: An introduction to the legal systems of Western Europe and Latin America.* 2nd ed. Stanford, CA: Stanford University Press.

Milaré, Édis, ed. 1992. *O Ministério Público e a defesa do meio ambiente.* Document written in the Meeting of Environmental Prosecutors in Goiânia on Aug. 21, 1991, reprinted in *Revista do Ministério Público, Rio Grande do Sul 1 (27): 243–46.*

————, ed. 1995. *Ação civil pública, Lei 7347/85—reminiscências e reflexões apos dez anos de aplicação.* São Paulo: Revista dos Tribunais.

————. 2001. *Direito do ambiente.* São Paulo: Revista dos Tribunais.

Montanye, Dawn, and Carol Welch. 1999. The IMF: Selling the environment short. Washington, DC: Friends of the Earth.

Moraes, Raimundo de Jesus Coelho de. 2005. Judicialização do licenciamento ambiental no Brasil: Excesso ou garantia de participação? *Revista de Direito Ambiental* 10 (38):204–37.

Moraes, Raimundo de Jesus Coelho de, and Edna Maria Ramos de Castro. 1998. Curso de especialização: Direito ambiental e políticas públicas. Belém: Universidade Federal do Pará, Ministério Público do Estado do Pará, Programa Piloto para Proteção das Florestas Tropicais do Brasil.

Mueller, Bernardo. 2006. *Who enforces enforcement? Can public prosecutors in Brazil break the endless regress?* Brasilia: Department of Economics, University of Brasilia.

Mumme, Stephen P. 1998. Environmental policy and politics in Mexico. In *Ecological policy and politics in developing countries: Economic growth, democracy, and environment,* edited by U. Desai. Albany: State University of New York Press.

Nef, Jorge. 1995. Environmental policy and politics in Chile: A Latin-American case study. In *Environmental policies in the Third World: A comparative analysis,* edited by O. P. Dwivedi and D. K. Vajpeyi. Westport, CT: Greenwood Press.

Neves, Estela Maria Souza Costa. 2006. A política ambiental e os municípios brasileiros. Doutorado, Curso de Pós-Graduação em Desenvolvimento, Agricultura e Sociedade, Universidade Federal Rural do Rio de Janeiro, Rio de Janeiro.

Nonet, Philippe, and Philip Selznick. 2001. *Law and society in transition: Toward responsive law.* New Brunswick, NJ: Transaction Publishers.

Norgaard, Richard B. 1994. *Development betrayed: The end of progress and a coevolutionary revisioning of the future.* London and New York: Routledge.

O'Donnell, Guillermo A. 1993. On the state, democratization, and some conceptual problems: A Latin American view with glances at some post-communist countries. *World Development* 21 (8):1355–69.

————. 1999a. Horizontal accountability in new democracies. In *The self-restraining state: Power and accountability in new democracies,* edited by A. Schedler, L. J. Diamond, and M. F. Plattner. Boulder, CO: Lynne Rienner.

————. 1999b. Polyarchies and the (un)rule of law in Latin America: A partial conclu-
sion. In *The (un)rule of law and the underprivileged in Latin America,* edited by J. E.
Méndez, G. A. O'Donnell, and P. S. d. M. S. Pinheiro. Notre Dame, IN: University of
Notre Dame Press.

————. 2003. Horizontal accountability: The legal institutionalization of mistrust. In
Democratic accountability in Latin America, edited by S. Mainwaring and C. Welna.
Oxford and New York: Oxford University Press.

Ohlin, Lloyd E. 1993. Surveying discretion by criminal justice makers. In *Discretion in
criminal justice: The tension between individualization and uniformity,* edited by L. E.
Ohlin and F. J. Remington. Albany: State University of New York.

Passos de Freitas, Vladimir. 2003. The importance of environmental judicial decisions
in the Brazilian experience. Paper read at the Symposium of judges and prosecutors
of Latin America: Environmental compliance and enforcement, Sept. 23–24, 2003,
Buenos Aires.

Pazzaglini Filho, Marino. 2000. Princípios constitucionais e improbidade administrativa
ambiental. *Revista de Direito Ambiental* (17):112–22.

Pérez-Perdomo, Rogelio. 1995. Corruption and political crisis. In *Lessons of the Venezuelan
experience,* edited by L. W. Goodman, J. Mendelson, M. N. Forman, J. F. Tulchin, and
G. Bland. Washington, DC: Woodrow Wilson Press, Johns Hopkins University Press.

Peritore, N. Patrick. 1999. *Third World environmentalism: Case studies from the global
south.* Gainesville: University Press of Florida.

Pozzo, Antonio Araldo Ferraz Dal. 1990. Reunião Geral dos Membros do Ministério
Público. *Justitia* 52 (152):364–77.

————. 1993. 1990–1993: Um relatório de reformas. *Justitia* 55 (164):163–89.

Prillaman, William C. 2000. *The judiciary and democratic decay in Latin America: Declining confidence in the rule of law.* Westport, CT: Praeger.

Proença, Luis Roberto. 2001. *Inquérito civil.* São Paulo: Revista dos Tribunais.

Raz, Joseph. 1979. *The authority of law: Essays on law and morality.* Oxford: Oxford University Press.

Remington, Frank J. 1993. The decision to charge, the decision to convict on a plea of
guilty, and the impact of sentence structure on prosecution practices. In *Discretion
in criminal justice: The tension between individualization and uniformity,* edited by
L. E. Ohlin and F. J. Remington. Albany: State University of New York Press.

Rios-Figueroa, Julio, and Matthew M. Taylor. 2006. Institutional determinants of the
judicialization of policy in Brazil and Mexico. *Journal of Latin American Studies*
38:739–66.

Rodrigues de Souza, José Carlos. 1999. Improbidade administrativa e meio ambiente.
Revista de Direito Ambiental 4 (14):83–90.

Rosenberg, Gerald N. 1991. *The hollow hope: Can courts bring about social change?*
Chicago: University of Chicago Press.

Rosenn, Keith S. 1971. The jeito: Brazil's institutional bypass of the formal legal system and its developmental implications. *American Journal of Comparative Law* 19:514–49.

———. 1998. Judicial reform in Brazil. *Nafta: Law and Business Review of the Americas* 4:19–37.

———. 2000. Judicial review in Brazil: Developments under the 1988 Constitution. *The Southwestern Journal of Law and Trade in the Americas* 7:291–320.

Rowat, Donald Cameron. 1965. *The ombudsman: Citizen's defender.* London: Allen & Unwin.

Sachs, Wolfgang. 1992. *The development dictionary: A guide to knowledge as power.* London: Zed Books.

Sadek, Maria Tereza. 1995a. A crise do judiciário vista pelos juízes. In *Uma introdução ao estudo da justiça*, edited by M. T. Sadek. São Paulo: IDESP, Editora Sumaré.

———. 1995b. Institutional fragility and judicial problems in Brazil. In *Growth and development in Brazil: Cardoso's real challenge*, edited by M. D. A. G. Kinzo and V. Bulmer-Thomas. London: Institute of Latin American Studies.

———. ed. 1995c. *O judiciário em debate.* Série Justiça. São Paulo: IDESP, Editora Sumaré.

———. 1995d. A organização do poder judiciário no Brasil. In *Uma introdução ao estudo da justiça*, edited by M. T. Sadek. São Paulo: IDESP, Editora Sumaré.

———, ed. 1995e. *Uma introdução ao estudo da justiça.* Série Justiça. São Paulo: IDESP, Editora Sumaré.

———. 1997. *O Ministério Público e a justiça no Brasil.* Série Justiça. São Paulo: IDESP, Editora Sumaré.

———, ed. 1999. *O sistema de justiça.* Série Justiça. São Paulo: IDESP, Editora Sumaré.

———, ed. 2000. *Justiça e cidadania no Brasil.* São Paulo: IDESP, Editora Sumaré.

Sadek, Maria Tereza, and Rosangela Batista Cavalcanti. 2003. The new Brazilian public prosecution: An agent of accountability. In *Democratic accountability in Latin America*, edited by S. Mainwaring and C. Welna. Oxford and New York: Oxford University Press.

Salles, Carlos Alberto de. 1999. Entre a razão e a utopia: A formação histórica do Ministério Público. In *Ministério Público II: Democracia*, edited by J. M. M. Vigliar and R. P. Macedo Júnior. São Paulo: Atlas.

Sanches Filho, Alvino Oliveira. 1999. Instituições, cidadania, e movimentos sociais: O papel do Ministério Público da Bahia. *Cadernos de CEAS* (182):47–65.

Santiso, Carlos. 2003. Economic reform and judicial governance in Brazil: Balancing independence with accountability. *Democratization* 10 (4):161–80.

Santos, Boaventura de Sousa. 2000. Law and democracy: (Mis)trusting the global reform of courts. In *Globalizing institutions: Case studies in regulation and innovation*, edited by J. Jenson and B. d. S. Santos. Aldershot, UK: Ashgate.

Santos, Roberto A. O., and Wolf Paul, eds. 1995. *Amazônia perante o direito: Problemas ambientais e trabalhistas*. Belém: Universidade Federal do Pará.

Sarat, Austin. 1981. Book review: Access to Justice. Mauro Cappelletti, General Editor, vols. 1–4. *Harvard Law Review* 94:1911–1924.

Schedler, Andreas. 1999. Conceptualizing accountability. In *The self-restraining state: Power and accountability in new democracies*, edited by A. Schedler, L. Diamond, and M. F. Plattner. Boulder, CO: Lynne Rienner.

Scholz, Imme, Daniel Dräger, Isabelle Floer, Constanze Neher, and Julia Unger. 2004. Sociedade civil e política ambiental na Amazônia: Os casos da barragem de Belo Monte e da rodovia federal BR-163. Bonn: German Institute of Development.

Scholz, John T. 1984. Cooperation, deterrence and the ecology of regulatory enforcement. *Law and Society Review* 18:601–46.

———. 1994. Managing regulatory enforcement in the United States. In *Handbook of regulations and administrative law*, edited by D. H. Rosenbloom and R. D. Schwartz. New York: Marcel Dekker.

Selznick, Philip. 1992. *The moral commonwealth: Social theory and the promise of community*. Berkeley: University of California Press.

———. 1999. Legal cultures and the rule of law. In *The rule of law after communism: Problems and prospects in east-central Europe*, edited by M. Krygier and A. W. Czarnota. Aldershot, UK: Ashgate.

Selznick, Philip, Philippe Nonet, and Howard M. Vollmer. 1969. *Law, society, and industrial justice*. New York: Russell Sage Foundation.

Shaman, David. 1996. Brazil's pollution regulatory structure and background: World Bank, New Ideas in Pollution Regulation (NIPR).

Shapiro, Martin M. 1988. *Who guards the guardians? Judicial control of administration*. Richard B. Russell Lectures, no. 6. Athens: University of Georgia Press.

Sieder, Rachel, Line Schjolden, and Alan Angell, eds. 2005. *The judicialization of politics in Latin America*. New York: Palgrave Macmillan.

Silbey, Susan S. 2002. Legal culture and legal consciousness. In *International encyclopedia of the social and behavioral sciences*, edited by N. J. Smelser and P. B. Baltes. Amsterdam and Miamisburg, OH: Elsevier, ScienceDirect online.

Silva, Catia Aida. 2000. Brazilian prosecutors and collective demands: Bringing social issues to the courts of justice. Paper read at the Meeting of the Latin American Studies Association, March 16–18, Miami.

———. 2001. *Justiça em jogo: Novas facetas da atuação dos promotores da justiça*. São Paulo: Universidade de São Paulo.

Skocpol, Theda. 1985. Bringing the state back in: Strategies of analysis in current research. In *Bringing the state back in*, edited by P. B. Evans, D. Rueschemeyer, and T. Skocpol. Cambridge, UK: Cambridge University Press.

Soares Júnior, Jarbas. 2003. The action of the public prosecutor's office on river basins and the experience in Minas Gerais. Paper read at the Symposium of Judges and Prosecutors of Latin America: Environmental compliance and enforcement, Sept. 23–24, 2003, Buenos Aires.

Sobrane, Sergio Turra. 1999. A lei de improbidade administrativa e sua utilização para a proteção das florestas brasileiras. *Revista de Direito Ambiental* 4 (16):49–55.

Spradley, James P. 1979. *The ethnographic interview*. New York: Holt, Rinehart & Winston.

State of Pará / SECTAM. 1999. Relatório de Atividades, 1995–1998. Belém: SECTAM.

———. 2002. Atividades desenvolvidas pela Diretoria de Meio Ambiente no período de 1995 a 2001. Belém: SECTAM.

State of São Paulo / SMA. 1992a. *Brasil 92: Perfil ambiental e estratégias*. São Paulo: SMA.

———. 1992b. *São Paulo 92: Environmental profiles and strategies*. São Paulo: SMA.

———. 1998. *Quem somos e o que fazemos*. São Paulo: SMA / CED.

Tate, C. Neal, and Torbjörn Vallinder. 1995. *The global expansion of judicial power*. New York: New York University Press.

Taylor, Matthew M. 2005. Citizens against the state: The riddle of high impact, low functionality courts in Brazil. *Brazilian Journal of Political Economy* 24 (4):418–38.

———. 2006. Veto and voice in the courts: Policy implications of institutional design in the Brazilian judiciary. *Comparative Politics* 38 (3):337–55.

———. 2008. Judging policy: Courts and policy reform in democratic Brazil. Stanford, CA: Stanford University Press.

Taylor, Matthew M., and Vinícius C. Buranelli. 2007. Ending up in pizza: Accountability as a problem of institutional arrangement in Brazil. *Latin American Politics and Society* 49 (1):59–87.

Thornton, Dorothy, Neil Gunningham, and Robert A. Kagan. 2005. General deterrence and corporate environmental behavior. *Law and Policy* 27 (2):262–88.

Tomazi, Luiz Roberto. 1981. Ministério Público e defesa do meio ambiente. *Justitia* 43 (113):135–42.

Topan, Luiz Renato. 1994. O Ministério Público e a ação civil público ambiental no controle dos atos administrativos. *Justitia* 56 (165):46–55.

Tulchin, Joseph F., and Ralph H. Espach. 2000. *Combating corruption in Latin America*. Baltimore: Johns Hopkins University Press.

Twining, William. 2004. Diffusion of law: A global perspective. *Journal of Legal Pluralism* 49:1–45.

———. 2005. Social science and the diffusion of law. *Journal of Law and Society* 32 (2):203–40.

Ungar, Mark. 2002. *Elusive reform: Democracy and the rule of law in Latin America*. Boulder, CO: Lynne Rienner.

Valente, Luiz Ismaelino. 1988. A legitimação ativa na ação civil pública. *Revista do Tribunal de Justiça, Estado do Pará* 32 (45):54–59.

————. 1994. Defesa do meio ambiente e justiça ambiental no Pará. *Revista do Tribunal de Justiça, Estado do Pará* 38 (62):5–29.

————. 1995. Atuação do Ministério Público em defesa do meio ambiente na Amazônia. In *Amazônia perante o direito: Problemas ambientais e trabalhistas*, edited by R. A. O. Santos and W. Paul. Belém: Universidade Federal do Pará.

Valery Mirra, Álvaro Luiz. 1989. A defesa do meio ambiente em juízo. *Revista dos Tribunais* 645:40–46.

————. 1999. O problema do controle judicial das omissões estatais lesivas ao meio ambiente. *Revista de Direito Ambiental* 4 (15):61–80.

Vandenbergh, Michael P. 2003. Beyond elegance: A testable typology of social norms in corporate environmental compliance. *Stanford Environmental Law Journal* 22:55–145.

Veríssimo, Adalberto, Carlos Souza Jr., Danielle Celentano, Rodney Salomão, Denys Pereira, and Cíntia Balieiro. 2006. Areas para Produção Florestal Manejada: Detalhamento do Macrozoneamento Ecológico Econômico do Estado do Pará. Belém, Pará: IMAZON.

Vieira de Andrade, Filippe Augusto. 1999. Algumas reflexões sobre vinculação e discricionariedade em matéria ambiental. In *Justiça Penal–6*, edited by J. d. C. Penteado. São Paulo: Revista dos Tribunais.

Viola, Eduardo, and James W. Nickel. 1994. Integrando a defesa dos direitos humanos e do meio ambiente: Lições do Brasil. *Novos Estudos* 40:171–84.

Vogel, David. 1986. *National styles of regulation: Environmental policy in Great Britain and the United States.* Cornell Studies in Political Economy. Ithaca, NY: Cornell University Press.

Voigt, Stefan. 2006. Power over prosecutors corrupts politicians: Cross country evidence using a new indicator. Law and Economics Workshop, University of California Berkeley, Year 2006, Paper 6. Sept. 25, 2006. Posted at the eScholarship Repository, University of California, http://repositories.cdlib.org/berkeley_law_econ/Fall2006/6.

Vorenberg, James. 1981. Decent restraint of prosecutorial power. *Harvard Law Review* 94 (7):1521–73.

Watson, Alan. 1976. Legal transplants and law reform. *Law Quarterly Review* 92.

————. 1993. *Legal transplants: An approach to comparative law.* 2nd ed. Athens: University of Georgia Press.

Werneck Vianna, Luiz, Maria Alice Rezende de Carvalho, Manuel Palacios Cunha Melo, and Marcelo Baumann Burgos. 1997. *Corpo e alma da magistratura brasileiro.* 3rd ed. Rio de Janeiro: Revan.

————. 1999. *A judicialização da política e das relações sociais no Brasil.* Rio de Janeiro: Revan.

Wiecko V. de Castilho, Ela, and Maria Tereza Sadek. 1998. *O Ministério Público Federal e a administração da justiça no Brasil.* Série Justiça. São Paulo: IDESP, Editora Sumaré.

Wolcott, Harry F. 1995. Making a study "more ethnographic." In *Representation in ethnography*, edited by J. Van Maanen. Thousand Oaks, CA: Sage.

Wood, B. Dan, and Richard W. Waterman. 1991. The dynamics of political control of the bureaucracy. *The American Political Science Review* 85 (3):801–28.

World Bank. 1996a. *Brazil: Managing environmental pollution in the state of Rio de Janeiro.* Vol. 1: *Policy report.* Natural Resources, Environment and Rural Poverty Division, Country Department I, Latin America and the Caribbean Region, Report no. 15488-BR. Online at http://siteresources.worldbank.org/BRAZILINPOREXTN/Resources/3817166-1185895645304/4044168-1185895685298/025pub_br7.pdf.

———. 1996b. *Brazil: Managing environmental pollution in the state of Rio de Janeiro.* Vol. 2. Natural Resources, Environment and Rural Poverty Division. Country Department I, Latin America and the Caribbean Region, Report no. 15488-BR.

———. 1998. Brazil: Managing pollution problems, the brown environmental agenda. Brazil Country Management Unit, ESSD Sector Management Unit, Latin American and Caribbean Region.

———. 2000. *Greening industry: New roles for communities, markets and governments.* Oxford: Oxford University Press.

Wright, Ronald, and Marc Miller. 2002. The screening/bargaining tradeoff. *Stanford Law Review* 55:29–50.

Zaelke, Durwood, Matthew Stilwell, and Oran Young. 2005. What reason demands: Making law work for sustainable development. In *Making law work: Environmental compliance and sustainable development*, edited by D. Zaelke, D. Kaniaru, and E. Kruzikova. London: Cameron May.

Index

Page numbers followed by *f*, *m*, or *t* indicate figures, maps, or tables, respectively.